"Our modern world, the Front Porch Republic essayists in this volume rue, is a world of big government, big corporations, concentrated power, globalizing and scaled-up markets; and these latter-day conditions tend to produce rootless, restless, job-hopping, unhappy individuals. Might there be ways to inspire renewed commitments to localism without lapsing into libertarian recklessness, invidious tribalism, or priggish provincialism? Here is a thoughtful and arresting manifesto about building a new kind of republicanism for the twenty-first century."

—JOHN SEERY, George Irving Thompson Memorial Professor of Government, Professor of Politics, Pomona College

"American localism is like the little man upon the stair: it seems it isn't there—but it won't go away. This important volume bears witness to this long and honorable tradition, points to paths not taken that could have averted many of our present discontents, and suggests some ways to reverse our course toward centralization, standardization, and dreary uniformity. Let us pray that it's possible."

—JOHN SHELTON REED, author of *The Enduring South: Subcultural Persistence in Mass Society*

"Why reorient our lives toward local communities, economies, farmlands and forests? Because that's where you can be a citizen rather than a consumer, where you can see a need and help to meet it, where kinfolk might gather not just to visit but to live, where flesh-and-blood neighbors can offer one another aid and companionship, where public officials must answer for their actions, where you can grow food when the trucks stop rolling, where sun and wind offer free energy, and where you can protect and restore a piece of Earth. If anything in that list appeals to you, then you'll be stirred by this book—a bold reimagining of our lives and our places."

—SCOTT RUSSELL SANDERS, author of *Staying Put: Making a Home in a Restless World* and other books

"If each of these essays is a gem—and it is—then coming upon them all in one place is what it must feel like to come upon a streak of emerald in a layer of shale. To find them embedded in one place, in a manifesto that is a paean to place itself, is a sight, and a site, for hope. Singly, they bring us—with equal parts humor, humility, and gravitas—to new vantage points from which to glimpse tantalizing glints of an alternative to today's creed of greed and gain. Together, they construct a non-military equivalent of a phalanx— with equal parts criticism, common sense, and ideals—against destruction of the particular local places and bonds that give us our lives. Only such patient words and intricately argued bridge-building can help us withstand the ravages of expansion without limits, exploitation without renewal, and social and political polarization without thoughts of perpetuity."

—ELISABETH LASCH-QUINN, Syracuse University, author of *Race Experts: How Racial Etiquette, Sensitivity Training, and New Age Therapy Hijacked the Civil Rights Revolution*

"Among the few remaining signs of civilization these days is this smallish salon of wonderful writers and thinkers, the Porchers, as they call themselves. In well-tuned prose, they celebrate rootedness and that elusive notion, a sense of place. Not to mention a sense of the truly human."

—ELIAS CRIM, editor and founder, Solidarity Hall

"This is a book of serious ideas, well parsed, and rather brave considering the pervasive intellectual perversity elsewhere on the American scene. But mostly it is a lot of really good writing."

— JAMES HOWARD KUNSTLER, author of *The Long Emergency* and other books.

"For over 30 years we have heard lamentations from across the political spectrum about the decay of community. Most sound quaint now, for we have lost so much more than community. We've lost contact with reality as we move through an environment of abstractions and, worse yet, appeals for even more unreal abstractions. Even our most "real" and tangible institution, family, has come perilously close to being little more than an emotionally charged set of freely chosen and temporary affections bound only by fragile allegiances. *Localism in the Mass Age* is not just about local communities, but about the local context in which real things are either made or discovered. Localism isn't a political creed or a reactionary abstraction: it is an affirmation of the most human of things, in all their messy and colorful expressions. This collection of essays is about real things, including human needs, and ought to be the starting place for our national conversation of rebuilding a nation of free republics. Free republics are constructed of gnarled oak, not Formica uniformity and clean simplicity. Gnarled oaks may be found locally, the individualized products of real life situated in a real place. A better future is found here."

—TED V. MCALLISTER, Pepperdine University, author of *Revolt Against Modernity: Leo Strauss, Eric Voegelin, and the Search for a Postliberal Order*

"Any seeking a way through the barren strait of Fox News and CNN will find in this volume a seaworthy, storm-tried vessel. Responding point by point to the easy assumptions and begged questions of our day, these writers engender a rare quality of mind: the diminishing of melancholy and the presence of hope."

—ERIC MILLER, Geneva College, author of *Hope in a Scattering Time: A Life of Christopher Lasch*

"This indispensable collection of essays brings together the most important thinkers advocating the decentralization, diffusion, devolution, and dispersal of government power. Anyone concerned about the size, scale, and scope of the current form of the nation state will find here the maturity, wisdom, and common sense necessary to cultivate virtue, prudence, modesty, and restraint. In a noisy age of ephemeral controversies, the contributors to Front Porch Republic represent plain living and high thinking."

—ALLEN MENDENHALL, Associate Dean, Thomas Goode Jones School of Law

"This book is a welcome respite from the vulgar reality show of contemporary American politics and culture, and a wholesome reminder that life according to reality—place, limits and embodiment—is a lot more fun. In insightful and entertaining essays on topics ranging from economics to art, the Front Porch Republicans show why pessimism does not have to be world-weary and why humor is a mark of sanity and hope."

—NATHAN SCHLUETER, Professor of Philosophy and Religion, Hillsdale College

Localism in the Mass Age

A
Front Porch Republic
Manifesto

Localism in the Mass Age

A
FRONT PORCH REPUBLIC
MANIFESTO

edited by
Mark T. Mitchell
and Jason Peters

Front Porch Republic *Books*

LOCALISM IN THE MASS AGE
A Front Porch Republic Manifesto

Copyright © 2018 Mark T. Mitchell and Jason Peters. All rights reserved. Except for brief quotations in critical publications or reviews, no part of this book may be reproduced in any manner without prior written permission from the publisher. Write: Permissions, Wipf and Stock Publishers, 199 W. 8th Ave., Suite 3, Eugene, OR 97401.

Cascade Books
An Imprint of Wipf and Stock Publishers
199 W. 8th Ave., Suite 3
Eugene, OR 97401

www.wipfandstock.com

PAPERBACK ISBN: 978-1-5326-1443-9
HARDCOVER ISBN: 978-1-5326-1445-3
EBOOK ISBN: 978-1-5326-1444-6

Cataloguing-in-Publication data:

Names: Last, First. | other names in same manner

Title: Book title : book subtitle / Author Name.

Description: Eugene, OR: Cascade Books, 2018 | Series: if applicable | Includes bibliographical references and index.

Identifiers: ISBN 978-1-5326-1443-9 (paperback) | ISBN 978-1-5326-1445-3 (hardcover) | ISBN 978-1-5326-1444-6 (ebook)

Subjects: LCSH: subject | subject | subject | subject

Classification: CALL NUMBER 2018 (print) | CALL NUMBER (ebook)

Manufactured in the U.S.A.   MARCH 29, 2018

The strength of free peoples resides in the local community.
—ALEXIS DE TOCQUEVILLE, *DEMOCRACY IN AMERICA*

Table of Contents

List of Illustrations xv

Preface xvii
Mark T. Mitchell

Introduction: A Republic of Front Porches 1
Patrick J. Deneen

PART ONE: DEPARTURE AND RETURN

Look Homeward, Angels (and Others) 13
Bill Kauffman

Birthright 25
Katherine Dalton

The Orphans of Success and the Longing for Home 32
Jason Peters

PART TWO: POLITICS AND ECONOMICS

Federalism, Anti-Federalism, and the View from the Front Porch 45
Jeff Polet

The Quest for the Common Good:
Political Economy on the Front Porch 60
John Médaille

Opposition to Crony Capitalism: A Truly Bipartisan Opportunity 69
Andrew V. Abela

Agrarian Politics and the American Tradition 77
Jeff Taylor

American Foreign Policy and Modest Republicanism:
The Great Rule Reconstituted 89
Michael P. Federici

The Demise of Virtue in Virtual America 99
David Bosworth

PART THREE: THE HOME ECONOMY

Work, Death, and the Romantic Agrarian 107
Mark T. Mitchell

The Productive Home vs. The Consuming Home 115
Allan Carlson

Killing the Animals We Eat 124
John Cuddeback

PART FOUR: ART AND EDUCATION

"A New Magnetic North": 39 Theses on Education 131
R.J. Snell

Reimagining the University with Wendell Berry 141
Jack R. Baker and *Jeffrey Bilbro*

Art, Beauty, and Communal Life 151
James Matthew Wilson

PART FIVE: CIVIC LIFE

A Land Like No Other:
American Exceptionalism and the Problem of Scale 163
Richard Gamble

Do-It-Ourselves Citizenship 171
Pete Peterson

Luxury and Buying Local 184
David Cloutier

PART SIX: THE URBAN CHALLENGE

Chicago 2109: The Metropolitan Region as Agrarian-Urban Unit 195
Philip Bess

Port City Confidential 208
Susannah Black

PART SEVEN: PHILANTHROPY

Satan Was the First Philanthropist 223
Jeremy Beer

Philanthropy's War on Community 235
William A. Schambra

PART EIGHT: TECHNOLOGY AND POPULAR CULTURE

Technology, Mobility and Community 243
Christine Rosen

Our Hookup Culture 250
Susan McWilliams

PART NINE: BEYOND THE CORRUPTION OF MOTH AND RUST

Life Under Compulsion:
Rejecting the Glorious Liberty of the Children of God 261
Anthony Esolen

Defining Conservatism Down 273
D.G. Hart

Imagination and Memory Deformed: The Gnostic Resentment of Embodied Life and its Limits 281
Mark Shiffman

Afterword 295
Jason Peters

Contributors 301

Illustrations

FIGURE 1: The Chicago Metropolitan Region | 197

FIGURE 2: *Plan of Chicago* (1909) Plate 1 | 198

FIGURE 3: *Plan of Chicago* (1909) Plate 107 | 199

FIGURE 4: The World's Population, Concentrated, from persquaremile.com (used with permission) | 201

FIGURE 5: Metropolitan Chicago Developed Land Existing (2009) and Projected (2109) | 202

FIGURE 6: Hamlet / Village / Town / City | 202

FIGURE 7: Western Metropolitan Chicago | 203

FIGURE 8: Town settlement meets agricultural landscape in metropolitan Chicago | 203

FIGURE 9: Chicago's historic center viewed from the southwest, 2109 | 204

FIGURE 10: Proposed new high-rise city hall and boulevard fronted by sacred buildings | 204

Preface

Mark T. Mitchell

The conception, gestation, and birth of this book are framed by two great disruptions: the economic collapse (or near collapse) of 2008 and the presidential election of 2016, which featured Republican and Democratic candidates who were both spectacularly unpopular. Both events signal something about the general ill-health of the republic, but at the same time they provide, as crises so often do, opportunities for reflection and, if one is attentive, glimmers of hope.

In the spring of 2009, when the economic crisis of the previous year was unfolding, a group of academics and other writers joined forces to form the Front Porch Republic website. At that time I described the situation in the following terms:

> Here we can see the curious state of affairs in our waning republic: Democrats tend to be suspicious of big business but they trust big government to rein in abuses; Republicans express suspicion of big government but trust economic centralization to solve market instability. Both are half-right but half-blind. Here is a principle that we would do well to grasp: concentrations of power in any form are a threat to liberty. It may be too late for this generation to see this vital truth or, if seeing, to do anything about it. But nothing is inevitable, and there are hopeful signs that people are beginning to think seriously about the importance of localism, human scale, limits, and stewardship, the very things woefully lacking in the current spending orgy. While a return to these ideals is still only in its infancy, change is afoot. This represents a glimmer of sanity in a world succumbing to the apparent security promised by centralization.

> Nevertheless, we are facing the specter of a strange new phase in our nation's history. Through massive spending we are embarking on an age of concentration, an age where economic and political power are not only allied but centralized, an age where the two will become increasingly intertwined and difficult to distinguish. The long courtship is over. The ill-starred marriage has been consummated. The Wall-Street bailout and stimulus package are the grotesque progeny of this unholy union.

Although FPR launched in March 2009, the seeds of the project had been germinating for some time. In 2007, Jeremy Beer, then the editor-in-chief of ISI Books, organized a conference in Charlottesville, VA, titled "Liberty, Community, and Place in the American Tradition." Speakers included Bill Kauffman, Patrick Deneen, and Jason Peters, along with Dan McCarthy of *The American Conservative* and Jesse Walker of *Reason*. The conference also provided an opportunity for some future FPR writers to meet and discuss matters that would be of central concern to the FPR project.

For the academic year 2008-09, I was on sabbatical at Princeton University under the auspices of the James Madison Program. During the fall of 2008, as the country descended into economic uncertainty, I became increasingly frustrated by what was clearly an inadequate response to the crisis. I called Jeremy Beer, who had left ISI and co-founded American Philanthropic, to discuss the matter. We decided to establish an on-line magazine that would provide an outlet for writers whose ideas did not fit comfortably into the neat and inadequate Left/Right dichotomy or the blue-state/red-state opposition that characterizes so much political writing in America. Others quickly joined the enterprise. Patrick Deneen (then professor of Government at Georgetown, now at Notre Dame) was also on sabbatical at Princeton at the time. His office was just down the hall from mine. He immediately saw the merits of the project. Writers such as Bill Kauffman, Caleb Stegall, Katherine Dalton, Daniel Larison, and Rod Dreher, along with academics such as Jason Peters, James Matthew Wilson, Susan McWilliams, Allan Carlson, Mark Shiffman, and Russell Arben Fox, quickly joined.

FPR sought to promote human-scale institutions and associations against a steady consolidation of political, economic, and cultural power. With the tagline "Place, Limits, Liberty," FPR writers set out to articulate a critique of the current situation and to provide a theoretical alternative as well as provide practical examples of how this alternative could be implemented in particular settings. While no litmus test has ever existed, FPR writers are generally oriented by the broad tradition of Christian humanism and, in promoting the idea of human flourishing born of that vision of human affairs, they have promoted such ideals as political decentralization, economic localism, cultural regionalism, and the dignity of both individuals and local communities. Key thinkers who serve to inspire and inform many FPR writers include Wendell Berry, Christopher Lasch, E.F. Schumacher, Wilhelm Röpke, Russell Kirk, Hilaire Belloc, G.K. Chesterton, and Alexis de Tocqueville.

Within the first year of operation, FPR was incorporated as a non-profit in the state of West Virginia, and in 2010 FPR Inc. was issued a 501c3 status by the IRS. This non-profit status opened the door for tax-deductible donations, which, though generally modest, provided the means to finance conferences and other occasional expenses.

In the fall of 2011 FPR held the first of its annual conferences. The site was Mount St. Mary's University in Emmitsburg, Maryland. About 150 people converged on the campus to hear a variety of FPR writers—including a keynote address by Bill Kauffman—and others discuss various aspects of human scale and the human good. At least half of the attendees were students from colleges and universities in the region. The success of the conference demonstrated that FPR's appeal could support a successful conference. Since then we have held a conference each year at various venues across the country and have featured keynote addresses from such figures as Dana Gioia, James Howard Kunstler, and Wendell Berry.

One of FPR's main objectives almost from the beginning was to have its own imprint and therefore the means by which the broader FPR vision could be articulated in print. This objective was realized in 2013 when FPR Books was established as an official imprint of Wipf & Stock Publishers. Our modest goal of producing a handful of books each year, despite having to do so as a kind of after-hours unpaid extracurricular avocation, has so far proved manageable.

When FPR began, "localism" as a movement was only in its infancy. Today localism is an idea with a wide array of adherents from academics to hipsters, from city planners to organic farmers. It is becoming increasingly clear that many people across the political spectrum have come to question the wisdom of centralization in all its many guises. While there are plenty of discrete reasons for hope, the conventional wisdom in so many quarters, especially among the "intellectual class," is generally still in the direction of the centralized, super-sized, and homogenized.

But, as I said in that original post, change *is* afoot. The Brexit vote in July of 2016 followed by Donald Trump's "surprise" win in November of the same year should be understood as part of the same movement that, while not a tsunami, represents a clear challenge to the liberal cosmopolitan agenda—found on both the Left and the Right—that champions internationalism over nationalism, that celebrates an abstract global community over concrete local affiliations, and that rejoices in the inevitability of globalization. That globalization has suffered a series of recent setbacks must be galling (not to mention confusing) to those convinced of its inevitability.

The vulgar billionaire from Manhattan, now President of these United States, is an odd messenger of the working class burned by trade treaties and economic policies that have lined the pockets of Wall Street investors but all too often decimated local communities, uprooted citizens, and led many to question whether what benefits the purveyors of abstractions is equally beneficial to the rest. It goes without saying that Trump is no localist messiah. However, his America First campaign rhetoric apparently struck a chord that has long remained unsounded by national leaders. His emphasis on securing the nation's borders pushes against the cosmopolitan dream of a world without borders where citizens of the world (and therefore of nowhere in particular) wander the globe seeking wealth, pleasure, and diversion without impediment. His refusal to submit to the strictures of political correctness has endeared him to many (or at least earned him the grudging respect) of those who intuit that sanity rooted in common sense and (ironically) common decency has fled the field under an onslaught of powerful and self-righteous individuals and institutions hell-bent on compelling all citizens to conform to standards that grow increasingly bizarre.

In short, the rise of Trump and Trumpism, whatever their manifest flaws, appears to represent a reaction against forces openly hostile to local communities, local authorities, and local idiosyncrasies. It represents, however inchoately and inarticulately, a rejection of ideals that have animated a class of social elites lacking strong local or even national affiliations in favor of an alternative rooted in patriotism, national pride, and perhaps even a commitment to living in and loving a particular place. A return to the scale of the nation-state is surely a move in the right direction, for it suggests a repudiation of the global village nonsense and, perhaps—just perhaps—opens the way to creative thinking about communities built to human scale. To be clear, there is little evidence Trump thinks in these terms. However, it may turn out that his election, in spite of Trump himself, opens the door to possibilities that would not have been as likely had his opponent won: less central planning by those convinced they know best and more power accruing to local governing bodies, less hostility to religious beliefs that run counter to the prevailing enthusiasm for liberation from all constraint, and perhaps less bellicose behavior abroad, even if Trump's persona does not exactly provide a recipe for tranquility at home.

Herein lies the gambit. Humans, individually and corporately, tend to overreact. Thus this movement in the west (for this trend is not limited to the U.S. and Britain but includes much of Europe as well) is fraught with danger. We already hear of the rise of ultra-nationalist parties, of neo-Nazism, and violence against immigrants in certain European countries. Many of the most ardent opponents of Trump argue that the same forces are incubating here in the U.S. and have been nourished by Trump's victory. To be sure, a new tribalism characterized by xenophobia, violence, and suspicion of "the other" is a possibility.

However, we are not *necessarily* doomed to the equally dismal alternatives of liberal cosmopolitanism and xenophobic tribalism. There is a third way, and although mainstream Republicans and Democrats generally fail to see beyond their false dichotomies and on-going animosities, it is just this alternative that animates the FPR project. What we might call "humane localism" appreciates the variety of local communities and resists the homogenizing impulse that is so strong in modern liberal democracies. It recognizes that the language of the global village represents an abstraction that will never satisfy human longings. Humane localism is characterized by a love for one's particular place, yet at the same time it is not animated by fear of the other, for by an act of imagination it sees through the inevitable differences and recognizes the common humanity we all share. It recognizes that we are all living souls with needs and longings that bind us together even as the particulars of our own places remind us of our distinctness. In short, humane localism is rooted in respect, not in homogeneity, in a recognition that liberty is sustainable only alongside respect for limits, and in the realization that human flourishing is best realized in the company of friends and neighbors sharing a common place in the world.

This collection of essays represents a cross-section of writers and ideas associated with FPR and the vision that FPR seeks to articulate. The essays provide an introduction to the rich cultural, political, and economic vision associated with the FPR project. All of the authors have written for the FPR site or spoken at an FPR conference. Some of the pieces are based on conference presentations. Some were written expressly for this volume. All provide a slice of the human-scale vision that has characterized FPR from the beginning. While much progress has been made toward articulating this alternative to the left/right stalemate, there is still much to be done. The rhetorical battle has been more successful than we had hoped. However, changing the actual economic, political, and cultural reality is a much longer process. The essays compiled here will help readers see the possibility of a world where human affairs are conducted as if place really matters, where economic affairs are conceived as if limits really matter, and where political power is exercised as if liberty really matters.

Introduction

A Republic of Front Porches

Patrick J. Deneen

What Happened to all the Front Porches?

Names are important, and few can be more significant than what a publication calls itself. Perhaps at first sight the name "Front Porch Republic" will give pause, causing the reader to think momentarily about what it means, how it came about, what its creators intended. After a time its explicit meaning will fade into the backdrop (and so it did, becoming fondly known as "FPR"), becoming a label that is rarely reflected upon, barely registered, but that still confers meaning—increasingly implicit—both for the undertaking and for those who originally named it, or who write under its banner. A name such as "Front Porch Republic" deserves some reflection before it fades into that subconscious space.

I can think of no better text by which to explore the meaning of "Front Porch Republic" than an old essay—one few have encountered and even fewer still would remember—that I read during my freshman year of college in a course taught by the man who became my mentor and best companion, though he has passed from this vale: Wilson Carey McWilliams. I've never forgotten the essay. It influenced me then and remains with me still. It was written by a man named Richard Thomas and was entitled "From Porch to Patio," published in 1975 in *The Palimpsest*, the journal of the Iowa State Historical Society. It had such an effect on me not only because of what it taught me but because so much of my childhood and young adulthood had involved being in various ways on our big front porch where I grew up in Windsor, Connecticut. This essay was more than mere theory; it taught me about who I was and why that was so.

In this simple but profound essay Thomas explores the social implications of building houses with front porches and the eventual abandonment of this architectural practice in favor of patios out back.[1] As with any central feature in our built environment, this is more than merely a passing fashion or a meaningless design change: the transition from porch to patio was one of the clearest and most significant manifestations of the physical change from a society concerned with the relationship of private and public things—in the Latin *res publica*—to one of increasing privacy. The porch, as a physical bridge between the private realm of the house and the public domain of the street and sidewalk, was the literal intermediate space between two worlds that have been increasingly separated in our time, and hence increasingly ungoverned in both forms.

Thomas expresses clearly some of the social dimensions of the porch and contrasts them with the patio. The porch, he wrote, "presented opportunities for social intercourse at several levels":

> When a family member was on the porch it was possible to invite the passerby to stop and come onto the porch for extended conversation. The person on the porch was very much in control of this interaction, as the porch was seen as an extension of the living quarters of the family. Often, a hedge or fence separated the porch from the street or board sidewalk, providing a physical barrier for privacy, yet low enough to permit conversation. The porch served many important social functions in addition to advertising the availability of its inhabitants. A well-shaded porch provided a cool place in the heat of the day for the women to enjoy a rest from household chores. They could exchange gossip or share problems without having to arrange a "neighborhood coffee" or a "bridge party." The porch also provided a courting space within earshot of protective parents. A boy and a girl could be close on a porch swing, yet still observed, and many a proposal of marriage was made on a porch swing. Older persons derived great pleasure from sitting on the porch,

---

1. I've discussed this transition in relation to the film *It's a Wonderful Life*, specifically in comparing Bedford Falls to Bailey Park. See "Awakening from the American Dream," in *Conserving America: Essays on Present Discontents* (South Bend, IN: St. Augustine's Press, 2016), ch. 4.

watching the world go by, or seeing the neighborhood children at play.²

The patio, by contrast, reflected both new settlement patterns and the increasing desire for privacy and withdrawal from interaction with one's neighbors. "In communities with high rates of mobility, one did not often want to know his neighbor. The constant turn-over of neighbors worked against the long-term relationships which are essential to a sense of belonging." The patio, it was believed, was a symbol and practical expression of our independence, our liberation from the niggling demands of neighbor and community. Yet Thomas insightfully notes that it was just as much a symbol and reality of a new kind of bondage, the bondage especially to the automobile and to the grim necessities of mobility, including long commutes and increasing isolation from a wide variety of bonds. It was too soon, perhaps, to note that this form of living also symbolized our increasing bondage to "foreign oil," though at the time he wrote it we Americans had just recently passed the apogee of oil production (allowing for a brief beguiling spike from fracking) and would forever become dependent on foreign powers—particularly tyrants—for our purported liberation through energy and would eventually fight a series of wars in a region far from where we should have any real concerns. The house, Thomas wryly noted, housed fewer people but more cars, and it was our new inanimate occupant that "both freed us and enslaved us."

In a microcosm, the forces that led to the decline of the porch as a place of transition between the private and the public realm have eviscerated both those domains of their capacity to educate a citizenry for self-government. The porch—as an intermediate space, even a sphere of "civil society"—was the symbolic and practical place where we learned that there is not, strictly speaking, a total separation between the public and private worlds. Our actions in private are not merely "private" but have, *in toto*, profound public implications. The decline of courtship and marriage proposals within earshot of kin, for one instance, has led to ever greater "privatization" of our intimate lives and a proportionate decline of the societal and public investment in undergirding families and the communities that foster them.³ Our private actions of driving ever greater

---

2. Richard H. Thomas, "From Porch to Patio" in *The Palimpsest* 56 (1975), 120–27; 122.

3. For more on this important aspect, see Beth Bailey's *From Front Porch to Back Seat: Courtship in Twentieth Century America* (Baltimore: Johns Hopkins, 1989).

distances in our automobiles have resulted in devastated landscapes, fostered deep dependence of foreign powers, and given us tract housing inimical to real community.

Meanwhile, our "public" world is increasingly shorn of the voices of citizens, wholly attenuated in the decline of the capacity of localities to govern their fates. For me, there was nothing more symbolic of this fact than the herd of state governors who rushed to serve the Obama administration, a sad pathetic revelation that governing a state is less significant for most of our leaders than becoming a functionary in the national bureaucracy. Our states, not to mention our localities, are less a kind of "porch," that transition from the world of the home to the public realm of community and eventually state and nation. Instead, as wholly "private citizens"—or, to invoke the preferred term, "consumers"—accustomed to houses that are places of private retreat, we see only one public entity of significance—the national state—but find it difficult to see ourselves a part of it. We regard the state as a distant and mysterious entity, occupied either by our team or their team but in either case an organization so vast, complex, and dizzying that we regard it as anything but the locus of our practice of shared self-governance. With each passing day we are less a republic, because with each passing day we perceive less of what our common or public things—our *res publica*—are. Without the literal spaces where we come to know what we have in common through speech, habit and memory, we regard politics as a competitive spectator sport and government as a distant imposition—in any event, anything but self-rule.

Tocqueville already anticipated the forces that would lead simultaneously to the retreat of individuals into a "small circle" of friends and family on the one hand and the rise of the "tutelary state" on the other. Tracing the logic of democracy, he foresaw a time when

> no man is obliged to put his powers at the disposal of another, and no one has any claim of right to substantial support from his fellow man, [at which point] each is both independent and weak. These two conditions, which must be neither seen quite separately nor confused, give the citizen of democracy extremely contradictory instincts. He is full of confidence and pride in his independence from his equals, but from time to time his weakness makes him feel the need for some outside help which he cannot expect from any of his fellows, for they are both impotent and cold. In this extremity he naturally turns his

eyes toward that huge entity which alone stands out above the universal level of abasement. His needs, and even more his longings, continually put him in mind of that entity, and he ends by regarding it as the sole and necessary support for his individual weakness.[4]

We rarely consider the ways that our built environment—even something so simple as a front porch—constitutes some of the necessary conditions for self-government. Thinking of ourselves in ways that can only be described as simultaneously disembodied (by means of our technology) and wholly embodied (albeit as monadic individuals only), we ignore the way spaces shape us, even prepare us for lives of responsible citizenship, community, and the proprieties of private life. Instead, we simultaneously crave a retreat into the purported liberties of the private realm yet regard the only public entity worthy of our attention to be a distant and inaccessible government. For those who would stand and defend the future of the republic, a good place to start would be to revive our tradition of building and owning houses with front porches, and to be upon them where we can both see our neighbors and be seen by them, speak and listen to one another, and, above all, occupy an intermediate space while still being firmly *in* place.

What Is to be Done?

Building a Republic of Front Porches is a start, but what else is to be done? There is the vexing question whether the many threads of argument in these pages and on the FPR website are not simply so much nostalgic longing for a bygone era (or, alternatively, a fantasy for an era that never existed), and whether the longing, while charming and interesting and even at times exciting in its counter-cultural resistance, nevertheless is finally irrelevant to the main debates that lie at the heart of the real world of a globalizing, free-market liberal system that is here to stay.

For some, the answer is simple: live the life you are given here. Wendell Berry is the touchstone for many of FPR's authors, not only because he has articulated well an alternative vision to the dominant cultural, political and economic presuppositions of this nation of "boomers," but because he has *walked the walk*, leaving a promising academic career in

---

4. Alexis de Tocqueville, *Democracy in America*, ed. J.P. Mayer, trans. George Lawrence (New York: Harper Perennial, 1969), 672.

New York City to take up a life of greater "complexity"—as he puts it—on the farm in Henry County, Kentucky. To greater or lesser extent, this is the example also on display here not only in the words but also in the deeds of many of the contributors. In living lives of deep commitment to places that are at once *home* and *outside the cosmopolis*—even in some cases (as at least two essays here show) tending to the land in those places—they are living demonstrations of their words. Some contributors have, more than once, expressed misgivings about writing for a website, because to do so draws them away from the very actions we all write about here. There is something inauthentic about propounding, on the internet, a life of localism and community, however magnificently and persuasively that life is propounded.

Most here acknowledge living lives deeply enmeshed in the world shaped by an itinerant economy and rootless journeymen. Particularly the academics among us have emerged from a system that is designed to foster the very opposite of the ethic that is being articulated and defended at FPR. It has been noted on more than one occasion that most of us writing here lack the *authenticity* of the likes of Berry. Because of this, we can be dismissed all the more easily as, at best, intellectual romantics of a Rousseauian mien and, at worst, as hypocrites who would call on others to live a life that none of us has ever shown any real capacity to live.

My own response, however, takes several parts. First, those among us who have emerged from the experience of graduate education designed, above all, to create deracinated and rootless intellectuals who theoretically could work anywhere but who generally crave to live and teach in one of a half-dozen cosmopolite cities in the world, have come to understand with crystal clarity the deepest presuppositions of the liberal ethic. While we doubtless expose ourselves to the easy charges of hypocrisy, I suspect that for many of us—for me, certainly—our opposition to the dominant ethos comes largely as a result of this particular education and the contradictions and ultimately the distortions that it forced most of us here to confront.

Those of us in this "itinerant" category are, in some ways, well-positioned to speak to so many of our fellow countrymen who find themselves in a similar pass. Many of us—whether because of circumstance, such as our professions, or because of background and upbringing—cannot easily make choices that would demonstrate our full commitment to a more rooted life in a small town or even our home town. There is no "going home again" for many of us because many of us come from places that cannot properly be called home. And, for many others of us, it is perhaps the ultimate irony that a society so deeply defined by choice and mobility makes the choice for rootedness difficult. Whereas the default was once to become a country doctor or town lawyer or one-team baseball player, now the defaults are set in an opposite mode.

I'll give one personal example of this. Shortly after I finished my Ph.D., I received an invitation to interview at a college that was quite close to where I had grown up. I was inordinately excited at this possibility, thinking that it might work out that my wife and newborn son and I might be able to settle close to family and childhood friends. When asked about accommodations during my interview, I proudly informed the college that I would be staying in my bedroom that night—my childhood bedroom, that is. During the two day interview I related in every conversation that I was native to the area and had a longstanding relationship to the campus, having attended its plays, movies, and used its library for many years. I believed my local connection would make me an especially attractive candidate, sure in the knowledge that a school would be attracted to someone who already had deep roots in the community and was likely to build a long life and career in that place.

I was incredibly naïve. I learned later that this proud display of my nativeness went over badly—it was discerned as a compromise of what should have been my true and only motivation for seeking employment at that institution, which was its objective and universal academic excellence. And, more generally, it is now almost universally the case that institutions will not hire faculty who have been trained at the same institution, or even an institution in the same state. Any such hiring would be suspected of nepotism—or, worse, "in-breeding"—as if there are not positive features of such connections having to do with particular institutional identity and loyalty and memory. However, academia, no less than the international and global economy, is now an international "marketplace" as well, and we only become valuable when we enter the stream of international intellectual commerce that is at once nowhere and everywhere.

Most of us, then, live in "the real world" as it is and as it will continue to be for the foreseeable future. Yet I think all of us genuinely struggle with second-bests: how to put down roots where one is; how to introduce a different ethic into a profession and way of life now defined by the dominant liberal ethic; how to raise good families amid the wreckage of this culture; how to live in ways larger and, more often, smaller, that reflect a resistance to the dominant culture and that support the sustenance or renewal or even creation of communities.

Second—for most of us, I think—the process of coming to an understanding of what was wrong with our current way was an "intellectual" discovery. Speaking personally, while I grew up in a small town and was catechized in the faith of my fathers—and imbibed the values that were embedded there—I was also unconsciously raised to accept the dominant presuppositions of mid- and late-20th-century American liberalism. For me, the process of reconciling (or ultimately properly ordering) those two parts of my upbringing ultimately was assisted by books and thinkers who had made various parts of that journey long before I was born. Much of this discovery has been remarkably and even regrettably recent, with much of the foundation having been laid long ago, but somehow the scaffolding only having been erected in recent years through a prolonged encounter with the writings of Berry and others and reverting to the faith of my fathers. More than ever, many of our countrymen will not have had the experience of growing up in small towns or on farms, or visiting grandparents or friends in such settings, as ever-more Americans lose all contact with a way of life now disreputable and transcended. Increasingly, those who seek to understand what is wrong in the world they inhabit, or even articulate vague misgivings, will first need the words to guide them to some possibility of an experience they will not have personally stored. And here, I and others hope, FPR is a forum, and a lasting one, in which some of those articulations and arguments can be made.

Third—and this is by no means a matter on which Front Porchers agree—I am of the view that not only are the actions of individuals needed, but ultimately a change in culture *and* politics is needed, and not necessarily or solely in that order (or in the reverse order), but mixed together. The connection between culture and politics is too mysterious and complex for me to unravel, but for many of us here it is clear that for too long "conservatism" *qua* the Republican party has emphasized "politics" at the expense of culture. It is the view, I think, of every author here that culture is ultimately the foundation of a society's mores and folkways, the source of its values and virtues. To turn to a Tocquevillian insight, "moeurs" ("mores," or culture) shape the law, and, thus, politics is derived at the deepest level from the culture. However, Tocqueville also observed that "moeurs" are in turn shaped over time by changes in the law. It's a mysterious process and one that can be excavated only with the care and attention akin to that of archaeology. What we *say* and believe can and likely will ultimately have an effect on how we act. Thus, Tocqueville observed that, while Americans justify most of their actions in terms of "self-interest," they frequently *act* out of altruism and public-spiritedness. He observed that Americans "do more honor to their philosophy than to themselves"—they are officially Lockeans, but practically Christians. Over time, however, our self-understanding will influence even our "unofficial" behavior, and just so, over time, the nation has become evermore officially and practically Lockean. How we understand ourselves consciously works itself ultimately into our unconscious actions as well.

So FPR is at least this much: an effort to change our self-understanding—of the selves we are, the selves we might be, and the communities we inhabit or aspire to inhabit. Many observe rightly that FPR's arguments are almost everywhere and always paradoxical, if not contradictory—arguing on behalf of communities and a culture in which choice and escape and individual self-assertion is subordinated, yet urging the embrace of these ways as a matter of choice and self-assertion. This paradox is forced upon anyone making these arguments by a culture that renders everything into a choice. Still, ultimately a people persuaded by the wisdom of such a course will begin to enact some of its basic presuppositions into law, and thus slowly create a "virtuous circle" in which the law emanates from culture, and culture is in turn strengthened by law. Some of us will act as individuals within communities, stepping out of the mainstream to preserve or create a distinctive alternative for our families or small communities of families. Others of us—and here I would include myself—will call for citizens to consider public acts large and small that will begin to offer us a different way to live.

Small changes might have large effects over time. Changes to zoning laws, requiring more mixed-use space—commercial, residential, educational, religious and otherwise—would begin to make possible a re-integration of the various central activities of human life. Demotion of the automobile is a major desideratum, and here a great coalition between the environmental Left and traditionalist Right is possible. Libertarians, Catholics, and traditionalists can make common cause in demanding more economic and legislative subsidiarity, although libertarians must chasten their dogmatic individualism and understand that the best restraint upon large-scale centralized institutions is not the individual but the community. Robert Nisbet's call for a "*laissez-faire* of groups" comes to mind. There is no "free market"—it is the fantasy of ideological purists—but there are markets that leave us more free as members of communities and relatively more immune from large-scale centralized institutions (public or private) than others. People might be persuaded to call for a different finger to be put on the legislative scales: not the one that now gives advantage to large-scale organizations, but one that gives advantage to smaller companies, family businesses, and local enterprises whose bottom-line is not the benefit of absentee shareholders but the life and fabric of local communities. Libertarians are right that onerous regulation is to be rejected, but *not* because it represents an imposition upon profitability; they are right because it is desired by *both* big government and big business as an obstacle to the entry of smaller players. Perhaps something so inventive as a dual regulatory system could be conceived, in which smaller businesses bear a lighter burden. Incentives to *smallness* and *localism* should become the norm and default, and they should replace the current set of incentives that favor the creation of entities that are "too big to fail." Anyone who believes that the years since 2008 demonstrate our greater "freedom" needs to have his pulse checked.

There are many other things that could be done, large and small. Front Porchers are not (at the moment) particularly well-versed in the kind of public policy that would be needed to help effect, or to support, a change in our current ways (and not all of us agree that a sane path includes a political or legislative dimension). I would think a fundamental change in subsidization of the automobile and trucking industry would be a good place to start (along with our more profound and troubling military and our imperial subsidizing of "cheap" oil), but I don't know exactly what that would look like. Before any legislative proposals can be launched, however, a change in mind must take place. And this is what I think needs to "be done" first, before any real political action of significance can get off the ground. Indeed, if we do our job well here, then I fully expect some much more interesting legislative and public-policy debates to follow (not the impoverished debates between proponents of "big government" and "big business"—as if they were really at odds). For the moment, what is being done here on the pages of this book—thought that resists the consolidating and dehumanizing spirit of the age—is the very thing that needs to be done. Read it while sitting on your front porch.

Part One

Departure and Return

To its fugitive children, Grand Republic will forgive almost anything if they will but come back home.

—SINCLAIR LEWIS, *CASS TIMBERLANE*

Look Homeward, Angels (and Others)
Bill Kauffman

THERE ARE FEW THINGS more presumptuous or annoying than strangers bearing advice. But I'll do it anyway. Well, perhaps this is not advice, exactly; I have an aversion to telling people how to live their lives. But I will suggest an option that runs counter to every popular notion of "success" in America. And that is: look homeward. Stay put. Or, in Booker T. Washington's marvelous phrase, cast down your bucket where you are.

That is a warning shot across the bow that I intend to wax, if not wane, autobiographical, but then, if I don't mythicize myself, who will? This is much easier to do when far from home. I live in Genesee County, New York, the rural county in which I was born and raised, in which my ancestors were born and lived and died, and there is a kind of "truth squad" effect of living in one's homeplace. You can't play the fey aesthete or the otherworldy artist when everyone remembers you as a snot-nosed kid misplaying a grounder in the Little League playoffs (it was a bad hop) or as Count No-Account, as his neighbors in Oxford, Mississippi called William Faulkner.

About ten years ago, I wrote a book titled *Dispatches from the Muckdog Gazette*, which is, megalomaniacally, a memoir about my repatriation to my hometown of Batavia. But it's also about the way that Batavia—and by extension all the Batavias from sea to dimming sea—have struggled to maintain a distinct identity, a character, rather than just becoming another washed-out blur in the great American nowhere.

This book reads as an angry love letter from a native son who desperately loves his hometown, who returned to live in, or just outside, that hometown, but who hates what has been done to it in his lifetime. Imagine watching, as a boy, as the center of your town is just knocked down, destroyed by the wrecking ball of federally sponsored urban renewal and a misguided faith in "progress," which is the one religion Americans are never permitted to mock. Batavia's city fathers were like the character in the poem by Robert Frost:

> To him the love of country means
> blowing it all to smithereens
> and starting all over again.

I am not from what you'd call a book-reading family, but I was blessed in that I grew up with a sense that my place, Batavia, had a history, a culture, an accent all its own. It was ravaged, it had often been mistreated, outsiders might think it a flavorless dump, but to me it had pith and soul and was a source of endless fascination. My dad used to tell us the stories, many of them libelous, behind the houses: we'd go around town and he'd say that's where the town whore lived (the fact that it was a distant relation complicated matters); that's where Father Kelly's fife and drum corps practiced; that's where Vinny the bookie set up, a guy who never did a day's work in his life. Parenthetically, there's a friend of mine who's a musician, also a repatriated native son. He and I say that's our ambition: that when we're old men we'll be walking down the street and fathers will point us out to their sons and say, "those two guys never did a day's work in their lives."

Ah, dare to dream.

Anyway, I grew up with the knowledge that Batavia contained the stuff of myth and drama and tragedy and farce—every story you could ever hope to tell. I knew that where I was from mattered, even if the corporate media relentlessly pound into the skulls of every kid who doesn't live in LA or Manhattan or DC the message that your life is a joke, it's trivial, why even bother to live if you're not smoking dope with Lindsay Lohan or talking Dianetics with Tom Cruise? In the warble of Belinda Carlisle, "This town is our town/It is so glamorous/Bet you'd live here if you could and be one of us."

Bet not.

I had always felt an intense homesickness no matter where I was. So in 1988, I persuaded my wife Lucine, a Los Angelena, that we should come home for what I said would be a one-year experiment. That year, it turns out, is measured in Old Testament terms, à la Methuselah. We're up to about March 4th.

I had worked prior to that as a legislative assistant to the legendary Senator Pat Moynihan and as a magazine editor in DC and Southern California before a vague suspicion that I had nursed since college concretized into a massive and unshakeable conviction: that a life lived anywhere but in my natal place would be insubstantial, evanescent, meaningless. So we went back.

(I should mention parenthetically that my Moynihan daze coincided for a couple of years with those of a recently canonized saint, Tim Russert. Oscar Levant said that he knew Doris Day before she was a virgin, and I knew Saint Timothy when he was a genial, backslapping, good-hearted but deadly serious political operative who picked off Moynihan's hapless Republican challengers like he was shooting aliens in a video game. He played hard and, if necessary, he played dirty. No one would have thought to fit him for a halo. It calls to mind Ambrose Bierce's definition of a saint as a dead sinner revised and edited.)

According to the pop-culture definition of success, going home is the act of a loser. Home may be where the heart is, but the body is usually long gone. In the typical American success story, the heart is the only organ that is *not* transplanted. These poisonous assumptions are even embedded in our language. Consider a pair of colloquialisms: "he'll go far," approving elders say of promising youngsters, the assumption being that success can be measured in terms of the distance one has travelled from home. If, on the other hand, we say of a boy, "he's not going anywhere," we are not praising him for his steadfast loyalty but damning him as an ambition-less sluggard. To stay loyal to one's little postage stamp of ground—there's no percentage in that. To abandon it, to trash it, to forget it—that's the freeway to American success. We are expected to look away, to prize the distant over the near-at-hand, to care more about Hollywood and Vine than Oak Street.

Well, absence may make the heart grow fonder, but love's truest, greatest expression, I have come to believe, is immobility. Fixity. Staying, not straying.

Yet the mobile rule.

The men and women who run the corporations, who tax and bomb from their Washington offices, who finance and make the films and TV shows and CDs from which so many of our children learn what is expected of them—they're the most hypermobile class there is. They haven't any ties to a particular place. Our ruling class is thoroughly deracinated—and there are consequences. Boy, are there consequences.

Our former president, lauded in 2008 as the "world candidate," was born in Hawaii, a state that is only in the union because of its military significance. (Hawaii's annexation, I'm proud to say, was vigorously opposed by that greatest of post-Civil War presidents, the corpulent Grover Cleveland of Western New York. Grover Cleveland: just another alcoholic Buffalo lardass sitting on a barstool cursing the Bills? I don't think so.) To my knowledge, when asked for favorite books, bands, etc., President Obama has never mentioned a Hawaiian writer or artist. Raised also in Indonesia and at various times resident in Los Angeles, New York City, and finally Chicago, Barack Obama is a "cosmopolitan," which by some lights means a sophisticate but which a character in Henry James's *Portrait of a Lady* defined as "a little of everything and not much of any. I must say I think patriotism is like charity—it begins at home." (The man Obama defeated in 2008, John McCain, is if anything even more placeless: a virtual poster boy for the manifold pathologies of the military brat.)

Why does this matter? What's wrong with electing competent but rootless people to public office? Because just as one cannot love the "human race" before one loves particular human beings, neither can one love "the world" unless he first achieves a deep understanding of his own little piece of that world. America is not, as the neoconservatives like to say, an idea: it is a place, or rather the sum of ten thousand and one little individuated places, each with its own history and accent and stories. A politician who understands this will act in ways that protect and preserve these real places. A rootless politico will babble on about "the homeland"—a creepy totalitarian phrase that, pre-Bush, was never applied to our country.

People lacking strong identifications with specific places—a block, a village, a city, a state, a region—will transfer their loyalties to abstractions. Woodrow Wilson, a displaced Southern minister's kid, renounced the traditional American practice of neutrality and tossed the First Amendment in the scrap heap in his crusade to "make the world safe for democracy." George W. Bush, the Texan-cum-Yankee prep-school cheerleader, wasted astronomical sums and thousands of lives in a campaign whose ostensible purpose was to "rid the world of evil." The costs of such grandiose schemes may be measured in trillions of dollars and acres of corpses. In addition, political power is centralized, citizens are uprooted, and the economy undergoes wartime distortions. But democracy was no safer despite the First World War, and I daresay evil will exist long after

U.S. troops come home from Iraq and Afghanistan. If they ever come home.

People with local attachments, by contrast, will ask the question that *never* gets injected into national debates over war and peace: What are the domestic costs of this crusade? Loving their block, they will not wish to bomb Iraq. Loyal to a neighborhood, they will not send its young men and women across the sea to kill and die for causes wholly unrelated to local life.

But don't mind me: I'm just an isolationist. I have no place in a national political discussion whose limits are defined by Arthur Schlesinger's ghost and Bill Bennett's ghostwriter.

Lincoln Colcord, the Maine novelist, saw his country losing itself as it took its place on the world stage. If America was everywhere, then it would be nowhere. To Colcord, home was Searsport, Maine, and his encomium upon it might stand as the creed of the whole Little American tradition: "It's not a bad place, much like many others, but the secret of our love for it lies in…[this]—we know it intimately. This is the lesson I get from Thoreau. Love your own pond. All are beautiful. Be contented where you are. Content!—a lost word in our America. This restless ambition—I cannot feel the truth of it. I cannot follow there."

Lacking "restless ambition." Loving your own pond. Being content. What a loser.

I'm not saying that one must stay in his or her hometown, though 'twould be nice if more stayed put. But I am saying that for a country or a place to be healthy, citizens need to have some attachment to it. Take some responsibility for it. If enough folks think that one place is pretty much the same as the next, and no place has any special value, then eventually you get a world in which that comes true—in which all places look alike, and streetscapes and idiosyncrasies and even sins descend to the same drab level of uniformity.

I seem to have strayed from autobiography and into sermonizing, but perhaps it is just as well. False memory syndrome is the occupational hazard of the memoirist. When I was writing *Dispatches from the Muckdog Gazette,* I seemed to recall my high-school days as a blur of four-touchdown games and passionate couplings with the head cheerleader. But I think I was remembering someone else's past.

We now live five miles north of Batavia in Elba, apt address for an exile. Lucine, my wife, is our town supervisor—and I like to think she may be the nation's highest ranking Armenian-American elected official, or at least she is until the voters of California send Kim Kardashian to the U.S. Senate. I should add that, as first husband, my role model is Mamie Eisenhower, not Hillary Clinton.

The local Republicans are indulgent of Lucine's non-Republican husband, but then in a healthy society politics plays so small a role in our lives that who really gives a damn how others vote? Cold ideologies melt in the warmth of daily communal life. I think of the local civic organizations in which, say, Assembly of God churchgoers and Daughters of Bilitis work side by side in the cheerful labor of neighbors. They can be friends because they are, to each other, rounded and fully dimensional persons, not caricatures. They are people, not cartoons. This is nigh impossible in larger places, where such disparate folk would never meet, and would exist to each other only on the flat screen of the TV set. Instead of Dave and Karen they would be "Right-wing Religious Nut!" and "Homo!" How numbing. How lifeless. How very Red & Blue.

Dana Gioia, the excellent California poet who by some strike of lightning became the chairman of the National Endowment for the Arts—appointed by George W. Bush, the least poetic president since . . . Bill Clinton?—anyway, Dana Gioia has a poem in which he walks through a California cemetery—depressing, treeless, stoneless, griefless places; no wonder people out there want to live forever. The poet hears the voices of the dead—the rootless dead:

> We lived in places we never knew.
> We could not name the birds perched on our sill,
> or see the trees we cut down for our view
> what we possessed we always chose to kill.

These shades—shades that cast no shadow—ask the poet, with a kind of despairing insistence:

> Become the voice of our forgotten places.
> Teach us the names of what we have destroyed.

Teach us the names of what we have destroyed.

It is our responsibility, our ennobling duty, to those who have gone before and those who will come after, to say the names, to tell the stories that attach to those names, to embroider those stories, to make poetry of the prosaic.

"America, turn in and find yourself," urged the Iowa poet Paul Engle. We are going to have to do this on our own, without any help from the TV networks, the newspaper chains, the corporate muzak labels. DIY, as the old punk rock ethos went: do it yourself. Community supported agriculture. Home brewing. Homeschooling. As we live through the early stages of the collapse of this rotten American Empire that is the enemy of the Little America, the soulful America, people are doing it themselves.

I'll give you an example or two from God's country. Batavia's not-so-favorite literary son was the 1970s novelist John Gardner, among the last American writers to grow up on a farm. Gardner had something of an ambivalent relationship with his hometown. When asked by an interviewer what function Batavia served in his fiction, he replied that it was "a good symbol . . . of the decline of western civilization."

It's kinda hard for the chamber of commerce to put *that* on a brochure.

Nevertheless, Gardner was ours. As another Upstate New York writer, the drunken scamp Frederick Exley, once said of his birthplace, "Watertown is not in my marrow—it *is* my marrow." So, too, with Gardner. And so every October we have an evening of Gardner readings in his favorite diner, the unselfconsciously funky Pokadot, outside which now sits our purple and yellow John Gardner bench, upon which you all are invited to sit your literate selves when next you're in our fair town. (Because Gardner's novel *The Sunlight Dialogues* begins with a wild man being arrested for painting LOVE at Batavia's Thruway exit, we were going to emblazon LOVE on the bench, but we feared that the passionate and randy youths of our amorous town might take it a bit too literally.)

I also wrote and played a role in our county's bicentennial play a few years ago. As an actor, I have all the emotional range of Desi Arnaz Jr., but few things have ever given me as much satisfaction as doing that play to packed houses, honoring our forbears, making myth of their lives at the same time we tried to celebrate the everyday moments of holiness in their—and our—lives.

These are small, person-to-person acts, I know. But I don't see how anything larger is practically possible or, should I say, desirable. You end up with a forest but no trees. As the painter John Sloan replied when asked if he favored a Federal Bureau of Art, "Sure, it would be fine to have a Ministry of the Fine Arts in this country. Then we'd know where the enemy is."

Bob Dylan's favorite poet, the South Carolinian Henry Timrod, commanded:

> Poet! if on a lasting fame be bent
> thy unperturbing hopes, thou wilt not roam
> too far from thine own happy heart and home,
> cling to the lowly earth, and be content.

Well, that's easier said than done, I suppose. Or maybe not. Maybe it's easier done than said. America, the legend goes, is a land of perpetual motion, of restless pioneers striking out for the west—or, in our time, of restive television addicts lighting out for Las Vegas with the mini-set in the SUV playing "Two and a Half Men" DVDs so that, unlike the Joads, members of this fambly don't have to talk to one another. We are, supposedly, always moving, never stopping, consumed by what William Cullen Bryant called "the vain low strife that makes men mad." And yet the best American writers—even those who follow their characters on rafts down the Mississippi, even those who title books *On the Road* or *You Can't Go Home Again*—are almost always attached to a place. Not simply a mailing address or a home page but a real, palpable place that's different from any other place on earth. Sarah Orne Jewett in South Berwick, Maine. Sinclair Lewis in Minnesota. Wendell Berry in Henry County, Kentucky. Thoreau in Concord. The list goes on and takes in every state, every region, and if it doesn't, alas, include every hill and vale in our lovely land, well that's all the more invitation for young writers to stake their claims. Write about *your world*—it matters.

I was very much struck by an incident a few summers ago, when we spent a day in Columbus, Mississippi, hometown of Tennessee Williams, a city of beautiful antebellum homes untouched by the war. The first place we stopped was a little restaurant. I am a hopeful romantic and expected to find wise old men, white and black, whittling on benches, and laconic loafers playing checkers and drawling wittily on courthouse steps, and tomboyish Nell Harper Lee hiding in the bushes, taking it all down. Eh, not quite. The first Columbian we encountered was a sullen youth from teenage central casting, playing the usual corporate schlock on his boombox. We entered the eatery and were seated behind four ladies with lovely and mellifluous Mississippi accents. They spent the next half hour recounting the plot of the previous night's episode of *Friends*, that smuttily witless show by which archeologists of the 23rd century will condemn our civilization. I wanted to confront them, to plead with them: "Look, here you are, daughters of a poor reviled state which is nevertheless one of the culturally richest states in the union; your home gave us the Delta blues, Eudora Welty, Shelby Foote, William Faulkner, Muddy Waters, and yet you consume the commercial products of cocaine-addled greedheads in Manhattan and Los Angeles, people who hate your guts, who despise you as ignorant crackers and stupid rednecks. Get off your knees, Mississippi! There are new Robert Johnsons and Eudora Weltys in your midst; support them. Look inward; look homeward. With a little help, the flowers in your own backyard will bloom a thousand times more brilliantly than anything on your high-definition TV set."

Well I didn't say this, being a polite Western New Yorker. But I wanted to. The tools of our revivification are at our feet, if we'd just look down. Look around. Every Main Street and Oak Street and Elm Street deserves its own record, its own poem. So where are they?

And now, as Lawrence Welk might say, a special message for the young people. If you have a kid and you sit him in front of the idiot box watching *The View* or MTV or CNN for hours at a time every day, the odds are he's going to grow up stupid and vulgar, a totally docile consumer, putty in the hands of advertisers, a patsy easily taken in by the wiles and lies of politicians. A subject of the empire, not a citizen of the republic. So give the kid a book or a baseball or a paintbrush or some seeds and a shovel or a field guide to the stars or the birds or the flowers. Give him a chance, for God's sake. (I speak here, of course, in the usual condition of semi-hypocrisy, knowing, as I do by heart, the words to the theme songs of both *The Brady Bunch* and *The Partridge Family*.)

Give the kid a baseball.

Batavia is a charter member of baseball's New York-Penn League, founded in 1939, one of the oldest minor leagues in the country. My dad was a batboy in the '40s. I grew up one block from Dwyer Stadium, named for the kindly Irish Catholic shoe store owner whose labors of love kept baseball alive in Batavia. It's been a gathering place across the generations, a place of fellowship and good cheer, and as vice president of the Batavia Muckdogs, a club perennially on the financial ledge, I'm trying to keep it alive now for those who'll follow, so that my daughter, with whom I have shared hundreds of soft summer nights in the third-base bleachers, may one day do the same with her children. It's those dreams of continuity that sustain one. Or sustain me, anyway. When I look out over the crowd I see the dead as well as the living. G.K. Chesterton spoke of a democracy of the dead. The presence of those who've gone before—it's not an annoyance, or a grimly obligatory pull. It hallows the places we live.

This is not to say they're Edenic. In fact, when you're living in a place rather than idealizing it at a distance—which is easy to do, and I've done it; as Lord Acton said, exile is the nursery of nationalism—you see, you even embrace, the imperfections. Consider our ill-fated Baseball Poetry Night, or as we called it, Shoving Culture Down Fans' Throats Night. Muckdogs President Brian Paris and I misconceived the idea a couple of years ago; with the recitative assistance of my daughter Gretel and our friend Pat Weissend, we filled the between-innings air of a game against the Auburn Doubledays with baseball verse by everyone from Charles Bukowski to Grantland Rice. My favorite was Bukowski's "Betting on the Muse," which begins, "Jimmie Foxx died an alcoholic in a skidrow hotel room." I thought of it as a cautionary tale for the boys.

Baseball Poetry Night was a catastrophe. My Batavia, God bless her, is poetry in repose to me, but as for poetry response . . . let's just say that when Brian asked the fans over the p.a. system, "Do you want another poem or a song?" the shouts of "Song!" rivaled the New Testament crowd's cry of "Free Barabbas!"

Or I think of a recent season when the team unwisely scheduled "Bill Kauffman Day." I thought every day was Bill Kauffman Day, but . . . I had to throw out the first pitch that night. A friend of mine who was a top aide to George W. Bush—friendship *always* trumps ideology—told me that Bush told him that *nothing* made him more nervous than throwing out the first pitch. Not massacring Iraqi children; not defecating on the Bill of Rights—nothing. Anyway, I shambled out to the mound, told the crowd over the mike that my brother had promised to buy everyone in the stands a beer if I threw a strike, and I threw a fastball right down the pipe. I think the radar gun clocked it in the low 80s—others estimated the mid-40s.

That night my daughter Gretel and her friend Megan sang the national anthem, and canorously. During the seventh-inning stretch, now unfortunately scored in so many ballparks by that empty cloud of bombast "God Bless America," the girls ignored post-9-11 protocol and instead sang my favorite, "America the Beautiful."

Gretel and Megan weren't past "Oh beautiful" when a heckler started in from the beer deck: "Wrong song! Wrong song!" The girls got a huge kick out of it. How many singers have ever been jeered during "America the Beautiful"?

So Batavia reminds me every day that it's an imperfect world. Flawed. But why are we here if not to love the damaged, the marred, each other? And how can we love each other unless we know each other, and how can we know each other unless we live in small communities, face to face? Otherwise we're just passin' through, man.

In Chesterton's wonderful novel *The Napoleon of Notting Hill*, a character explains his attachment to a seemingly ordinary neighborhood:

> I was born, like other men, in a spot of the earth which I loved because I had played boys' games there, and fallen in love, and talked with my friends through nights that were nights of the gods. And I feel the riddle. These little gardens where we told our loves. These streets where we brought out our dead. Why should they be commonplace? Why should they be absurd?... Why should anyone be able to raise a laugh by saying, 'the cause of Notting Hill?'—Notting Hill where thousands of immortal spirits blaze with alternate hope and fear.

Why indeed?

Notting Hill. Batavia. Our world is healthy only insofar as these places mean something. I saw the distinct identity—the meaning—of my own place fading and that's why I raised my voice.

Each of us needs a home, a place where we feel connected, feel a part of something bigger than just ourselves. Seldom does this home look like paradise; oft-times, as with my Batavia, perhaps with your piece of ground, home has been bent, folded, spindled, and mutilated almost out of existence. Self-mutilated, even. Home can seem, to outsiders, an unlovable place. But it is our task to love the unlovable, to find the sacred in the everyday.

I suppose there's a sense in which my books are a kind of voice of the forgotten America, the untelevised America, the America that the talking heads smugly assure us is dying, or deserves to be mercy-killed, the America of eccentric hicks and place-bound losers, rural Christians and working-class Catholics, neighborhood bars and people who live, or dream of living, in the house that they grew up in.

But maybe everything that dies someday comes back. We're behind 27–1 in the bottom of the eighth, but hey, ya never know. It ain't over till it's over. Someone might start the rally with a bunt single. And besides, maybe it's a doubleheader. I wouldn't switch teams even if I could. After all, our side is country churches and sandlot baseball and volunteer fire departments and backyard gardens and homemade beer. And home. Their side is bombs and tanks and television. How can we lose?

Birthright
Katherine Dalton

Every Memorial Day my husband, Mark, takes our children to visit family who lie in three cemeteries in Henry County. We take some grass from the farm for a great-grandfather, rhubarb for a great-grandmother, peonies and roses and whatever else is blooming. With these my daughters decorate the graves of family members that go back six generations. Someday perhaps we will discover where Conrad is buried, and then they will decorate a seventh.

As we drive around, my husband points out where all the extended family's farms have been over the years. In Campbellsburg's Masonic Cemetery we lay flowers on Cousin Kathryn, who told us so many family stories, and who is now a story herself. At the Antill cemetery, Mark realigns a broken stone and repeats again, in the hope it will sink into the girls' minds eventually, the line extending from Conrad to them.

My own dead are not here. But I too have deep roots in this state, and in cemeteries in Wayne County lie my father's parents and their parents and grandparents. Though I was born elsewhere, I have spent the bulk of my life here, in this state where so many other Daltons have lived, and I know one of the reasons I care about Kentucky is that Kentucky is where I belong.

Some people never leave home. Others go and then never return. But for me, as for many, it was love that called me back. This is the sort of argument that either needs no explaining or is inexplicable, but those who have ears can hear it: I had missed my family and old friends. I'd missed my grandfather's farm in Shelby County, and my old neighborhood outside of Louisville, and the way spring comes. I'd missed the manners here, and the things unsaid, and the idioms of my neighbors, and the dry humor my friend Bob Sexton has perfected—you can come home to language, too. I wanted to be around to hear Dr. Bob tell again about the blue Fugates and the blind Fugates, and to serve my great-grandmother Zona's pumpkin pie at Thanksgiving. I wanted to be closer to some of the people I'd buried. All of these things were tied up together in a great Gordian knot that I understood, finally, held me tight.

I could take an ax and sever it. I had tried to, the fall I moved away to college—because if I have always felt most at home here, I certainly haven't always known it. When I went off to Connecticut, I went shaking the dust of Kentucky off my feet. None of my plans included Kentucky, and in my mind the place I was going was like a garden in March: all potential and no weeds. But if travel is broadening to the mind, what broadened for me was my affection for what I had left. Living up north, I came to realize as I never had at home what was valuable back in Kentucky, and what was unreproducible elsewhere, and just where it was I was from.

Moving back to the place where you've grown up gives you an instant increase in what sociologists call social capital—the academic term for the web of associations that bind people in a community to each other. A strong social network has practical benefits and will generally make you happier, and it brings both understanding and a sense of fittingness. You are in a place that is culturally familiar. You're living in a landscape that, if not overbuilt and polluted, will feel right because it was imprinted on your brain when you were a child. Perhaps most importantly, you will pick up the thread of lives of many people you already know. We need to live a long time in one place in order to understand people at all, and surely one of the points of living is to acquire the charity that can come with such understanding—the charity that begins at home.

That doesn't mean rootedness will make you a better or wiser person in and of itself, but it does offer an ordering to the mind, a sense of belonging and a (mostly) willing sense of obligation that might make you saner. I think it's enriching, too. Every community has its own cultural diversity, which it keeps only if it can hold onto its people. Memory is one of the things that makes us most human, but to move is to lose touch with so much of it: family anecdotes, old associations with places, local stories, children's rhymes and games, knowledge of the soil and how the land lies, history, recipes. If we move away, we can only maintain those things artificially and with effort, and generally we get busy, and there is no one to remind us how the great-uncles fell out, or whether the Battle of Perryville was fought in the spring or the fall, or the way the cousins cooked ham, and so we lose lots of this community- and family-specific culture of ours. Many young adults move away expressly to become more original, only to find they become less of what they are. When someone leaves it is not just the neighborhood that is diminished but the individual. The best people are not made from scratch.

I am not alone in my desire to raise a glass to the "stickers" (as Wallace Stegner called them), but I am alone enough. In the national press we hear relatively little about the gains of staying home, and lots about the negatives. Ours is a culture that either celebrates all the possible pluses of moving, or shrugs its shoulders at the assumed necessity, and there is no question the economic deck is stacked against any place that isn't hip or large or both. The argument is often couched in economic and so-called quality-of-life terms, as if our income and our entertainment were the essential deciding factors of the value of our lives. In *Who's Your City,* Richard Florida spends a few pages acknowledging the value (to some) of remaining rooted, but devotes the rest of the book to describing the best places for your type of personality at your particular stage of life. His assumption is we can happily leave most human relationships behind, or squeeze out all their juice in an annual visit. But our ties to a certain place and certain people are not so easily compressed or replaced.

If the argument for moving away is that you must "Be All That You Can Be," well, that's the slogan of the Army, one of the great deracinating institutions of modern life, whose organizational purpose—whatever its necessity and merits—is to kill people. If we're picking slogans here, I much prefer (with thanks to writers Bill Kauffman and Caleb Stegall, revivers of the phrase) Cast Down Your Bucket Where You Are.

Of course there are some people who don't have a place to go home to. They had Navy officers or corporate nomads for parents, or their small town or family farm or city neighborhood has been hollowed out or developed or urban-renewed beyond recognition, and the neighbors are gone, too. But most people move because there's a new job in that city by the sea, or the old job demands that they go, or the children now live in Texas, and not because there is nowhere to return to. After a few years of wandering, perhaps some of these people will make one last move and stick. It is not a terrible thing, to move and resettle. Every civilization (and every barbarity) has had its share of homesteaders. You can take hold in a new place and dig in, and certainly sticking where you've moved is the next-best choice to staying where you're from.

But I would argue it's only a next-best. You can't choose your roots any more than you can choose your gene pool. If you are from somewhere, that's where you're from. No one becomes a Bostonian by moving to Boston—your children may be able to assert the title, thinly, but not you. If you move, you start over, for a clean slate has nothing on it. And it will take the rest of your life in your new place to build the web of relationships you had as a free birthright in the old place. Plus you'll never get your family back, unless by some luck they all follow you out.

That is the fate—often freely chosen—of a lot of people, including a lot of people I love. Few of them are miserable. Some of them would say they feel more at home in the new place, and some have moved to their wife's or husband's home, and in any case it is not my wish to argue with anyone on so personal a matter. As Elizabeth Bennett said to her father, I am complaining not of peculiar but of general evils. I do think a people that celebrates newness over roots is at risk of losing whatever culture it has managed to retain. I also think those who resettle best are the ones who follow the advice Wendell Berry gave a man who asked him, years ago, where a person who has no hometown should go. Mr. Berry told him to stay put.

As for those of us fortunate enough both to have a hometown and to live in it: I don't want to overstress the "free" before birthright. Birthright is a gift the way a free horse is a gift—there's going to be plenty of work involved, and it may get expensive. Wes Jackson called one of his books *Becoming Native to This Place*, and I believe part of what that native Kansan meant by the title was earning his roots. Belonging to a place is never a one-way relationship, in which it gives and you get. Belonging requires involvement, and it must mean also all the rights and obligations of what we used to call citizenship, before politicians generally identified us as "the American people" (a passive term) or marketers targeted us as "consumers" (to our belittlement).

In Mr. Jackson's case becoming native has meant years of farming, biological research, and political involvement, focused in Kansas but extending a good ways beyond it. How well can you be a citizen of a place that's new to you? Those who have done it have done it by staying, and I think real citizenship is hard until the new place has become an old place. When I lived in New York City, I never voted in a local election. What did I know about the city council, and what had I learned to care? Even then I felt that whatever my legal right to vote was, I didn't have much of an ethical one. I was too new and knew too little. If I had stayed in New York, I'd know something by now. But the ability to be a moderately informed voter, or neighbor, doesn't come with a change of address card.

In *I'll Take My Stand* and *Who Owns America?* the Southern Agrarians argued again and again about the importance of real property—by which they meant something like a piece of land or a business, which is under a person's control to make or mar, and not something like a stock, which is property in the much more limited sense of something that can only be bought and sold. For them the important connection was between real property and liberty. When Andrew Lytle wrote the essay "The Small Farm Secures the State," he was arguing that only real property brings the economic independence that makes for a free citizen. A man who earns a salary works at someone else's pleasure and under someone else's thumb. A farmer (or a small businessman) works and votes for himself.

The corollary to that argument is that real property is a rooted thing—again, as opposed to a stock or bond, which exists as a promise on a screen and whose ultimate connection to some touchable asset may be splintered and nearly impossible to determine. Small businesses move, but not so often, and typically not far. Farmers move, but even less often, and most farmers will consider long and hard before leaving behind years of soil-amending and fence-building: farming is perhaps the quintessential "sticker" profession. And from such stickers come (be they farmers or not), in towns both large and small, the majority of city councilmen and school board members and civic volunteers. The new people, however virtuous they are, are still figuring things out, and finding the grocery, or deciding if they really want to stay.

Kentucky, bless her, is a relatively unpopulous, provincial, and unprogressive state. But even she is in the midst of a sea change in her makeup and her thinking that has everything to do with the incredible mobility of Americans and with immigration. It has become un-American—and puts you in some danger of being called intolerant—to argue that a spanking-new Kentuckian recently imported from another country or even from nearby Indiana is less Kentuckian than someone with roots here. And given this national chariness of ours, you will look high and low before you find someone to contradict publicly the notion that the Kentucky point of view—Kentuckianness, if you will—is either something one acquires quickly upon entry and residence, or just doesn't matter very much. This really does signify an important cultural change here, for this has always been a state terribly proud of its rough childhood, its Indian raids and Indian blood, its Long Hunters and river towns, its veterans from both sides of the Civil War and all the other wars, its burgoo and horses and coal, its songs and storytellers.

But let's flip that argument over and ask: if a Hoosier becomes a Kentuckian instantly upon arrival, does that mean that years of living in one place have no effect on a person's view of himself as part of that place? No effect on his affections or his loyalties, or—even if he still hates the town, after twenty years' residence—no effect nonetheless on his ties to it and his understanding? No one would argue that. To argue that is to argue that our experience of living has no meaning for our lives.

That won't prevent some people from telling you till they're as blue as a Fugate that cherishing the idea of rooted Kentuckianness is just so much sentimentality. Yet if there is anything living in one place will cure you of, it's sentimentality. I have lived in Kentucky much too long to be misty-eyed about it. No intimate relationship with a person or a place is ever simple or in any way static—for good or ill. No one is ever fully at home in the sense of being fully at ease, and we can't say we weren't warned of that, either: I will not try to speak for other faiths, but Christians are reminded frequently that at its best this world is only a partial answer to hope.

Living fully and open-eyed in one place is like sticking to one church: often Sunday morning is less a source of comfort than it is an exercise in charity, patience, and (if we can keep the beams out of our eyes) the acknowledgement of our own pride and fault Yes indeed, there may be a pulpit or a place out there that is in some senses "better." But it may not be better for us. Or it may simply not be the place where we've been called. If you are going to love your neighbor, you must know your neighbor, and to know your neighbor you have to stick around. You can wish a stranger well, but wishes are cheap, while love—an active verb in the demanding sense intended by the Christian understanding of "charity"—is the real coin.

The Greeks, restless as they were, understood all about home. They imagined Odysseus, who journeyed for years and abandoned a goddess to return to a wife who was no longer young, and to a small and rocky island. They also imagined Antaeus, who grew weak when he could no longer touch his own Mother Earth. For them ostracism was a serious matter, a kind of social death, and they hated it. In the Louisville newspaper a while back, a professor praised Socrates as one of the first "world citizens." Good Greek that he was, he was precisely the opposite. He might be a "world citizen" in the sense the whole world wishes to claim him now, but while he lived he himself only claimed Athens, and he lived and died under obligation to his native city. Offered a chance to escape after being condemned for impiety, he preferred to stay to drink the hemlock because, he argued, having grown up and flourished under Athens' laws, he would not flout them even when they ordered his execution. He was a man so tightly bound to the city he had pricked and prodded all his life that he was content to let her put him to death. It would be a worse death, he said, to leave.

That is an extreme view, and an extremely virtuous view. But surely it is the right idea, that we should spend our lives in the place that nurtured and made us, and where we would be happy both to live (prodding away) and to die.

The Orphans of Success and the Longing for Home

Jason Peters

> *Home is where one starts from. As we grow older*
> *The world becomes stranger, the pattern more complicated*
> *Of dead and living. Not the intense moment*
> *Isolated, with no before and after,*
> *But a lifetime burning in every moment*
> *And not the lifetime of one man only*
> *But of old stones that cannot be deciphered.*
> —T.S. Eliot, "East Coker"

ONE OF THE DIREST consequences of that great liberal affliction known as hypermobility is that many parents must raise their children in the absence of grandparents, uncles, aunts, and cousins. Familial ties are so attenuated, and familial influences so muted, that children scarcely know *who* they are, much less *where* they are.

That such ties and influences can be problematic I fully acknowledge. I certainly don't share all the views of the kinfolk and the in-laws, who for all I know think of going to the polls not as a civic duty but as a way to cancel out my vote. But to say that familial ties and influences can be problematic is simply to say that all ties and influences can be problematic, just as they might also be salutary. So add to the list of permanent things parental vigilance and the daily task of debriefing the children.

But I do think it is socially injurious that so many people—and they are usually considered very "successful"—raise their children in the absence of their extended families. And I expect the consequences of this to be more devastating than we've yet imagined—and more devastating still if it turns out that we are too myopic to notice them. To be blind and not know it is to be doubly impaired.

Such perhaps was I on the day my elder son appeared in the rear-view mirror, nine years old and crying in the back seat. We were leaving to go "home," and he was crying because, as he said, he was "going to miss everyone so much"—where "everyone" meant the grandparents and cousins we had driven four-hundred miles to visit. Later that evening, still in the thrall of his grief and shaken by it and wondering how to name it, I began to think of my son as an orphan of success, an orphan among many such orphans, including his siblings. And then things began to pile up; the file of evidence against me began to thicken.

For example, there was the opportunity I had a year or so later of sharing over cigars and drinks several stories about my grandfather with my dad and his older brother. What I know about my grandfather, who died when I was a boy, has been sketched and colored by the stories and yarns that I am the lucky auditor of, most of which have been told to me by the three sons my grandfather sired, stories about building the milk house and driving the team and crossing the river to retrieve stray cows from a neighbor's field and the thousand other natural shocks a farmer's heir to. But under my own domestic arrangements at the time of this symposium, arrangements characterized by a professorship far from home, I realized how unlikely it was that my children would know their uncles as I have known mine, and this would certainly mean that their knowledge of their grandfather would also be limited. That my own sons would ever duplicate this story-telling session with my brother and me seemed unlikely, as unlikely as their knowing their grandfather not just immediately but also through the same or similar forms of mediation, which are not merely supplemental but necessary.

For at the time my brother was also far away: one branch of the armed forces had done an exemplary job of keeping him loyal to a powerful abstraction. His talent, like my mine, had been needed elsewhere, so elsewhere we both had gone. For twenty years he and I spoke infrequently and saw each other even less. My sister too had been sent away, though indirectly, following her husband as our deracinating State Department moved him from one foreign country to another. Bureaucratic monsters are just clever enough to know that if you move a man every two years he'll have little choice but to swear his fealty not to any place but to an uncle known as "Sam"—"Sam," who has never smoked a cigar, sipped a bourbon, or told a joke; he has no father or grandfather; he never built his own milk house or walked behind a team or retrieved a stray cow.

If the forces that conspired to pull us apart were legion, they were each attended by justifications—"at least you have your careers"—that only a rootless technocrat could dream up. One, predictably, is that the market compensates us; another, equally predictable, is that technology performs this sacred compensatory duty. My response to the first is that anyone who falls for such a ruse is a few evolutionary stages shy of walking upright—and in consequence not fully suited to contemplate the heavens. It is not for nothing that Mammon is the "least erected Spirit that fell / From Heav'n."[1] My response to the second is that a man has an array of dissenting authorities he might appeal to, from Socrates to David Kline. Even Freud wrote tellingly of that "factor of disappointment" we tend to experience in the "technical application" of the sciences;[2] "mankind has made an extraordinary advance" and "established his control over nature in a way never before imagined." But men "seem to have observed that this newly-won power over space and time, this subjugation of the forces of nature, which is the fulfillment of a longing that goes back thousands of years, has not increased the amount of pleasurable satisfaction which they may expect from life and has not made them feel happier." Freud anticipated a few objections: that there is both pleasure and happiness in being able, whenever you want, to hear your child's voice from hundreds of miles away. And there is the longevity we enjoy because of improvements in medicine—to this day a favorite with the statisticians preaching liberty to the regressive captives. But "here the voice of pessimistic criticism makes itself heard," Freud said. It calls these enjoyments "cheap." They are like

> putting a bare leg from under the bedclothes on a cold winter night and drawing it in again. If there had been no railway to conquer distances, my child would never have left his native town and I should need no telephone to hear his voice.... And, finally, what good to us is a long life if it is difficult and barren of

---

1. *Paradise Lost*, I.679–80.

2. Sigmund Freud, *Civilization and its Discontents* in *The Complete Psychological Works of Sigmund Freud* (London: Hogarth, 1961), Vol. 21, 87.

joys, and if it is so full of misery that we can only welcome death as a deliverer?[3]

I will return to this presently, but for the moment all I wish to say is that, although I make a comfortable living and live a life made comfortable by the "technical application" of the sciences, and although I am the grateful beneficiary of this application, the compensatory powers of money and technology do not impress me much. They make an appeal far beyond their merits. And they could hardly be regarded as transcendent values for someone who had this to show for his success: parents, four of them well into life's fifth act, wondering who would look after them in the coming uncertain years.

For this was now on my mind, thanks to another event that got me thinking about the consequences of raising the orphans of success. It occurred a few years after that story-telling session with my dad and uncle, but it harkened back to a conversation I had with a friend and former colleague of mine who once asked me whether my parents had anyone to look after them in their old age. I told him that, were I to do it, I would probably have to leave the teaching profession. His response to this was swift and unequivocal: he said I should be willing to pay that price for them.

He said this because, nearing retirement himself, he was alone in the world: no parents, no siblings, and, being a bachelor, no children. Handing himself over to the institutions was on his mind, which was then still very keen.

Nearly two decades after he gave me his swift unequivocal response, my wife and children and I were again visiting our families in late August when both my mother and my mother-in-law became seriously ill. My wife, a nurse, having the benefit of useful knowledge, proposed that she stay in Michigan to help put things in order, that I return to Illinois to get the children back in school, and then prepare for the start of my own school year. And that is what we did.

Our mothers pulled through, but this episode got us thinking about things we had put off thinking about, save at the odd moment when I would mention a piece of land I'd seen—I'd been wanting something like my grandfather's farm for many years—and my wife would wisely put the matter to rest by saying she wasn't going to go through the trouble of

---

3. *Ibid*, 87–8.

moving again until we moved home, where four parents, who deserved our attention, were for all practical purposes like my friend and former colleague: childless and in their downward years.

The episode also got us thinking about other matters: not only what a terrible thing it is to raise children in the absence of their grandparents, but also what a terrible thing it is to deprive your own parents of the company of their grandchildren. The list of reasons to think of our children as the orphans not of success but of failure grew longer, and grew apace.

Then a small run-down farm looking for all the world like a meth lab came available. It was a ten-minute walk through the woods from one ancestral house and fewer than four miles from the other. The place was a mess—I would end up gutting the house—but also so cheap that we felt as if we were losing money if we didn't buy it. And so in a kind of Byzantine fashion we cobbled together enough money to buy the place—and then did.

And then we moved. After a fashion. For I did not leave the profession or quit my job or do anything else that a person might point to as evidence of full-blown lunacy. But this did inaugurate slightly new living arrangements: for nine months each year, minus holidays and most weekends, I am the very emblem of the modern condition, which is to be away from home, a localist living a life of hypocrisy, my hypocritical life unrelentingly on Red Alert thanks to the 80–94 corridor in northern Indiana, save when I make use of a passenger rail system that, as Jim Kunstler says, the Bulgarians would be ashamed of.

Not that the return has been without abundant recompense. My son, the one in the rear-view mirror, attends our high school and has a legitimate shot at breaking his old man's scoring record, now into its fourth decade. And making Methlehem livable was and continues to be great fun. It's work I enjoy and, because of my schedule, have time to devote to. But there have been complications. For example, there is the shock, after a long exile, of family-in-concentrate. Life can seem a bit like an unending family reunion, and a family reunion, as everyone knows, is one of those gatherings at which you must listen politely for long stretches of time to people who are utterly defenseless against bad politics and worse religion.

And it turns out that if you know how to do things, then notwithstanding your own chores you end up working for a lot of people for free, though of course it was in order to be useful that we made this move in the first place.

Then there are the little irritants of placelessness and hypermobility. I find myself in the uncomfortable—but, I hope, temporary—position of opposing in theory what in practice I now have little choice but to enact.

And there is the question of whether otherwise normal adults should deprive their children several days a week of contact with both parents—especially if the parents are already outnumbered and have to back off each morning into a zone defense—or whether a marriage should endure such a breach, a breach that is clearly not that expansion like gold to airy thinness beat of which John Donne wrote.

And if you think of what you do not as a career but as a vocation, as I try to do, especially allowing the word its full theological significance, and notwithstanding the changes that significance suffered, at least in its American career, from John Cotton to Benjamin Franklin, then it is no small matter to "leave the profession," as I put it so long ago. And if the decision to do one thing somewhere instead of another thing somewhere else introduces an indifferent kind of calculus to the matter, I think the math should at least be honest. Most of us have known people who couldn't wait to leave home and who couldn't stay gone long enough: the professor, for example, who hails from a small town but who learns at college to despise the place. Perhaps he leaves because he hates its pervasive mulishness or endemic racism, and good for him for condemning them. But let us not forget that the place has been abandoned by someone who might have done it some good—even though the same person may now be doing good of a different kind elsewhere. *All* of this has to go on the books. And if a Ph.D. candidate in philosophy, realizing what a professorship will mean for his children—namely, their uprooting—decides instead to study law so that he can practice it nearer his extended family, there will, very likely, be losses and gains all around. And all of those must go on the books if he is to calculate on honest net gain.

And this is why, *mutatis mutandis*, the problem of vocation proves difficult: we tend to think of the *what* in isolation from the *where* and *for whom*—of lawyering simply, not of lawyering *somewhere* to serve *these people in particular*—and thus we ignore, if not beg, certain questions, perhaps even questions of priority. We do this as if the meaning of *vocation* had not been hammered out long before the rootless succeeded the meek as inheritors of the earth. If the philosopher-lawyer has a mind to allow for such a thing as a calling, and therefore a Caller as well, then he won't be the sort of man who simply lets the answering machine pick up: "If you are calling to offer me this job for this amount of money, press 1." For in all likelihood the person who does that will leave both the *where?* and *for whom?* unanswered, maybe even failing in the process to allow for the freedom that comes from within and the disruptions that obtrude from without. He has gone from being John Cotton to Benjamin Franklin. He has a career instead of a calling, and he is in danger of being found dead in the wrong thing.

But if the philosopher-lawyer answers not only to what he has been *called* to do but also to where he believes he has been called to *be*, and to what he has *chosen* according to his best lights to do there, and for *whom*, then he has, I think, demonstrated a capacity to be supple- and large-minded about vocation. He has dignified it by refusing to simplify it. He has also preserved his own dignity by honoring the human capacity to answer—to *reply*—instead of just letting the machine pick up. I once heard a Trappist monk talk about his calling, and he put it this way: "it was as if God were saying to me, 'I won't require you to be a priest, but of course I would be very pleased indeed should you choose to be one.'" This monk took, I think, a proper accounting of how vocation must be tempered by human freedom. And as for the lawyer, his children may "lack opportunities," of course, and those must go on the books, but his children might not have to suffer as orphans of success. And that too must be a part of the bookkeeping.

For I would come round again to the orphans. Say I am fulfilled as a professor. Good for me. Say my students benefit from my "answering a call." Fine. These are measurable—and perhaps immeasurable—gains. But they are gains offset by losses, losses that my children and their grandparents and uncles and aunts and cousins (and I) incur. They may even be losses that my students incur, for who knows what better talent might have stood at the front of my classrooms? It's not as if we aren't, all of us, playing a kind of numbers game. To some extent we are.

But while we're at play, inattentive as usual, it does seem as if a thing called "grace"—by definition unmerited—is also at play. That's the lucky part. That's the *saving* grace. And so the real question, given the rampant hypermobility I both deplore and practice, is whether we careerists are content to put our own personal "gains" ahead of the losses of many others, including our children's and parents'. That is what still bothers me. It bothers me that, whatever the gains in our current arrangements, material or otherwise, there remain these orphans of success.

Which brings me back to Freud, who at the very least was making a gesture in the direction of the kind of honest bookkeeping I am talking about. Yes, we enjoy train travel and long distance communication and longevity. But what about the fact that "we do not feel comfortable in our present-day civilization"?[4] I would like to see an exacting and honest bookkeeping brought to bear on *all* things, as much to the problem of vocation as to progress and civilization itself.

So home-going comes with complications. My wife and I sometimes look at each other and marvel that two otherwise sensible people could have gone and done something so patently stupid.

But I wish to say plainly that we wanted to go home, that the reasons for going home and the opportunity to do so aligned, like Jupiter and Mars in the age of Aquarius, and that we had what was necessary to do so: the means, the guts, the wherewithal, and the stupidity. So we did it.

And then a couple of years into all this my father died—at home, surrounded by his family. Our children therefore had two years of close association with him, and he with them, that they would not have had apart from our being so gutsy and stupid. And because of those accruing benefits marked by one great loss, I have stopped worrying about repatriation. Not that any given decision extinguishes all moral examination, but I'm happy with the misery, except as often as twice each week on the Interstate Highway and Defense System—tenuously joining together what it first put asunder—where legions of lead-footed idiots on cell phones are trying to kill me.

That is all I want to say about the enterprise of repatriation as an actual event and a crisis of conscience. I now want to venture off into a brief flight of anagogy.

I've quit trying to convince myself that human action doesn't strike on another plane—call it a "higher" plane if you will. The Southern novelist Flannery O'Connor did, but then she had an analogical imagination. Nothing sank to mere idolatry for her; everything had something on the other side of it. Everything was an image. Likewise, St. Augustine did not think of the earthly city without thinking of its analog, the heavenly city—our true home, on his account—from which we are as it were

---

4. Freud, *Civilization*, 89.

exiled, and toward which our earthly pilgrimage takes us. Nor could St. Augustine speak of memory except in terms of how it alone reveals a pattern that we ourselves didn't weave and cannot, apart from memory, recognize. We may be looking and solving for pattern, but the patterns of a life may not be of our own making only. It is worth remembering that on this point Hamlet was insistent.

Now I share with the young Augustine of the pinched pear more than I share with St. Augustine of *The City of God*, but like him and because of him I am unable to think about homecoming without placing it in a larger story, without speaking of such amorphous but necessary things as *belonging* and *restoration* and *wholeness*, all of which had seemed to some extent missing from my life when my son appeared weeping in the rear-view mirror.

And for similar reasons I am unable to use the word "nostalgia"—a word that means "a hurt for home"—pejoratively, as apparently I'm supposed to. "Nostalgia," you may have noticed, must always be followed by the phrase "for a past that never existed"—even though that past did exist and still does in some places. My view is that we should hurt for home, for both the vehicle and the tenor of it, and that we should long for a past that did exist. And so I have endeavored to think of my whole homegoing enterprise as yet another effort to live on more than one plane of existence at a time.

I realize that I am very lucky to have been able to do what I've done. I realize that home is maybe not so place-specific for those who know *where* they are and know how to *be* where they are. But homegoing has been no small thing for us. To borrow from Emerson, it has been not whimsical but fatal—not indifferent but decisive. And it has brought considerable joy to three people, at one time to four, who qualify as "old," as I will in due time.

I also realize that there are people who regard all this analogical stuff, this living one life inside a larger one, as utter nonsense. They are the literalists and hard-headed realists who keep me from "leaving the profession." It is from them that I am trying to *rescue* the profession.

And, finally, I realize that most people would be utterly flummoxed by my premise: that raising children in the absence of their extended families will lead to consequences more devastating than we've yet imagined. And the perplexity stems, I think, from how fully reconciled we are to the rootlessness and hypermobility that characterize the age but that lack the benefit of time's imprimatur. My father, may he rest in soft peace, was fond of saying that it doesn't take long for the abnormal to seem normal. So I will say it again: I think the consequences of our new normality will be more devastating still if it turns out that we are too myopic to notice them. To be blind and not know it is to be doubly impaired.

I mentioned Flannery O'Connor a moment ago, so let us consider her on the topic of going home. In her first novel, *Wise Blood*, the narrator tells us that the hero, Hazel Motes, harbors a misery, but that the misery he has is a "longing for home"; it has "nothing to do with Jesus."[5] When the novel opens Hazel simply wants to go to his home town, Taulkingham, and he is journeying by train, somewhat restlessly, to get there. His longing, so far as he knows, has nothing analogical about it. But when we readers turn the final pages of the novel we know that Hazel is journeying to the heavenly city, even if he himself is only dimly aware of this. And by this point his longing has everything to do with Jesus, because, of course, he's been visited by grace—or, if you prefer, *victimized* by it, as seems to be the case with many of O'Connor's characters. Home is where you start from, as Eliot said, but in this novel, given the proper longing, it is also where you're headed.

Wise Blood is a repatriation story. It is a retelling, in a grim zoo-like world, of the old pilgrimage narrative, which we find in both the Old and New Testaments. It is also in St. Augustine, who stamped it on Western consciousness. It's in Homer, in Dante, in Chaucer, and Shakespeare; it's in the novels of Walker Percy, Evelyn Waugh, and Graham Greene. It's everywhere you find that sense of the comic structure of history. In that pilgrimage narrative the purpose of the journey—that is, the purpose of life itself—is transformation: being worthy of the destination. As Hazel Motes discovers—for he is being transformed—escaping it is difficult, even here in the post-Christian and post-literate West, where the Bible, for all its neglect, still somehow manages to assert itself. The Bible is a book that moves hopefully from chaos to order and ends, as comedies do, in a marriage feast—in a restoration of the social and even the cosmic order. And in O'Connor, who once reminded us that somewhere is better than anywhere, the longing for home is not merely a longing for home. It is that plus something else.[6]

---

5. Flannery O'Connor, *Wise Blood* (New York: Farrar, Straus & Giroux, 1952), 24.

6. I offer a fuller explanation of this in "'The Beginning of Something': *Wise Blood*, St. Augustine, and the Tradition of Catholic Comedy" in *Anamnesis* 6 (2017), 89–121.

If the longing for home isn't itself plus something else—if art is symbolic but a life is not—then, as O'Connor said in another context, "to hell with it!"[7]

---

7. "[N]ow she thought of it [the Eucharist] as a symbol and implied that it was a pretty good one. I then said, in a very shaky voice, 'Well, if it's a symbol, to hell with it.'" See O'Connor, *The Habit of Being*, ed. Sally Fitzgerald (New York: Farrar, Straus & Giroux, 1979), 125.

Part Two

Politics and Economics

Our centrist civilization, which has become more and more remote from man and human scale, has reached the point where its own continued existence is at stake.

—Wilhelm Röpke, *A Humane Economy*

Federalism, Anti-Federalism, and the View from the Front Porch

Jeff Polet

American cheerfulness and belief in unlimited progress augur against a tragic sense of history. At the heart of American exceptionalism is a denial of the pattern governing every other civilization: rise and fall, birth and flowering, each age objectively better than the one that preceded it. And so Americans are particularly suspicious of declension narratives. Such untrammeled optimism is bound to generate skepticism, the opposition to the progressive ideology being a supposedly conservative theory of decline. America was born correctly, the theory goes, but lost its way under the big government reforms of the 20th century, and the only way forward is the way back. To restore America to its original promise, which is to say its original greatness, requires a recovery of the ideas and beliefs of those who founded this country. If only we could read the Constitution in the light of the Framer's self-understanding, and govern ourselves accordingly, then America could restore its own luster and claim its presumptive place as the City on the Hill.

But is America's founding really that simple? And does the Constitution really work better if we understand it as the Framer's did? What if, rather than viewing the Constitution as a consensual monolith, we see it as the result of differing views of a political community, one view having largely won out over the other? And what if the "losers" had a better view? This essay considers that possibility. It supposes that the losers, whom history calls the Anti-Federalists, had a proper respect for place, limits, and liberty and the extent to which a healthy democracy depends on them. In other words, the political thinking that animates the Front Porch is not something new, but a hearkening back to classic American republican and localist ideas. These ideas were in some way incorporated into our political order, but also undone in other ways, by the combination of financial, military, and liberal interests that found a surer place for themselves under the Constitution than they did under the Articles of Confederation.

There is good reason to assume that even the most aggressive nationalist of the founding period could not have imagined the current configuration of American politics. What are the defining features of that configuration? Any list would have to include America's expansive military empire. It would have to include America's crippling fiscal problems and also an increasingly sclerotic social welfare system funded largely through public debt. It would also have to include the deepening of America's cultural problems: the dissolution of the natural family, increasingly contentious political rhetoric, the decline of free associations, and a lack of public spiritedness. It would have to include an economy that tends toward exploitation, concentration of wealth, and mismanagement of resources. It would have to account for widespread alienation.

Robert Nisbet identified the American propensity for war, bureaucratic centralization, and the advent of the "loose individual" as defining features of the age. These features, already visible in the mid-20th century when Nisbet wrote *The Present Age*, have become more pronounced.[1] In short, our contemporary crisis does not represent a change of course for America so much as a natural progression of American experience, which was sent into hyper-drive after the fall of communism.

One of the effects of the Roman victory in the Punic Wars was the eventual collapse of the Roman republic, its modest governmental structure designed for a city-state now forced to adjust to a large commercial and military empire. Carthage played a vital role in maintaining Roman limits. So long as Carthage presented an alternate political and economic power, it forced Rome to restrain its worse impulses toward financial profligacy, personal hedonism, and military conquest. It was left to those such as Cato, who didn't desire greatness or power, to understand that intemperateness would mean the end of liberty and ultimately the end of Rome itself.

---

1. Robert Nisbet, *The Present Age: Progress and Anarchy in Modern America* (Indianapolis: Liberty Fund, 2003).

The person perhaps most responsible for the defeat of Carthage, Cato the Elder (noted for celebrating the life of agrarian virtue), begot Cato the Younger, who was most responsible for trying to maintain Republicanism in the face of Caesarism. The latter became the subject of Joseph Addison's famous play.[2] Besides being the source of Patrick Henry's "liberty or death" speech, Addison's *Cato* argued for modesty in politics, piety in religion, and virtue in action. The play also reflected the waning tradition wherein "all our frugal ancestors were blest/In humble virtues, and a rural life."[3] Addison depicts Cato as the defender of liberty grounded in virtue and connected to a life of self-sufficiency and modest aims. "The conquered world" was Caesar's: the realm of untrammeled desire, conquest, lust, and civil war. Glory and history-making were juxtaposed to the charms of simple living, those pursuing the former comfortable with evil and those pursuing the latter seeking virtue.

Cato also became the pseudonym for one of the leading critics of the Constitution (likely George Clinton of New York), who summarized many of the arguments against consolidation.[4] The central issue involved Publius' claim, in favor of consolidation, that it was left to the fledgling Americans to reconcile personal liberty to an energetic government that was the friend of commerce. Publius would trump the adherents to the Articles of Confederation, who emphasized virtuous and small republics, in favor of an energetic and efficient government that would relocate power in a centralized administrative state over an extended territory.

Is such centralization the result of choice and reason, as Hamilton suggests in Federalist 1, or did it result from ineluctable historical forces? American historiography has thus far been kind to Publius. The continued endurance of the Constitutional regime, regardless of its permutations, argues for Publius' foresight. Changes in communications and transportation technology, as well as economic shifts, seem to validate the energetic creativity of administration (Federalist 68).

To be sure, the arguments against the variegated "Anti-federalists" seem plausible on the surface, given Publius' historical and comparative

---

2. See Joseph Addison *Cato: A Tragedy, and Selected Essays* (Indianapolis: Liberty Fund, 2004.) Washington had the play performed repeatedly for his troops, celebrating the play's emphasis on honor, virtue, and stoic self-reliance.

3. *Ibid*, IV.iv.137–38.

4. See *The Anti-Federalist Papers and the Constitutional Convention Debates,* ed. Ralph Ketcham (New York: Signet, 2003); also *The Federalist Papers,* ed. Clinton Rossiter (New York: Signet, 2003).

detail. The "petty Republics" of the past were susceptible to partisan strife and predatory foreign powers. These small republics filled the observer with "horror and disgust" as they vacillated between tyranny and anarchy. They couldn't provide the right platform that would give "lustre" to the "bright talents" that would allow these republics to emerge from "the gloom" (Federalist 9). Ancient Republics were "as short in their lives as they [were] violent in their deaths" (Federalist 10).

All these problems were related, in Publius' judgment, to issues of scale, misjudgments concerning human nature, and an absence of the newly emergent "science of politics " that understood government mechanistically. These "wholly new discoveries" would move the emergent union toward modern "perfection." But perfection in its nature can't be incomplete or partial: it strives toward universality and comprehensiveness. It looks outward and abroad. Since it couldn't be found in human beings—men not being angels—it had to be attained in the mathematical and physical basis of the political system. The complex machinery of government could correct the problems of human nature and democratic excess.[5]

Granted, Publius expected virtue to make an appearance. Republican government wouldn't be possible without belief in "other qualities in human nature," which are presupposed by a Republican government "in a higher degree than any other form" (Federalist 55). Legislators were expected to be men of "upright intention" and "sound judgment" (Federalist 53). Publius regarded it as fundamental to Constitutional democracy that only "men who possess the most wisdom to discern, or the virtue to pursue, the common good" should hold legislative office (Federalist 57). The structure of Presidential election provided a "moral certainty" that only men "endowed in an eminent degree with the requisite qualifications," only those who were "pre-eminent for ability and virtue," would hold the office. It would never fall in the hands of one with a talent for "low intrigue" or "the little arts of popularity" (Federalist 68). Likewise the courts by their very nature would ensure that only men who had united personal integrity with broad legal knowledge would ascend to the bench.

But if Publius expected virtue and wisdom, he paid scant attention to either their nature or the conditions necessary for their cultivation. Indeed, skepticism that they even *could* be cultivated consistently manifests

5. See Greg Weiner, *Madison's Metronome: The Constitution, Majority Rule, and the Tempo of American Politics* (Lawrence: University Press of Kansas, 2012).

itself in Federalist 10's famous argument that self-interest alone could provide a stable platform for political contestation and in 51's equally famous claim that only ambition could effectively counter ambition. Nonetheless, Publius could trade on "the vigilant and manly spirit" by which Americans could be counted on to defend their liberty. But if such a spirit ever conceded to bad laws, then the "people would be prepared to tolerate anything but liberty" (Federalist 57).

This spirit of liberty operated on the premise that an adversarial political process would provide liberty's surest protection. Even then, Publius averred, such contestation would take place largely among the yeomanry. Soon, however, the husbandman would give way to the industrialist, who will give "a variety and complexity to the affairs of the nation" (Federalist 56) that will, in turn, create a need for representatives less bound by local concerns or preserving traditional ways of life. Unity and stability, and with them national greatness, would be enhanced by the promotion of industry and trade over agrarian life.

Thus, Publius encouraged self-interest, ambition, and class divisions unmitigated by the ties of kinship, the warmth of hospitality, or the virtues of neighborliness. Jay may have averred in Federalist 2 that Americans were religiously, ancestrally, and politically homogeneous, but what wasn't true then is even less true now. Jay's claims were largely negated by Madison's subsequent arguments that our vast differences were the surest guarantees of our liberty. The more individuals can be isolated, the less powerful they become. Deracination, monetization of the economy, and social alienation could thus become useful in protecting liberty against the threat of the increasingly energetic central government Publius desired.

But men can't trust those they don't know. And, not knowing them, they can't commit to a common good. This distrust, if made pervasive, will fray the social fabric. Madison knew this, which is why he took pains to point out in Federalist 10 that one of the benefits of an extended society is that it would foment distrust, distance citizens from one another in ways other than geographically, and thus provide a surer protection of the liberty to think freely. Personal autonomy became both a legal and a social principle, generated through the weakening of traditional ties.

Madison was quick to point out that the seeds of distrust would be so thoroughly poisonous that they would render less likely the combination of interests into an oppressive majority, which—for Madison, at least—was the danger to be avoided. Not a military chieftain himself, but one greatly experienced in the tumultuous operations of state legislation, Madison was particularly interested in the way representative government might avoid the twin dangers of majority oppression and minority obstruction of public purposes. To achieve that, however, one sacrificed the common good. Justice may be desirable, but not if you have to give up liberty in its pursuit (Federalist 51).

Hamilton, on the other hand, seemed more interested in the ways that limited scale would undo the gains of the revolution. Unless the independent colonies could somehow consolidate their authority, they would forever be subject to the threat of each other or of foreign governments. Additionally, the young country had "reached the last stage of national humiliation," as manifest in its inability to manage its finances and secure its rightful territory. Military weakness left the government unable to "remonstrate with dignity," forming part of "the dark catalogue of public misfortunes," which created the "present melancholy." Perhaps worst of all, the young government was helpless to achieve the goals of being "a friend and patron of industry" and thus make America a "significant" nation (Federalist 15).

Without the greater efficiency and energy of government, America would never achieve its own promise of greatness, which included a prominent place on the world stage and a clipping of Europe's wings. For too long Europe had dominated the world and ruled it through its "arrogant pretensions." Publius argued that it belonged uniquely to the Americans to "vindicate the honor of the human race" by teaching Europe moderation (Federalist 11). This could only be accomplished by creating the great American system that would be superior to Europe and overcome the "little arts of little politicians" who, because they resisted economic and political growth in the name of local autonomy, were attempting to thwart "the irresistible and unchangeable course of nature" (Federalist 11). Nature as opposed to history, be it noted.

Publius connects desire and ambition to an abstraction: namely, America as "the most interesting" empire "the world has ever known." Rather than depending on "accident and force," the new Constitution would be grounded in "reflection and choice" that alone tracked the animating principle of political life: the formation of a commercial empire capable of preserving personal liberty. Publius thought he could square the demands of dispossession, national greatness, and liberty, and the key was the idea of union.

The abstract and indeterminate nature of this political union was held together by Publius' mechanistic assumptions about political order. A political community didn't have to be organically whole so long as the machinery of government operated according to its predetermined patterns. In that instance, virtually any community could be substituted in the place of the actual existent one, for government would operate independently of the culture itself.

The critics complained about this assumption in different ways. First, they believed that the machine that had been created was too complex and too remote to be amenable to the only guarantee of liberty: public control and oversight. Without such inspection the machine would get larger and more complex and powerful. This is why issues of representation and term limits played such an important role in the critics' writings on the proposed Constitution. Cato averred that in a republic both extended and adversarial there would be such a "complication of interests" that "the science of government will become intricate and complex" to the point where it would be "too mysterious for [citizens] to understand and observe" (Letter 3).

Second, the Federalist model, they argued, seemed to presume that government could for the most part eschew virtue. Given Publius' operative assumptions, the critics couldn't see how you could make a good government out of bad persons. Publius believed the breach could be filled by institutional arrangements alone, but the critics realized such arrangements could not be "neutral" in the social sphere. The key for Cato and others was not the belief that men were good by nature, but the more fundamental insight that men are moral by nature. Given this, the question was not whether men are good, but how to make men good. The law operates by coercion; but the free development of virtue emerges from men in their associative lives.

Third, machines operate independently of the material upon which they are operating. That is to say, a mechanistic government will reshape the political community rather than be an extension of a community's way of being. Political community begins with the household, and the farther away one moves from direct acquaintance with and attachment to it, the weaker becomes the principle of community that ties people together. Force rather than comity creates unity. Granted, Madison and Hamilton believed that the states were the location of political tumult, and that the federal plan provided the promise of better government because it would be better administered, this largely because of its superior ability to command resources (Federalist 27). An extended union can't possess the natural levels of unity to allow for a well-ordered and mutually compelling—because actually dependent—community life. Citizens become subjects of distant power. It seems that the best arguments Publius could muster would be that the people would eventually become acccustomed to federal intrusions (Federalist 27, 45).

Cato, meanwhile, asked his readers to consider the great variety of climate, territory, economics, interests, and commerce in the country and wondered whether this "dissimilitude of interest, morals, and politics" would mean that any government trying to unite them might succeed. The extant states had very different histories and cultures, and these had been in existence for over 150 years. These cultures, traditions and interests, despite their mutual commitment to democratic politics, could not easily be reconciled. The slavery issue alone was sufficient demonstration, and some of the Anti-Federalists complained bitterly about being saddled with a political system that gave slavery legal protection.

Again, this could only mean that the new government would establish its authority first by drawing its power away from local and domestic institutions and then by reshaping those very institutions in accordance with the government's implicit doctrine of rational progress, directed toward national greatness. Publius may have banked on the "vigilant and manly spirit" of liberty, but Cato worried that opinion and manners were "mutable" and couldn't be counted on as a bulwark against government encroachment.

Cato and some of his fellows further worried about the effects of Hamilton's commercial empire upon the fabric of American society. Cato and his ilk believed there was value in subsistence-plus living. It kept men hardworking and self-sufficient, each enjoying the "fig of his own tree and fruit of his own vine" (Letter 5). Since government has no resources of its own, it can grow only if it seizes for its purposes the resources of another. It would be difficult for government to engage in such seizing in a land-based economy. Only if an economy moved to a cash nexus could government easily skim wealth. A cash-nexus economy, however, becomes necessary only when economic transactions are impersonal. It also creates enormous problems of credit and debt, not to mention destructive financial speculation.[6] It creates a more pronounced inequality

---

6. Consider, for example, Aristotle's distinction between *oikonomia*, the economics of the household, which are natural, productive, and conducive to virtue, and *chrematistics*, which are unnatural, speculative, usurious, and conducive to vice.

of wealth. It creates luxury—"the parent of inequality" and the "foe to virtue," said Cato—which operates always beyond the limits of restraint (Letter 5). It now becomes possible for a remote government, unattuned to local needs, confiscating and relocating local wealth, to pursue projects contrary to the immediate interests of those paying for them.

One of the keys to the Anti-Federalist view was the conviction that people are shaped by and care for the particular places they inhabit. Individuals become attached to a place, to its local customs, habits, manners, and traditions. This place becomes vital in terms of identity-formation and sustenance, and the people in it would resent and resist intrusions on their ways of life. America would be free and good if such variety were cherished. A highly mobile population was one not to be trusted. An ethic of exploitation would supplant an ethic of care.

The deracinated are easily ensnared in grandiose schemes, for they don't care what happens to particular places because they are willing to pull up stakes at any time. They don't develop the habits of caring and sustaining a natural and social environment. Always on the move, they count on government to make their way easier. They long only for a world that is familiar to them, no matter where they reside, because it is homogenized, corporatized, and soulless.

Anti-Federalist fears were soon realized. The chartering of the Second National Bank in 1816, and its support by John Marshall's Supreme Court, was a decisive event in moving America away from the ideals of an agrarian republic and toward one dominated by financial, industrial, and commercial interests. One major effect was to dislocate small propertied farmers from their self-sufficient lands (as a result of market collapses) and place them in what William Blake called "dark Satanic mills."[7] Jefferson sadly noted that his vision of republican life was being undone by men "having nothing in them of the feelings or principles of '76, [who] now look to a single and splendid government of an aristocracy, founded on banking institutions, and money incorporations . . . riding and ruling over the plundered ploughman and beggared yeomanry."[8] By the age of Jackson, Alexis de Tocqueville saw the ways in which these dominant interests and this untrammeled individualism worked together to undermine liberty.

7. From a short poem, popularly known as "Jerusalem," in Blake's preface to *Milton*. See *The Selected Poetry of Blake*, ed. David V. Erdman (New York: New American Library, 1976), 187.

8. http://founders.archives.gov/documents/Jefferson/98-01-02-5771.

American exceptionalists, those who believe America embodies history's meaning and therefore will avoid its patterns, enjoy meditating on Tocqueville's observations concerning America's central role in "the coming democratic revolution," which it would be neither "possible nor prudent to resist." But they ignore Tocqueville's own qualification that the "entire book" was written "under the pressure of a sort of religious terror in the author's soul." Tocqueville squares the contradiction by offering *Democracy in America* as a way "to instruct democracy, if possible to reanimate its beliefs, to purify its mores, to regulate its movements, to substitute little by little the science of affairs for its inexperience, and knowledge of its true interests for its blind instincts."[9]

Such instruction is required because of the way egalitarian democracy with its materialistic impulse was undoing social institutions particularly conducive to human flourishing: the family, voluntary and localized associations, village life, and churches. It would undermine the cause of liberty, which he regarded as "the source of all moral greatness." And while on the one hand Tocqueville observed that Americans would have no tolerance for aristocracy, on the other he foresaw a new aristocracy emerging from the mists of democratic revolution: the industrial class. Tocqueville saw the formation of large-scale industry and a powerful centralized government as mutually supportive developments. Big government and big business need one another, and the lynchpin, as Tocqueville saw, was a centralized financial system whose main mechanism of control is debt.

In its irresistible movement to larger projects, government becomes the agent solely responsible for running the public sphere, while the population at large becomes ever-more dependent on it. "Centralization," Tocqueville wrote, "has grown everywhere in a thousand different ways. Wars, revolutions, conquests have served its development; all men have worked to increase it." And neither political party, he believed, had the imaginative or structural capacity to offer an alternative. Rather, while there may be superficial differences between heads of state, "all have wanted to centralize in some manner. The instinct of centralization has been almost the sole unmovable point in the midst of the singular mobility of their existence and thoughts."[10]

---

9. Alexis de Tocqueville, *Democracy in America*, trans. Harvey Mansfield (Chicago: University of Chicago Press, 2002), 6–7.

10. Tocqueville, *Democracy*, 659.

By slowly drawing from and thus draining the life and authority out of the mediating structures of society, this democratic movement was accomplishing the undoing of its animating promise: the preservation of individuals in their self-sufficient liberty. Indeed, Tocqueville plaintively observed that he could "not trust the spirit of freedom that seems to animate my contemporaries; I see that the nations of our day are turbulent, but I do not clearly find that they are liberal, and I fear that sovereigns, at the end of these agitations that make all thrones tremble, will be found more powerful than ever."[11] Once the protective canopy of associative life is removed, individuals have nothing to protect them from government intrusions. Burke called the weakening of these institutions traitorous.[12]

The rich tapestry of social life would be gradually unraveled. Individual human beings, previously enmeshed in distinctive local communities, would become estranged. Unlike in France, where "simplicity of taste, tranquility of mores, the spirit of family, and love of one's birthplace [are] great guarantees of tranquility and happiness for the state," in America "nothing appears more prejudicial to society than virtues such as these."[13] No longer bearing the meaning-giving authority of their place, their familial and filial relations, and their participation in guilds and local organizations, these individuals would be forced to structure their own identities, to find their own meaning, to posit their own values, and to make their way in the world on their own. This can only create anomie, isolation, and fear, the price of which may be the anesthetizing of oneself through consumption and mass entertainment, the closing of oneself to others in stable relationships of mutual obligation and openness, and an escape from freedom itself. It would also alter the nature of dependency: no longer able to depend on the attenuated social institutions, the individual comes to depend on the government.

---

11. *Ibid*, 660–661.

12. "To be attached to the subdivision, to love the little platoon we belong to in society, is the first principle (the germ as it were) of public affections. It is the first link in the series by which we proceed towards a love to our country and to mankind. The interests of that portion of social arrangement is trust in the hands of those who compose it; and as none but bad men would justify it in abuse, none but traitors would barter it away for their own personal advantage." See Edmund Burke, *Reflections on the Revolution in France* in *Select Works of Edmund Burke* (Indianapolis: Liberty Fund, 1999), Vol. 2, 136–137.

13. Tocqueville, *Democracy*, 272.

As the social sphere broadens and aridifies, these erstwhile citizens, Tocqueville observed, retreat into narrower and narrower circles until they get to themselves, resulting in a society dominated by egoists. Democracy erodes our capacity to love what is nearest and most particular, creating disconnected citizens who relate primarily by means of tolerance or cash relations. And over this type of citizen, Tocqueville says, stands the immense tutelary state whose task is to assure enjoyments while it keeps individuals in a state of dependency. It does not break the will of individuals, but softens, bends, unhinges and unsprings their wills and "finally reduces each nation to being nothing more than a herd of timid and industrious animals of which the government is the shepherd."[14] Likewise, Nisbet, in *The Present Age*, reflects on those individuals who "hang loose" on society. They are takers. They play fast and loose with others. They are anomic, narcissistic, and bored. Their looseness results in part from the social fraying brought about by the cash nexus. "The vast abundance of liquidity, of money, of cash and painless credit make the genuinely heroic, like genuine honor, trust, and fidelity, improbable to say the least."[15]

A saving grace for America, Tocqueville believed, was the absence of a strong capital city. "To subject the provinces to the metropolis," he wrote, "is therefore to place the destiny of the empire not only in the hands of a portion of the community, which is unjust, but in the hands of a populace carrying out its own impulses, which is very dangerous. The preponderance of capital cities is therefore a serious injury to the representative system; and it exposes modern republics to the same defect as the republics of antiquity, which all perished from not having known this system."[16]

Thus we enter, *pace* Spengler, the phase of decline in civilization, whose mantle had now shifted to America, bringing with it Caesarism and imperialism. The free culture-generating life of town and village, dominated by folkways and mutual formation, is gradually replaced by great cities that distort culture, replacing meaning-giving forms of life with irony, cynicism, money, and cosmopolitan dreams. Cities appear to be creative, artistic places, Spengler argued, but true creativity takes place

---

14. Tocqueville, *Democracy*, 663.
15. Nisbet, *Present Age*, 110.
16. Tocqueville, *Democracy*, 536.

in small towns and villages where individuals shape artistic expression in a communally nurturing fashion. Artists in the cities are bohemian: disaffected, hyper-ironic and cynical, interested in undoing the forms of life that are self-evidently good to those living outside the city. A look at America's "culture wars" does much to confirm Spengler's thesis.

As capital flows to large urban areas, highly educated and ambitious individuals will follow it, thus concentrating power and wealth in the hands of the most ambitious, and draining talent from town and village, whose denizens will increasingly be thought of as hicks and yokels. Politics will become nothing more than rent-seeking and a competition for spoils.[17] Plutocracy replaces democracy. Spengler wrote:

> we find in every Culture (and very soon) the type of the capital city. This, as its name pointedly indicates, is that city whose spirit, with its methods, aims, and decisions of policy and economics, dominates the land. The land with its people is for this controlling spirit a tool and an object. The land does not understand what is going on, and is not even asked. In all countries of all late cultures, the great parties, the revolutions, the Caesarisms, the democracies, the parliaments, are the forms in which the spirit of the capital tells the country what it is expected to desire and, if called upon, to die for.[18]

Increasingly dependent upon the State, individuals would be solely concerned about whether it secured their "rights." Essential to this process, Spengler believed, was the process of disassociation, "the rootless fragments of population [that] stands outside all social linkages." Not attached to place, an Estate, or a vocation, these persons are easily collectivized and eased into the power structure. The world is divided into "cosmopolitans and provincials." The city "sucks the country dry, insatiably and incessantly demanding and devouring fresh streams of men" in their labor, bodies, and war sacrifices. Money becomes the key, for once divorced from the "prime values of the land" it can be used to pay off the public. All political problems become problems of money. "Intellect rejects, money directs—so it runs in every last act of a Culture-drama, when the megalopolis has become master over all the rest."[19]

---

17. See also Max Weber's famous essay "Politics as a Vocation."

18. Oswald Spengler, *The Decline of the West,* trans. Charles Francis Atkinson (New York: Alfred A. Knopf, 1928), Vol. 2, 95.

19. Spengler, *Decline,* Vol. 2, 402.

Freedom of labor from the soil, freedom of thought from institutional or cultural limits, and freedom of money to go where it wills all serve the purposes of the state and run contrary to the spirit of liberty. Is such centralization the result of choice and reason or did it result from ineluctable historical forces? For the West, the consolidation of power and money into the state apparatus was its "destiny," and also its decline. Spengler understood this in terms of historical determinism, but one wonders whether such dislocations would have occurred had Americans chosen a different path in 1787, as they very nearly did.

The value of a political system is best deduced from the use to which it is put. The form of American democracy is not found in its mechanistic theories, as Publius suggested, but in its consolidation and extension of power, as the critics suggested. One need not accept Spengler's deterministic conclusions to look back at the American founding and see that something truly tremendous was afoot. Publius' own tendency to couch his theories in the language of natural inevitability may have contained more truth than he realized. If that is the case, America's hope may require rethinking our Constitutional beginnings, especially with regards to issues of economy and scale. A more modest sense of American possibilities in contrast to Publius' ambitions may not make America great, but it might make it good. It may not prevent decline, but it might make decline less catastrophic.

The concentration of power into the state, and the concomitant penetration of state power into religion, economics, family life, local life, and so forth, could only happen once function and authority were dislocated. The anti-Federalists feared that the liberty and authority natural to man, once lost, would not be regained but rather replaced by power and the need for security. The atomistic individualism of modern liberalism would attenuate meaning-giving associative living and devalue the attachments individuals developed to concrete relationships. Those whom one would rule, one should first isolate.

But perhaps Hamilton was wrong to see such progress as a force of nature. Unlike physical universes, the powers of civilization and history are not inexorable. We are not left with a Nietzschean embracing of our fate. The disastrous patterns of recent years are subject to arrest and reversal, if done by men of good will, clear vision, and honorable intent who are guided by the permanent things and not distracted by baubles and beads. The vision of a life that avoids monetization and commodification, that connects labor to the land and virtue to the community, is still available to Americans, if they will but recall these long lost voices that sang of them.

The Quest for the Common Good: Political Economy on the Front Porch

John Médaille

The Politics of the Madhouse

This was written in the midst of the silly season—that is, during a presidential election—a season that lasts for far too many seasons. I call such seasons "silly" because they turn on a series of arguments that are silly in themselves. And by "silly" I mean something quite specific: I mean arguments that are framed in such a way as to make their resolution impossible. I mean arguments that place complements in opposition to each other, arguments that take things necessary to each other and try to make them mutually repulsive. By these means arguments become silly, become absurd, whichever pole of the argument you take. It is, quite literally, the politics of the madhouse.

Further, in treating complementary terms as opposites we lose the middle term that reconciles these apparent opposites, a middle term we call "The Common Good." For all politics and, for that matter, economics must make a fundamental choice: they can either be a quest for a common good among diverse interests or a lust for power by which one faction seeks to dominate all the others.

So what kind of arguments do we have that pit complementary terms against each other? Let me take three that are (primarily) from the economic realm: the argument between "free markets" and "socialism," the argument between regulation and freedom, and the argument between competition and cooperation. In each of these arguments the technique is the same: place the terms in opposition to each other so that their differences can only be resolved by power; by these means the common good, along with the opposition, is eliminated. Now it may not be apparent to everyone that all of these terms are in fact complements, things that depend on each other, so I must elaborate.

Socialism and the Free Market

All of our political and economic discourse, or nearly all of it, treats these terms as opposites, even though this does not, and cannot, correspond with any reality we actually see, either today or at any time in human history. For the plain fact of the matter—that is, the fact we see always and everywhere—is that all markets depend on a pre-existing order that no market can create but that it can, through inattention, destroy. For it doesn't matter how good you are at making products; if there are no roads to take them to market, you will not be successful. If each entrepreneur had to dig his own latrine, drill his own well, provide his own police, educate his own customers and workers, or substitute for any of the hundred other services that have been socialized, he would have precious little time to devote to his business. The presence of socialized services does not *per se* crush the market but enables it. The less the entrepreneurs have to think about these things, the more they can think about providing useful goods and services and trying their hands and their wits in the hurly-burly of the market.

Some may object to labelling as "socialism" all expenditures on socialized services. But to argue this is to argue about a term and not about a fact. Call it what you will, the mutual dependence of the market on socialized services can neither be rationally denied nor historically confounded. In truth, there is no pure free market, nor any pure socialism. Socialism, if it is to work at all, can only work with a market economy; likewise, a market economy requires socialized services or else it cannot exist at all. And capitalism is entirely a creature of the state; on one level there is no point in complaining about "crony capitalism," since that is the only capitalism that has ever existed, or ever will exist. The great danger comes when one faction tries to displace the other to create a "pure" form; but any attempt to abolish one term in favor of the other can only destroy both. Pure socialism and pure capitalism can only be pure failures.

Recognition of this fact radically changes the political debate. The question is no longer one *or* the other but, rather, "what are the proper domains of each?" But this is a question that cannot be answered in advance; rather, it can only be answered from within the unique historical circumstances in which each society and age find themselves. For example, the answers given from within an economy where production tends to be gathered in huge corporate collectives is different from the answers that will be given in societies where property is widely dispersed and a large fraction of the populous always has the option of making its own way in the world by its own wits. So the markers are not fixed by some universal and inflexible rule but vary with actual conditions and the character of the people. For a people that is largely dependent on a few owners for something called a "job" will be radically different from a society of small independent producers. But if there is no universal formula to set the boundaries, is there a universal principle by which we may judge the results? More of this anon.

Regulation and Freedom

There seems to be an assumption that freedom is what happens in the absence of constraint, that man can live with coercion or with liberty but not with both. But in reality the opposite is true: freedom depends on coercion; otherwise, we will be ruled by war-lords and Nietzechean "supermen." Liberty depends on restraint; otherwise, it becomes license, and a licentious society is half-way to slavery. Only rules make markets possible, for no man would risk his capital in an unruly market.

Indeed, there will always be rules for every market; the only question is, "Who will get to make them: civil society or the strongest player in the market?" In the days of the Robber Barons, when the railroads were the latest and most indispensable technology, the Railroad Barons got together to establish the Rate Bureau, which cartelized the transportation market. Not wishing to risk their capital in potentially destructive wars of competition, they fixed the rates that each rail line could charge. By these means their interests were protected; the interests of producers and consumers, alas, were not. Everywhere the history is the same: if the civil authority does not make the rules, the biggest players in the market will make them, and they will do so for their own narrow advantage.

Nor is this something buried in our remote past. Today Wal-Mart controls so much shelf space that producers must come hat in hand to Bentonville, Arkansas, and make their case and hear the terms of their surrender. These terms will be dictated to them, because the producers have next to no bargaining power. They will be told what to make, how to package it, how to ship it, what the return policy for unsold goods will be, and a hundred other things besides. And they will be told the price. And when they say they cannot possibly meet these terms and prices, they will be directed to re-locate their production to China, where such prices can be met. Indeed, Wal-Mart functions as a branch of the Chinese Trade ministry.

There is little difference between taking orders from a civil servant in Washington and from a bureaucrat in Bentonville. Well, perhaps there is this difference: there is at least some chance of bringing political pressure to bear on the civil servant; there is no such chance with the Bentonville Bureaucrat. And we can instance many examples of this kind of private rule-making.

It has never been different; there is no "golden age" to which we can appeal. The medieval guildsman likely operated under as many rules as does a modern tradesman. But there is this difference: the guildsman had a hand in setting the rules; he was able to negotiate with his colleagues and with the other powers—the Church, the king, the nobles, the free cities, the commons—who had a hand in setting the rules. The rules were something that rose at least partially from within his own profession. Today the rules are likely to be imposed by alien and even hostile forces. The men of the same profession, therefore, often feel that they have no choice but to engage in "regulatory capture," and the cost of lobbying becomes a normal cost of doing business.

But once again we are faced with the same problem: what principle will allow us to regulate social and commercial life but at the same time prevent one group from imposing arbitrary power over the rest of us?

Competition vs. Cooperation

Perhaps no term excites the American imagination, both in business and in entertainment, as does the term "competition." Cooperation is for tree-huggers; real men want to prove themselves in fierce competitions. In the game of life competition means constant improvement in products, constant winnowing of the incompetent, constant growth of the economy. It is competition that assigns the beautiful woman to the strong man. Hence, competition is the mainspring of order and progress, while cooperation can lead only to the dull gray landscape of poverty and stagnation. If any two terms could be counted as opposed to each other—as *un*complimentary—surely these terms are.

But once again it is not so simple. For there are two kinds of competition, only one of which produces the promised benefits, while the other works to destroy them. The first is *agonistic* competition, whose exemplar is war, and the second is *cooperative* competition, whose exemplar is sports. The first kind, war-like competition, has as its object the annihilation of all competitors and hence the end of all competition. It is not bound by rules, except the rule that the end justifies the means.

Sports, however, are rule-bound and seek the continuation of the game. Nobody really loses; rather, the clock runs out before one team catches up. But we are assured that the losers will walk away and that there will be a new clock next year. When I wrote this, the Carolina Panthers and the Denver Broncos were preparing to take the field in less-than-mortal combat. I did not know who would triumph, of course, but of this I was sure: the losers would not be slaughtered, their city would not be destroyed, and their women and children would not be dragged off into slavery. At worst, the winners would thump their chests and the losers would say, "Wait till next year."

Sport, properly understood, is competition within an elaborate form of cooperation. Indeed, no one would step on the field were it not for the presence of officials who can blow the whistle and throw the yellow flag; if there were no penalties for grabbing a facemask, the mortality rate would simply be too high. It is cooperation, and cooperation alone, that makes the game possible. And when we look at the sport as a business, we find an enterprise in which men may become rich, but only through a rather strict form of income redistribution.

Socialism and the NFL

Football as a game is often regarded as the quintessentially American sport, but it is also the quintessentially American *business*: The game itself seems to be modeled on corporate practice. It is rather sedate by the standards of other team sports, such as basketball, soccer, or rugby, all of which involve long periods of continuous action. An NFL football game, by contrast, averages only 11 minutes of action, total, between snap and whistle; it is a succession of brief periods of intense action separated by planning meetings, a mode of life familiar to every corporate drone in his cubicle.

As a business model it is a peculiar combination of socialism, capitalism, and government subsidy. The success of each franchise depends on the success of the League as a whole. Income is redistributed from stronger teams to weaker ones through revenue-sharing for income from TV, sales of team gear, and 40% of the ticket sales. The labor market for players is tightly controlled by the draft and free-agency. There is a salary cap, which means no team can outbid the others for players as a whole and that each team must make tough decisions about how to allocate the capped funds.

Market entry—that is, the granting of franchises—is highly limited, as is movement from one city to another, and both are controlled by a city's willingness to subsidize the team through tax abatements and support for building stadiums and other infrastructure. All in all, it would be hard to find a better model of socialized business than the National Football League.

Football as a Political Economy

Why is it that the wealthier teams are willing to subsidize their weaker members and willing to limit their own freedom of action in so many areas? The answer is obvious: the owners have identified a *good* that is common to all of them. That good is making the game as competitive as possible by insuring that no team, no matter how wealthy its market or loyal its fans, will be able to dominate the league for any length of time. Former NFL commissioner Bert Bell stated the *summum bonum* of the League: "On any given Sunday, any team in the NFL can beat any other team." This competitive parity insures that the interest of fans in all regions of the country will remain high, for their teams will have at least some hope of a playoff slot, perhaps even a Super Bowl berth.

In the light of competitive parity, the internal politics and economics of the NFL can be rationalized; it is a political economy in which all arguments and all economic arrangements must appeal to the same principle. So while there are, I imagine, many internal disputes, there is a common rule by which to resolve them.

The Quest for a Common Good

Note that while the NFL identifies a good common to all the owners, it is in no sense *the* common good, for it includes only incidentally, if at all, the good of the other participants in the game: the players, the fans, and the cities that give them so much support. The implicit belief of the League is that, if it takes care of its owners, the benefits will trickle down to all the other participants. But this is a doubtful proposition at best. For example, it is not the good of the owners that forces the League to take note of the health problems of the players after their brief moments of fame; rather, it is only public outrage over the physical and mental problems of the players that forces this concern on the League.

A *common good* must be just that: a good common to all the participants, one that allows for the flourishing of each member of the society. So when we turn our attention to social and economic order, what is this common good? Clearly, it is the health of all the associations that make up the fabric of society, primarily the family but also the communities and the religious, social, professional, and artistic associations through which all societies are what they are. It is only through the family that we come to be at all, and from which we receive our language, moral notions, nationality, and all the other things that provide the raw material for the formation of our personalities. And it is only through all these associations that we develop our skills and our character. Therefore, the rule or measure of all economic and social activity must be, first and foremost, the health and stability of the family and its surrounding community. We should be able to judge the success or failure of the economic order by the strength or weakness of the family, and this before we apply any other measure.

Every society adopts some rule or measure of its success, and our society has adopted one similar to that of the NFL: the good of the owners of society, as measured solely by profit maximization. It is thought that by constantly enriching the owners we insure that the benefits will trickle down to the rest of us. But of course the opposite is true. Everywhere we look, we see the family structure weakened and communities stripped of their assets. This is a natural consequence of substituting the good of a few for the common good.

Economics and Political Economy

The NFL is a political economy properly speaking, a system by which economic decisions are rationalized not by an appeal to an abstract theory but to the practical necessities of insuring competitive parity. Through this measure it is able to reconcile the seeming opposites of free markets and socialism, rule-making and liberty, cooperation and competition. But since it lacks a notion of the common good, the results are in many ways perverse. This too, is a model of what happens in the larger economy.

The 19th century knew nothing of "economics"; it knew only *political economy*. Political economy assumes that every actual economy is embedded within a network of laws, property rights, social expectations, concepts of justice, and a notion of the common good, and that no actual economy can be understood apart from these things, which are the ordinary considerations of any humane science. But throughout that century there was a movement to create a pure "economics" that would produce a "physical" science valid for all times and places. Hence, it split the heretofore unified science of political economy into the supposed "sciences" of politics and economics.

However, the new "science" of economics depended more and more on "stylized facts" that bear little resemblance to reality. For example, the *homo œconomius*, the creature who makes all decisions based on a comparison of bundles of utilities rooted in pure self-interest, is as much a mythical creature as the minotaur or the unicorn; starting with this mythical creature, you can only create a mythical economics. In splitting political economy, 19th-century theorists did not create two new sciences but rather two crippled disciplines incapable of describing events within their respective domains, because in reality there is only one domain with two aspects. It is impossible to describe any economy apart from the political matrix in which it exists; likewise, it is impossible to understand any politics without an understanding of the economy that supports it. Thus you have two groups of "scientists" who are continually mystified by the events they are paid to understand.

Political Economy on the Front Porch

Our mythical economics has produced mythical free markets: markets that appropriate the language of freedom but in which all production and distribution actually take place within large corporate collectives. This is because capitalistic competition is *agonistic*; it seeks always to absorb or eliminate the opposition until only a few large collectives are left and the "competition" becomes a show rather than a reality. And wherever we look that is what we see. Be it beer or banking, retail or restaurants, food or pharma, production is gathered into large corporate entities tending to monopoly or cartels; it is the opposite of a free market.

Those of us who view things from the Front Porch have a love of community and hence a loathing for collectives, be they Soviet or corporate. Hence, we wish to free production from globalist collectives and return it to the localities and their regions. We seek to restore truly free markets by restoring productive property to as many hands as are willing to take it up to provide useful goods and services to their neighbors and their communities. And we seek the restoration of the good of the family and the community—the common good—to the center of economic and political life. And by this we seek to unify the complementarities of free markets and socialized services, rules and freedom, competition and cooperation.

But there are those with a vested interest in eliminating a common good so that the complements become dichotomies, dichotomies that can never be resolved by reason but only by a contest of power. They believe, quite correctly, that in such contests they already own all the heavy artillery. But in truth, when they are unrestrained, they cannot run things. All they can do is run them into the ground. This is what we see happening today, right before our eyes. And when they have completed their ruinous task, and everything is in ruins, each community will have to rebuild itself from the ground up. And the best vantage point to oversee this task of rebuilding is neither the corporate boardroom nor the governor's mansion but, rather, the Front Porch.

Opposition to Crony Capitalism: A Truly Bipartisan Opportunity

Andrew V. Abela

While the United States remains deeply divided between liberals and conservatives, with little hope of reconciliation, they share one major source of concern. Liberals resent the power of major corporations and banks over the rest of society, while conservatives oppose the government handouts and bailouts to those same banks and corporations.

True, one faction imagines that the solution involves making the government more powerful, while the other argues for less government intervention in business. Yet both sides must come to the realization that the problem is neither big government nor big business *per se*. Instead, the real worry is when the two act together in what has come to be called "crony capitalism."

Crony capitalism is an economic system in which the relationship between business and government leaders plays an important—if not the most important—role in achieving business success. How does crony capitalism arise, and is there anything we can do about it?

According to the Austrian Economist Friedrich Hayek, what we now call crony capitalism arises because the institution of private property has been severely weakened. Speaking about Hayek and private property is not likely to win over contemporary American liberals, but in *The Road to Serfdom* (1944) Hayek credits this argument to English author Hilaire Belloc. Written some three decades before Hayek's work, Belloc's *The Servile State* (1912) championed an economic system he called "distributism." With its emphasis on widely distributed property, Belloc's distributism provides some useful insights for how to move beyond our current apparent deadlock.

Hayek and Belloc both make the case that the form of capitalism in which the ownership of the means of production becomes concentrated into a small number of hands—because of the tight relationships between business and government—is not compatible with a society based on principles of freedom and equality. When wealth—and therefore power—is concentrated in a few hands, the majority of the population do not feel particularly free or equal. Although Hayek wrote sixty years ago and Belloc one hundred, it is remarkable how well their argument explains the causes of the popular unrest that has arisen over the past few years.

Because of the inherent instability of crony capitalism, Hayek and Belloc argue that unless broad property ownership can be achieved, the system will predictably continue towards further concentration of property ownership, leading ultimately to totalitarian government.

Unfortunately, once a point of highly concentrated ownership is reached—as is the case in America today—it becomes extremely difficult to restore widespread property ownership. Concentration of property is self-perpetuating because people cease to rely on their own property for their security. What is it we ask of our politicians—and what do they offer us—from both sides of the aisle? "Jobs." Not the freedom and opportunity to make our own way, but a wage in someone else's establishment. Thus, there is no way out of crony capitalism without a renewed understanding of the importance of self-reliance and therefore of the essential role that private property plays in human liberty.

Today there exists a serious misconception about property. Property is stuff, a source of pleasure and comfort: what rich people have. The original idea of property—as the foundation for a free and independent life—needs to be recovered. One of the strongest and most consistent defenses of this view of property can be found in Catholic Social Doctrine, the teaching of the Catholic Church on social matters.

The Second Vatican Council of the Catholic Church (1962–65) affirmed that private property is "wholly necessary for the autonomy of the person and the family." The wording is interesting: the Council did not say that *because* we are free, we have the right to private property. Instead, the emphasis is on the reverse: private property itself is *necessary for* the exercise of freedom. This is not simply because property helps provide for our daily material needs. For, as the *Catechism of the Catholic Church* asserts, it is private property that guarantees the "freedom and dignity of persons." A property owner is free in practice, not just in theory. For example, if you find yourself in an unacceptable situation at work—say you're being pressured to do something unethical—if you have no property, then your freedom to walk away and find some other work is much more limited (especially in a weak economy) than if you have some productive property that could support you while you look for another position.

In earlier days, a family's security was largely based on the property that it was able to accumulate and put to work. In the twentieth century, however, we moved from relying upon private property for our security to relying in large part upon government transfer payments. When times are tough, or when workers retire, they depend less on their property and more upon unemployment support, welfare, or social security.

Underlying this shift is a fundamental—and false—assumption: that *property* and *income* are equivalent. At first blush they certainly appear similar: property can be invested to generate income; income can be saved to accumulate property. But this assumption only holds if the purpose of private property is solely to help provide for material goods, which it isn't. Unlike private property, income from government transfer payments does not facilitate the *exercise of freedom and responsibility*. With private property, you have the freedom to decide how much to save, how and where to invest, and when to draw from savings. Your Social Security "contributions," on the other hand, are compulsory; you have no say in how they are "invested," and the amounts and timing of both contributions and withdrawals are determined for you. A government transfer payment doesn't foster responsibility: it arrives monthly, and all the recipient does is cash the check. Private property, on the other hand, requires care, work, and thoughtful investment—owners must work *with* their property in order to ensure that they are getting a good return on it. Nobel economist Amartya Sen is famous in part for his work on how unemployment benefits are an acutely inadequate substitute for real work, because of the loss of dignity, personal development, and responsibility associated with unemployment. Transfer payments are likewise an inadequate replacement for property ownership. Private property enables freedom and encourages responsibility. Government transfer payments do neither.

How did we forget this critical role of private property? When we exchanged our reliance on private property for our economic security, and came to depend instead upon government transfer payments, we relinquished both freedom and responsibility. However, we still *maintain our natural desire to acquire property*. This desire, fueled by mass marketing, is redirected in part towards luxury or status goods. But luxury or status goods do not provide either of the benefits of private property: they don't create the opportunity to exercise our freedom and responsibility, nor do they efficiently support our material needs. Primarily, they provide pleasure: a vacation home is a source of pleasure, while a rental property is a source of income and independence; a yacht gives me pleasure, but a charter fishing boat gives me security and food.

To be sure, the purchase of luxury goods represents an *exercise* of one's freedom, and so there is no suggestion here that somehow we should restrict or tax them. What is important, though, is the recognition that certain kinds of purchases encourage freedom and responsibility while others don't. Yachts and vacation homes are not evil things. Each in its own way can help spread joy among families and friends. The point is simply that when we think about private property today, we tend to think about luxury goods or status goods. The largest and most imposing image in one issue of the *Wall Street Journal* was not of some remarkable new technology or product, but of a $19 million private home in Aspen.

We need to restore the idea of private property as *productive property*, which is so essential for liberty because of the security it provides. Goods such as rental housing, shares in a business, tools and equipment—these are true private property, for they represent *productive* property. But when the majority of people come to depend on government for their security rather than on their own property, then the natural desire for productive property is perverted towards luxury goods. At that point the institution of private property itself becomes difficult to defend. If private property is conceived simply in terms of yachts and vacation homes—a luxury of the rich rather than the foundation for the security of the many—then we should not be surprised at all to see more attacks on the right to private property and on "greedy capitalists."

Hayek and Belloc warn about the dangers of the concentration of wealth and power, which is to say, of crony capitalism. Supporters of the free market are deeply suspicious of, and generally hostile to, concentration of power in government. But according to Hayek and Belloc, the problem starts with concentration of power in *both* business and government. For the past several decades, free market advocates have been blind to half of the problem. While well aware of the dangers of concentration of power in government, these advocates are apparently unaware of—or unconcerned about—the perils arising from the concentration of power in business.

This blind spot is perhaps due to a certain discomfort among free market champions with any criticism of big business. Isn't a big business, after all, nothing other than an especially successful small business? Isn't criticism of big business a criticism of the market? Not necessarily. After reaching a certain size, some companies choose to move outside the free market to apply political power to defend and enlarge their businesses. Economies of scale and scope take you so far. Beyond that, the temptation to grow or protect profits in ways that are anti-competitive proves, in many cases, too great to resist.

Perhaps the clearest example of this attempt to cheat the market is the phenomenon of "regulatory capture," when government regulation is turned, over time, to favor those it is intended to regulate. Regulatory capture happens because companies have a substantial interest in how the government regulates them. Large companies are also relatively small in number, so they can easily organize to influence regulation. And they usually succeed in their efforts, because consumers are generally too busy with the details of their daily lives to provide any effective countervailing efforts. For example, how much time did *you* spend in the last year thinking about the price of electricity in your municipality or organizing your neighbors to lobby your regulator about it? How much time and effort do you think your electrical utility spent on the same question?

Catholic Social Doctrine helps here also. In opposition to concentration of power in both government and business, the Church proposes the principle of subsidiarity: the principle that larger organizations should not interfere with the legitimate functioning of smaller ones. What is the moral justification for this principle? It is not, as some think, one of efficiency—that societies function more efficiently when decision-making is widely decentralized. While it is true that subsidiarity promotes efficiency, this is not the primary moral rationale for it. The primary rationale for the principle of subsidiarity is *liberty*. The *Catechism of the Catholic Church* explains it as follows: "The way God acts in governing the world, which bears witness to such great regard for human freedom, should inspire the wisdom of those who govern human communities." In other words, if God rules us with such profound respect for our freedom, then our human rulers should do likewise.

The principle of subsidiarity is perhaps best known as a general principle underlying the law of the European Union. This association is perhaps unfortunate, because the EU does not always apply the principle authentically: in general, the final authority for determining whether EU institutions are violating subsidiarity remains with those EU institutions. Further away from Brussels, though, there are encouraging applications of subsidiarity in Europe. The northern Italian province of Lombardy, for example, has been actively and successfully applying the principle of subsidiarity to its social and economic development programs for the past fifteen years.

Though the word was only coined in the twentieth century, "subsidiarity" has held an important place in the American system since the founding; the 10th Amendment, and arguably the War of Independence itself, provide instances of it. Another example is what Professor Luigi Zingales of the Chicago Booth School of Business calls a "populist anti-finance bias," which "led to many political decisions throughout American history that were inefficient from an economic point of view, but helped preserve the long-term health of America's democratic capitalism." Americans valued freedom more than the supposed efficiency that would arise from consolidation of banks, because they feared the power that such large banking entities would wield. Zingales points to President Jackson's opposition to renewing the charter of the Second Bank of the United States, to numerous state-level banking restrictions, and to the Glass-Steagall Act, as examples of this populism. He admits that from a purely economic point of view, such restrictions are "crazy," but he also recognizes positive side effects. The fragmentation of the banking industry that resulted from such regulation led to the rise of a thriving securities industry and prevented the massive political power that banks now wield.[1]

Deregulation of the finance industry over the past several decades has overturned these restrictions. Was its re-regulation a move in the right direction—did the Dodd-Frank Act of 2010 promote subsidiarity? Not at all. We can divide regulation into two types, those that foster subsidiarity and those that hinder it. Glass-Steagall was largely of the former type; Dodd-Frank is of the latter.

Regulation that hinders subsidiarity tends to focus on activity and outcomes: you may or may not do this, that, or the other; if you do, you should do it in this way; and you should get these kinds of results, and not others. Environmental protection regulation is largely of this type.

---

1. National Affairs, http://www.nationalaffairs.com/publications/detail/capitalism-after-the-crisis.

Anti-trust regulation is too: it focuses not on the absolute or even relative sizes of firms, but on whether their market power is expected to affect consumers negatively. By its nature, regulation of activity or outcome requires a large bureaucracy to implement it, because one needs to monitor almost everything that firms do as well as the results they achieve. And so it is intrusive and hugely expensive: according to a 2010 report commissioned by the Small Business Administration Office of Advocacy, the total annual cost of regulation in the United States at that time was a phenomenal $1.75 trillion dollars.[2]

Regulation that fosters subsidiarity tends to focus instead on size and scope restrictions: you may not be bigger than x, you may not do business in an area wider than y, etc. It is much easier and therefore cheaper to monitor: you don't have to watch everything firms do; you just have to keep an eye on their size.

Because our current regulation is predominantly hostile to subsidiarity, we experience the perverse result that smaller enterprises—which typically violate regulations least—pay a disproportionate cost of regulation. Despite some attempts at regulatory relief over the years, in general, small business is still far more heavily penalized by most regulation. For example, businesses with fewer than 20 employees incur 44% more in per employee costs of regulation in total; for environmental regulation, they pay over 300% more. And yet, ironically, even though regulation costs these small businesses more, in many cases they need it less—usually because it is easier for small businesses to regulate themselves and to be scrutinized by the local community.

Agriculture is one industry in which regulation is particularly hostile to subsidiarity. Playing on fears of food safety, a handful of large firms promote regulation that favors them but burdens small farmers. One proposal (eventually defeated) required tagging of farm animals to help trace sources of disease: small farmers would have to tag each individual animal, while large factory farms need only one "tag" for an entire herd of thousands of animals. Yet where is food-borne disease most likely to arise, on a small family farm or in a huge animal confinement operation?

Some time ago my wife and I attended a Washington, DC, dinner on the occasion of the publication of a book by a popular organic farming

---

2. Crain, Nicole V. and W. Mark Crain, "The Impact of Regulatory Costs on Small Firms," Report Produced for SBE Office of Advocacy, September 2010. Available at https://www.sba.gov/sites/default/files/The%20Impact%20of%20Regulatory%20Costs%20on%20Small%20Firms%20(Full).pdf.

pioneer, Michael Abelman. There were about 60 people in the room, and Abelman did an admirable job facilitating a general discussion among the whole group after dinner. Reacting to one of the issues raised, a young woman who was evidently new to the group spoke up and said "Government should do something." I don't remember what the issue was, but I'll never forget the response: the entire room of small farmers and their supporters cried out as one: "No! Government *is* the problem!"— organic farmers become Reagan Conservatives.

If we could recognize that crony capitalism is the problem, and if we could realize that the solution to it is the restoration of private property and subsidiarity, we might find ourselves on the brink of a truly bipartisan moment in America.

Agrarian Politics and the American Tradition[1]

Jeff Taylor

Agrarianism is a political philosophy and way of life known and practiced among peoples of diverse nationalities and religions. While having ancient, medieval, and early-modern roots, agrarian politics blossomed most dramatically in America, during both its colonial and republican periods. Notable spokesmen for American agrarianism include Thomas Jefferson, William Jennings Bryan, and Robert La Follette. It has been in steady decline for the past century as cosmopolitan and centralizing forces have displaced tradition and smallness of scale. Still, there have been natural voices lamenting losses in the face of "progress": Distributists and Southern Agrarians, the Counterculture and the Green Party, Wendell Berry and Crunchy Cons.

The motto of Front Porch Republic is "Place. Limits. Liberty." While none of the three necessitates an agrarian context, each is a natural fit for rural life. Values such as community, self-government, and individual freedom are foundational to political decentralization. American decentralism has long been linked to agrarianism because widely-dispersed power includes a healthy dose of attachment to the land and to nature as a whole. Of course, it has made room for the benefits of urban life as well in the context of neighborhood rather than metropolis.

Geography matters. A sense of place has practical and political implications. There is less population density and more individual liberty in the country than in a city. Metropolitan life packs people closer together,

---

1. Portions adapted from *Politics on a Human Scale: The American Tradition of Decentralism*, by Jeff Taylor (Lexington Books, 2013). Used by arrangement with the publisher.

yet they are less likely to know one another than are rural residents. There are fewer formal constraints and a greater sense of personal responsibility on farms and in small towns. Paradoxically, freedom is maximized in such an environment, yet a sense of community also flourishes. Urban areas include their fair share of decentralists, and big-city anonymity provides liberty of a sort, but agrarianism remains foundational to the dispersal of power and independence from the state.

Early American Agrarians

The agrarian political culture of the United States has had many antecedents.

Benjamin Franklin became familiar with the thought of Physiocracy in the 1760s while in England. The physiocrats' "preference for agriculture over manufacturing and commerce accorded with his deepest convictions." Like Jefferson, Franklin championed the western frontiersmen of his colony, and, like Jefferson, Franklin was unusual among the founding fathers as an advocate of agrarian democracy.[2] Jefferson esteemed the physiocrat Turgot so highly that he placed a bust of the economist in the entrance hall of Monticello. Turgot's insistence on free enterprise and government frugality anticipated Jefferson's own national administration. However, Jefferson did not embrace the physiocrats' belief in political absolutism. For Jefferson, decentralization was linked to liberty and democracy. His vision was of a land populated by self-governing individuals. In the 1810s, his proposed system of ward-republics was an effort to decentralize and democratize the American republic as much as possible.

Of course, Thomas Jefferson's political philosophy was agrarian or farm-centered. His most famous tribute to farmers is in *Notes on the State of Virginia* (1782): "Those who labor in the earth are the chosen people of God, if ever He had a chosen people, whose breasts He has made His peculiar deposit for substantial and genuine virtue. It is the focus in which he keeps alive that sacred fire, which otherwise might escape from the face of the earth." Jefferson's desire to have more land in the West for farmers was one of the reasons he agreed to the Louisiana Purchase

---

2. Vernon Louis Parrington, *Main Currents in American Literature: An Interpretation of American Literature from the Beginnings to 1920* (New York: Harcourt, Brace, c1927, 1930), Vol. 1, 172.

despite constitutional scruples. Jefferson's much-quoted words concerning the urban masses suggest a pronounced anti-urban bias: "The mobs of great cities add just so much to the support of pure government, as sores do to the strength of the human body."[3]

While Jefferson's preference for farming is clear, his hostility toward urban workers and opposition to manufacturing should not be exaggerated. *Notes on Virginia* was written relatively early in his political career. During his three campaigns for president, Jefferson received considerable support from the laboring class in the eastern cities. He began to look favorably upon the idea of American factories even before the War of 1812.

One final point must be made concerning Jefferson's agrarianism. While he was a relatively wealthy Virginia farmer himself, Jefferson was a champion not only of the planters (large farmers) but also of the yeomen (small farmers). In his draft of the Virginia constitution of 1776, Jefferson attempted to create a more equitable distribution of land in the state through abolition of primogeniture (the practice of bequeathing all land to one's eldest son). According to Jefferson, "The small landholders are the most precious part of a state."[4]

Democrats vs. Aristocrats

Andrew Jackson of Tennessee was self-consciously in the Jeffersonian tradition. He was an agrarian and a populist. While, like Jefferson, he was a plantation owner, Jackson saw himself as the political voice of the common people, especially small farmers. Born in a log cabin, in the border area of the Carolinas, Jackson represented the nation's West—a growing region of small farmers and small businessmen. Jackson's first vice-president, John C. Calhoun of South Carolina, is famous as a spokesman for the Old South, but he was not a Jeffersonian and did not exemplify the best of the agrarian tradition in American politics. Calhoun and his aristocratic successors, the leaders of the Confederate States of America, were highly selective in their agrarianism. They represented a majority of the large, slaveowning farmers in the Old South. Plantation culture was not synonymous with southern agrarianism.

---

3. Thomas Jefferson, *The Life and Selected Writings of Thomas Jefferson*, ed. Adrienne Koch and William Peden (New York: Modern Library, 1944), 280.

4. *Ibid.*, 389–90.

During the Gilded Age, Henry George of California and New York was the most influential American agrarian. Author of *Progress and Poverty* (1879), journalist, politician, and economic theorist, George inspired an emphasis on land diffusion known as Georgism or the Single Tax movement. Targeting large, absentee landowners, George's system was designed to bring about wide distribution of land-use by abolishing private ownership of land and levying a single stiff tax on the rent of those with the most land (which would also lighten the tax burden on average members of society). James Weaver of Iowa was another important figure in agrarian politics during the era after the Civil War. A former Union general and Republican congressman, he was the presidential nominee of the Greenback-Labor Party in 1880 and the People's (Populist) Party in 1892. As the Populist candidate, he carried four states, ran second in eight states, and received over one million votes nationally. Building on a foundation of the Grange, Single Taxers, Greenbackers, the Farmers' Alliance, and labor union socialists, the Populist Party attempted to craft a transcendent populist coalition: North and South, white and black, rural and urban. It had some success as a third party in the South, Midwest, and West until it merged in 1896 with the anti-monopoly, pro-silver Jeffersonian revival within the Democratic Party. That revival was led by William Jennings Bryan of Nebraska.

A Century Ago

Bryan symbolized the culmination of dissatisfaction with the plutocratic and increasingly imperial status quo maintained by leaders of both major parties, who divided citizens through an emphasis on secondary wedge issues. Bryan's personal importance comes from his status as a three-time Democratic presidential nominee (1896, 1900, and 1908) and as leader of the national Democratic Party from 1896 to 1912. He went on to serve as U.S. Secretary of State under Wilson, eventually resigning in protest of the president's pro-war designs. Bryan, known as "the Great Commoner," retained influence within the party as a beloved figure for millions.

Late nineteenth-century agrarianism found a strong voice in Bryan. The aforementioned James Weaver supported all of Bryan's presidential campaigns, and most Populist leaders followed suit. A year before his death, Henry George backed Bryan for president in 1896. Bryan was deeply influenced by Russian agrarian Leo Tolstoy, especially in the area of foreign policy. Bryan was, first and foremost, an eloquent voice of the fifty-eight percent of the people of the United States who lived in the country and in villages having a population of less than one-thousand. An heir and enlarger of the agrarian revolt of the Gilded Age, Bryan was a friend of farmers.

Bryan believed that farm life was superior to city life for a number of reasons: it was a more independent way of living, it required less capital to begin work, the entire family could assist in work, it was more healthful, habits of industry and application were easily acquired, it cultivated hospitality and generosity, it increased parental influence, it emphasized the true basis of rewards, and it produced informed and independent voters. He later added three more reasons: contact with nature encourages belief in God, dependence on Mother Earth means the farmer is neither a parasite nor a pilferer, and the work schedule shields the young from those who profit from commercialized nighttime vices.[5]

Because of his commitment to rural life, Bryan looked to the noneastern regions of the nation for the bulk of his political support. It was difficult for Bryan to look kindly upon the East. The East was not only urban-based; it was home of America's economic elite (Wall Street) and intellectual elite (the Ivy League). In his Cross of Gold speech at the 1896 convention, he proclaimed, "You come to us and tell us that the great cities are in favor of the gold standard; we reply that the great cities rest upon our broad and fertile prairies. Burn down your cities and leave our farms, and your cities will spring up again as if by magic; but destroy our farms and the grass will grow in the streets of every city in the country." In contrast to Grover Cleveland's three campaigns, Bryan's carried no eastern state in its three runs for the White House. Like the Populists, Bryan was primarily a candidate of the farms and towns of rural America, but he did have some backing in the cities and did make overtures to organized labor. Still, Bryan's willingness to virtually write off an entire section of the country, and his inability to move much beyond his base, illustrates a potential weakness of agrarian politics—or at least a weakness of this particular practitioner.

Bryan's Jeffersonian counterpart in the Republican Party was Robert M. La Follette of Wisconsin. La Follette and his allies were responsible for many significant reforms and resistances during the Progressive Era.

---

5. William Jennings Bryan, *William Jennings Bryan: Selections*, ed. Ray Ginger (Indianpolis: Bobbs-Merrill, 1967), 75–78; Lawrence W. Levine, *Defender of the Faith: William Jennings Bryan: The Last Decade, 1915–1925* (Cambridge: Harvard University Press, c1965, 1987), 227–28.

After serving five years as an innovative governor of Wisconsin, La Follette went to Washington. Senator La Follette was a two-time national candidate for the GOP presidential nomination (1908 and 1912). He might well have run as a third-party candidate in 1912, but his support that year was largely co-opted by ex-President Theodore Roosevelt. In 1924, he finally bolted the Republican Party and received nearly 5 million votes as a third-party candidate for president. He is considered one of the historic giants of the Senate even though he was usually on the losing side during his nearly-twenty years in the chamber.

La Follette grew up on a farm in Wisconsin. His political philosophy was "profoundly influenced by the Granger and agrarian uprisings he had witnessed during his youth." La Follette was also influenced by the traditions of the midwestern wing of the Republican Party. From its founding in the 1850s, "there were tensions between two major components of the party: the aspiring industrialists of the urban Northeast, and the small farmers and traders of the West."[6] The urban eastern wing of the GOP was largely descended from the Hamiltonian wing of the Federalist Party, by way of Cotton Whigs and Anti-Masons. The agrarian midwestern wing was largely descended from the Adams wing of the Federalist Party and Jefferson's Democratic-Republican Party, by way of Conscience Whigs and Free Soil Democrats. Midwestern Republicans were considerably more Jeffersonian in their thinking than were their eastern counterparts. Eastern financial and industrial interests dominated both the party and the nation under Presidents Grant, Hayes, Garfield, Arthur, Harrison, and McKinley.

Political scientist Nicol Rae has made an important contribution to the understanding of history by clearly identifying two dissident streams within the Republican Party during the Progressive Era: eastern progressives and western progressives. Theodore Roosevelt exemplified the former; Robert La Follette exemplified the latter.[7] La Follette and most of his supporters were agrarian in orientation. They were certainly closer to Jefferson in their thinking than were Roosevelt, George Perkins, Frank Munsey, Henry Stimson, Charles Evans Hughes, Herbert Croly, Walter

---

6. Robert S. Maxwell, *La Follette and the Rise of the Progressives in Wisconsin* (Madison: State Historical Society of Wisconsin, 1956), 12; Nicol C. Rae, *The Decline and Fall of the Liberal Republicans: From 1952 to the Present* (New York: Oxford University Press, 1989), 11.

7. *Ibid.*, 15, 43–44.

Lippmann, and others identified with the eastern progressive wing of the party.

According to La Follette, "Nearness to nature, nearness to God, a truer philosophy, a keener human sympathy, higher ideals, greater individuality, will ever be stamped upon the life and character of the country home."[8] While they had an agrarian base of support, La Follette and the western progressives built bridges to city dwellers and urban laborers. La Follette's close association with the University of Wisconsin indicates that his political program was not confined to agrarian democracy. In 1924 his presidential campaign was relatively weak in the East. His popular vote percentages in all eleven eastern states were below his national percentage. Nonetheless, he did better than his national average in many of the nation's largest cities.

Although he tried to win the votes of city dwellers, La Follette never abandoned his agrarian base. He supported and was supported by the Nonpartisan League (NPL). His 1924 campaign speeches "were particularly vibrant when discussing the plight of farmers." When he was working on behalf of citizens who lived in rural areas, he was working on behalf of small, family farmers. La Follette was an opponent of what later became known as "agribusiness." He attributed the rise of the NPL in the Midwest partly to the influence of agribusiness. In 1924, he told an audience in Kansas City, "The railroads of the country are interlocked with the packers, with the millers, with the commission men, with the grain pits. Together they form an economic system, ruled from Wall Street."[9]

La Follette's allies in the U.S. Senate shared his perspective. Referring to this bloc in the 1920s, Nicol Rae writes, "Although they had adopted the Progressive label, the generally agrarian outlook of the Senate radicals bore little relation to the paternalist, urban, upper middle-class progressivism of [Theodore] Roosevelt and Herbert Croly."[10] La Follette Republicans William Kenyon of Iowa, Arthur Capper of Kansas, Peter Norbeck of South Dakota, and Charles McNary of Oregon were leading members of the senatorial Farm Bloc in the early 1920s. In the 1930s, the agrarian orientation of this pro-La Follette bloc contributed to tensions that arose between its members and the urban-oriented Franklin D. Roosevelt administration. Even when the New Deal addressed agricul-

---

8. Robert M. La Follette, *The Political Philosophy of Robert M. La Follette*, comp. Ellen Torelle (Madison: Robert M. La Follette Co., 1920), 282.

9. *Ibid.*, 288.

10. Rae, 23.

tural concerns, implementation of the programs was open to criticism. For example, the Agricultural Adjustment Act (AAA) disproportionately benefited large farmers and food processors, to the disadvantage of small farmers and sharecroppers.

The agrarian argument that the economic and political abuses of the monopolistic robber barons could be mostly curbed at the state and local level, and by conscientious application of federal antitrust laws, was rejected by President Woodrow Wilson in favor of federal regulation that often served to undercut more honest and progressive state attempts. As a result of grassroots discontent manifested in reform movements, labor unions, socialism, third parties, Bryan Democrats, and La Follette Republicans, the bipartisan Center moved toward corporate liberalism during the Progressive Era. Pressure from below resulted in a repackaging of policy from above. Corporate liberalism rejected both free enterprise and socialistic reform. Sophisticated, international-oriented businessmen and financiers created a partnership between big government and big business in an effort to neutralize opposition. FDR made this arrangement seemingly permanent by choosing to follow in the footsteps of Wilson and the first Roosevelt.

A less-domestic source of agrarian, decentralist thought arising during the Progressive Era was Distributism. Inspired by Pope Leo XIII's encyclical, *Rerum Novarum* (1891), which addressed the plight of the working class, distributists were Catholics in Britain who presented an alternative to both capitalism and socialism. The most important exponents were Hilaire Belloc and G.K. Chesterton. Although often addressing the modern plight of the proletariat, distributists were grounded in traditional agrarian values. The movement would influence Dorothy Day, Peter Maurin, and the Catholic Workers, who began their mission to the down-and-out in America's large cities in the early 1930s.

Around this time, the Southern Agrarian movement was brought to limited public attention through release of the book *I'll Take My Stand* (1930). A group of intellectuals and writers associated with Vanderbilt University in Nashville, the Twelve Southerners were not necessarily waxing nostalgic for the Lost Cause in the form of the planter aristocracy or the CSA. Instead, at least some were reaching further back to a less-tainted source: the independent yeomanry of Jefferson and Jackson. This is not to say that none of the Southern Agrarians were unsympathetic to the leaders of the Confederacy or that all were partial to racial equality. There was a common love of the land and its nurture, and of southern culture in general, but by the 1950s, at least one—Robert Penn Warren—publicly supported the Civil Rights Movement as a new manifestation of the old struggle against special privilege, while others were opposed. Herbert Agar became a friend of Chesterton's and helped to promote Distributism. Richard Weaver, a later Southern Agrarian, and Russell Kirk, a native of Michigan who received his MA at Duke University in North Carolina, were both admirers of John Randolph of Roanoke. Randolph was a cousin, supporter, and irritant of Jefferson—one of the Tertium Quids who were often more Jeffersonian than Jefferson during his presidency. Weaver and Kirk became fathers of modern American conservatism.

Agrarian Politics Today

Is agrarianism a real option today or is it simply a manifestation of nostalgia? Agriculture as a vocation and way of life was dealt a significant blow as early as 1917 when the U.S. entered World War I. The war helped to plant the seeds of destruction for family farming through the proliferation of modernization, expertization, agribusiness, and government domination. Subsequent decades did not arrest this trend. Between 1958 and 1967 alone, employment on farms—as a percentage of overall American employment—fell from 8.5 percent to 4.8 percent. The great champions of country folk had disappeared by this time. There were farm-state politicians in Washington who constantly pressed for more farm subsidies, but their primary interests lay elsewhere. Agricultural talk was more about reelection campaigns, corporate welfare, American Farm Bureau favors, and USDA hand-outs than about the farmers themselves.

Senator Hubert Humphrey of Minnesota can serve as a case study of what went wrong. As a fellow Midwestern liberal and rabble rouser, Humphrey is often mistaken as a populist in the vein of Bryan. He was not. Early in his career, when he was a Wendell Willkie Republican, Humphrey jumped into state politics and helped shove the genuine populists and agrarians aside through the merger of the Minnesota Democratic and Farmer-Labor parties. He became mayor of Minneapolis and co-founder of Americans for Democratic Action. His base of political support, both statewide and nationally, was primarily urban. He was a thoroughgoing Wall Street Democrat by the late 1960s—which, in the eyes of Bryan, would have made him thoroughly "unavailable" for the Democratic presidential nomination.

Some members of the U.S. Counterculture of the late 1960s and early 1970s were more consistently Jeffersonian in their approach. The exotic "lifestyle" trappings of the hippies seem a long way from the powdered wig of Jefferson, but there were important similarities under the surface, including decentralism and agrarianism. J.R.R. Tolkein's *The Hobbit* and *The Lord of the Rings* trilogy were published in the United States in new paperback editions in the mid 1960s. Salient themes in these books were the difference one person can make, attachment to one's home and its ways of life, and the dangerous nature of power. Rural values and ancient folkways were promoted as alternatives to the modern urban-commercial-industrial-scientific world. Describing hobbits, the publisher told readers, "They love peace and quiet and good tilled earth. They dislike machines, but they are handy with tools."[11]

The Hobbit and *The Lord of the Rings* influenced the Counterculture that, in turn, contributed to a new level of popularity for the books. Members of the Counterculture argued that the federal government had long been working in concert with corporations to destroy freedom, community, thrift, naturalism, and other traditional American values. By the early 1970s, many of those same people were agrarians who advocated going "back to nature," getting "back to the land." Far from arguing the impossibility and irrelevance of social change without government direction, they went out and created their own rural communes.

Humphrey's response during this period was much different. He remained a champion of agribusiness. From the days of the Grange and Nonpartisan League, the millers, bankers, and railroads headquartered in Minneapolis had been infamous for their exploitation of family farmers. Despite their illiberal reputations, these forces developed a close relationship with Humphrey. From the start of his career to its close he relied on support from Pillsbury, General Mills, Peavey, Minneapolis and St. Louis Railroad, Cargill, American Milk Producers Inc., and similar companies. Humphrey's close friend and financial patron, Dwayne Andreas of Archer Daniels Midland, personified agribusiness. There ought to be more options than either Hippies or Humphrey, and there are, but even semi-respectable voices on behalf of small farmers are hard to find in Washington today.

11. J.R.R. Tolkien, *The Hobbit, or, There and Back Again*, Rev. ed. (New York: Ballantine, c1937, c1966, 1973), 1.

Rooted in the West German Counterculture of the 1960s and 1970s, the U.S. Green Party began in the 1980s as a political offshoot of the American Counterculture. Borrowing their Ten Key Values and slogan "We are neither Left nor Right; we are in Front" from their German counterparts, American Greens had the potential of creating a broad populist coalition that might have recreated the popular appeal of the People's Party or the Bryan and La Follette insurgencies. In practice, they have been almost entirely Left and have been unable to rise above their loyalty to identity politics, their commitment to abortion rights, and their dislike of traditional Christianity's appeal to conservative populists. Conversely, their progressive ideological purity on democracy and peace has alienated the mass of more compromising liberals, who are willing to settle for the Democratic Party. While obviously supportive of nature, in the sense of ecology, the Green Party is not very agrarian. It has some support among hippie farmers but almost none among more traditional ones. In this way, it has not been successfully Jeffersonian.

During the G.W. Bush years, a countercultural variety of conservatism came to public notice with the publications of Rod Dreher's *Crunchy Cons* and Bill Kauffman's *Look Homeward, America* (both in 2006). While it was wide in scope, rooted in influences ranging from Burke to Bryan, agrarianism was one component of the new (or revived) movement. Among other things, it promoted local attachments, community-based economics, organic food, and a small-is-beautiful ethic. The writer Wendell Berry—long a favorite of "granola" progressives associated with Jerry Brown, Ralph Nader, and the Green Party on the Left—was also a favorite of this group on the Right. In both its life and politics, it could be described as Jeffersonian. Point number six of the Crunchy-Con Manifesto was "A good rule of thumb: Small and Local and Old and Particular are to be preferred over Big and Global and New and Abstract."[12]

Contemporary conditions are not encouraging. The horrors of factory farming, foremost for the animals but secondarily for human neighbors, continue largely unabated. The brave new world of Frankenfoods, engineered through an unholy alliance of the worst of commerce and the worst of science, offers GMOs, non-germinating seeds, monopolization of planting, cloning, patenting of life forms, and general hubris. It is one of the many ways in which the false religion of scientism has hurt society.

---

12. Rod Dreher, *Crunchy Cons: How Countercultural Conservatives Plan to Save America (or at least the Republican Party)* (New York: Crown Forum, 2006), 2.

The cult has fostered the neglect of history, philosophy, and theology as valid—and vital—methods of epistemology.

On the campaign trail, William Jennings Bryan made an important distinction between the God-made man and the man-made man, the human being vs. the corporation. As wonderful as many modern inventions are, and as helpful in many ways as industrialization has been, sometimes man-made products still rank as poor substitutes for the real thing. There is a difference between infant formula and breast milk, between air conditioning and a cool breeze. There is something to be said for convenience, but as we become ever more addicted to the artificial and superficial, we are losing touch with important parts of our culture and our reality.

Who speaks for agrarians today? For soil and plants and animals and breezes, both cool and warm? For farming rather than agribusiness? If we don't have a Jefferson, Bryan, or La Follette, at least we have a few Countercultural Greens, a few Crunchy Cons, a few Catholic Distributists, a few Contrarians in seats of political power. Wendell Berry still lives in Kentucky. Russell Feingold is back in Wisconsin, down but perhaps not out. Agrarian politics is a tough sell in a land where prisoners behind bars outnumber farmers on tractors, but things looked gloomy during the Gilded Age as well. Yes, that period gave rise to the Progressive Era with considerable harm done, but it also gave us some political victories that can still inspire. For some of us, moments enjoyed and insights learned on traditional farms during our youth can be passed on to the next generation. Even if Washington fails us, we can find hope in other places.

American Foreign Policy and Modest Republicanism: The Great Rule Reconstituted

Michael P. Federici

In the realm of foreign affairs there is a great divide between realists and idealists. Realists claim that politics is the art of the possible. In their view statesmen must learn how to use power effectively in order to promote national interests, security being paramount. Wishful thinking has no place in the cut-throat environment of world politics. The goal is to minimize threats and cut losses when things go awry. The prudent path often means choosing the lesser of evils. Idealists, by contrast, hope and believe that politics can achieve what realists regard as impossible. They place faith in international institutions that promise a new environment for international relations. Mutual interest, they say, can be used to forge a more peaceful and prosperous world. Common objectives like economic prosperity and concerns about climate change provide the foundation for cooperation among nations that might otherwise be at odds. Traditionally, these idealists are less willing than realists to use military force and they are less cynical about the possibilities of politics.

But the evidence of the last century suggests an interesting change in a least in one respect: idealists increasingly resemble realists in their willingness to use military force. But the paradoxical result in the context of American politics is that policy debates are largely competitions not between different types of realists but between different types of *idealists*.

If American foreign policy is to move away from the idealistic tendencies that inspired American involvement in WWI, Vietnam, and recent meddling in the Middle East, political leaders and the American people will have to reorient the way they imagine world politics. Given recent failures of American foreign policy in Afghanistan and Iraq, the circumstances are ripe for the emergence of a new realism—or for what used to be known as "modest republicanism."

Consider American adventurism in the Middle East. This is a brand of idealism that masquerades as realism. Tough talk, advocacy of larger defense budgets that fund increases in ships, planes, and soldiers, and a willingness to use military force in a unilateral way have been seen as characteristics of realism. Yet the escalation of American involvement in the Middle East during the George W. Bush administration was anything but realistic, even though it was not shy about using military force without the approval of the United Nations. In the aftermath of 9/11 the putative realists David Frum and Richard Perle compared the mistakes made by George W. Bush in Iraq to the mistakes made by George Washington in the American War for Independence. War, they said, is a messy business, and assessing the effectiveness of military intervention requires sober and realistic standards. From this one might assume that Frum and Perle are old-fashioned realists who chastise idealists for being unrealistic about the complexities of war. Yet elements of their argument do not comport with realism. Their rhetoric of using military force *and* acknowledging its imperfections is a mixture of both realist possibilities and idealist reaching. Consider the following comments as an example of this mixture:

> A world at peace; a world governed by law; a world in which all peoples are free to find their own destinies: That dream has not yet come true, it will not come true soon, but if it ever does come true, it will be brought into being by American armed might and defended by American might too.[1]

Here Frum and Perle sound like Wilsonian idealists, but they lack the commitment to collective security and multilateralism that would situate them neatly into the category. In fact what they do is fuse aspects of idealism and realism to form a kind of incoherence. It is worth noting that thirty-three international-relations scholars, all identified realists,

---

1. David Frum and Richard Perle, *An End to Evil: How to Win the War on Terror* (New York: Ballantine Books, 2004), 239.

took out an advertisement in the *New York Times* on September 26, 2002, arguing against an American invasion of Iraq.[2] *Traditional* realists were united in their opposition to American intervention in Iraq.

Frum and Perle are sensitive to the charge that they are advocating American empire. They refute such claims by assuring their readers that many small nations ask for America's help because they know that receiving it will not mean forfeiting their independence and sovereignty. Why is this the case? Because, they say, the U.S. is a virtuous nation. The point is crystallized in the statement that "America's vocation is not an imperial vocation. Our vocation is to support justice with power."[3] But there is more than a hint of American exceptionalism—the belief that there is something uncommon and great about the United States that other nations lack—in the argument. According to this doctrine Americans, from the inception of European settlements in North America, have been the chosen people of God meant to carry out the divine will in history. Even such thinkers as the nineteenth-century Catholic intellectual Orestes Brownson argued that "divine Providence has given us an important mission, and has chosen us to work out for the world a higher order of civilization than has hitherto obtained. We look upon ourselves as a providential people, as a people with great destiny, and a destiny glorious to ourselves and beneficent to the world."[4] Woodrow Wilson exhibited the characteristics of idealism when he told Congress that the war Germany was executing against the allies was "a war against all nations" and that it was a challenge "to all mankind." According to Wilson, the U.S. was entering the war for unselfish and humanitarian reasons. "We have no selfish ends to serve. We desire no conquest, no dominion. We seek no indemnities for ourselves, no material compensation for the sacrifices we shall freely make. We are but one of the champions of the rights of mankind." Wilson was clearly the voice of idealism, but he was also confident that military force would serve humanitarian ends. In this regard, American exceptionalism in various contexts fosters the very mix of realism and idealism that Frum and Perle represent.

But American exceptionalism has not always been ascendant. Alternative ways of thinking about American identity and foreign affairs were present in the Founding generation. In fact muscular idealism inspired

---

2. See http://www.bear-left.com/archive/2002/0926oped.html.

3. Frum and Perle, 239.

4. Orestes Brownson, "Mission in America," in *Brownson's Works*, ed. Henry F. Brownson, 20 vols. (Detroit: Thorndike Nourse, 1882–1887), Vol. 11, 566–567.

by American exceptionalism represents a radical *break* from an older American way of thinking about America's role in the world. Alexander Hamilton and George Washington articulated a modest role for the United States in international affairs, a role based on the Great Rule: that we should avoid involving ourselves in the conflicts of other nations. In short, America should mind its own business. Hamilton and Washington were not arguing for isolationism. They were strongly in favor of expanding and protecting American trade and building a military that could protect such interests. What they wanted to avoid was entanglement with European nations that would, they thought, lead to unnecessary conflict inconsistent with American interests. Hamilton in particular was opposed to the Jeffersonian inclination to support such ideological movements as the one in Jacobin France, which Jefferson considered part of a global revolution that would transform the world. There was something modest about Hamilton's and Washington's approach to foreign affairs that Jefferson's revolutionary idealism lacked. And the difference between them provides a more useful contrast than the one between realism and idealism that frames the current political debate.

Critics of a modest republican approach to American foreign policy argue that the older view and the Great Rule itself are antiquated relics of a past that is long gone. The United States ceased to be a small isolated republic before the end of the nineteenth century. By the middle of the twentieth century it was a world power and knee-deep in resolving the world's problems. The change in circumstances has meant that a modest approach to foreign policy based on eighteenth-century principles is imprudent. In the twentieth century the United States was called to greatness when it responded to the threats of German and Russian totalitarianism, and it is once again called to defend civilization from the new threat of global terrorism.

It may be possible, however, to apply the principle of the Great Rule to new circumstances in the same way that it is possible to apply to the twenty-first century such eighteenth-century American constitutional principles as the rule of law and the separation of powers. Change is inevitable in historical and political life, but adaptation to change can vary. Does the United States have to maintain a larger and more powerful military than it did in the eighteenth century? Of course it does. Does the United States have to be more involved in the world than it was in the eighteenth century? Of course it does, given the current circumstances. But modesty is a virtue that transcends time because, like all virtues, it is relative to context and circumstance. The parameters of conducting a modest foreign policy are different today from what they were in the eighteenth century, but such constraints exist. For example, the idea professed by George W. Bush in his Second Inaugural Address—that "the survival of liberty in our land increasingly depends on the success of liberty in other lands" and that "the best hope for peace in our world is the expansion of freedom in all the world"[5]—can easily lead to a foreign policy that is ideologically imperialistic and contrary to American interests. If Bush is correct, if regime-type determines the legitimacy of nation states and their commitment to such universal human values as liberty, then the United States has an obligation and a national interest in agitating for regime change around the globe. If the objective is global democracy, then non-democratic nation states must be pressured or forced to undergo democratic revolutions.

But if the formula for democratizing the world and making it peaceful is simple, the reality is complex, messy, and full of unintended consequences that ought to make us question the prudence of world-changing foreign policies, especially those that exceed human reach. Take Iraq as an example. The hope of the Bush administration was to invade a non-democratic nation, depose its leaders, and build a new Iraq based on democratic principles. Once Iraq was democratized, other non-democratic nations in the region would witness the wonders of democracy and freedom, overthrow their regimes, and institute democracy. There was at one time talk of an Arab spring that would transform the Middle East into a peaceful and economically prosperous community. Such idealism was buoyed by elections in Iraq and the ink-stained fingers of voters who ignored threats from anti-democratic forces and waited in lines for hours to cast their first votes for the new regime's leaders. At the time the dream of a peaceful democratized Middle East seemed to be unfolding. President Bush declared that "Iraqi democracy will succeed—and that success will send forth the news from Damascus to Tehran that freedom can be the future of every nation. The establishment of a free Iraq at the heart

---

5. George W. Bush, "Second Inaugural Address," January 20, 2005: http://avalon.law.yale.edu/21st_century/gbush2.asp.

of the Middle East will be a watershed event in the global democratic revolution."[6] But it is important to note that Bush's sentiments have more in common with the revolutionary idealists Jefferson and Wilson than with the modest republicans Hamilton and Washington.

Iraq and the Middle East look much different today from what they looked like during the early days of the Purple Revolution. The region is engulfed in war and disorder, and the threat of a larger conflict looms on the horizon. ISIS represents a global totalitarian movement that in some respects (but certainly not all) surpasses Nazi Germany in its inhumanity. The disorder and destabilization were caused, in part, by President Bush's idealistic foreign policy in Iraq and his dream of a transformed Middle East. Make no mistake about it: the pursuit of the impossible helped to cause the current mess in the Middle East. The pride that engenders American exceptionalism led Bush to believe that he could orchestrate the transformation of the Middle East. Modest republicans were not simply skeptical about such idealistic objectives; they were adamant in opposing such measures as imprudent, contrary to American interests, and likely to result in more harm than good.

However one classifies Bush's Iraq policy, it was not modest. It violated Washington's Great Rule because it was born from the pride of believing that American power is so great that it could destroy the Iraqi regime, create a new democratic Iraq, democratize the Middle East, and bring freedom and peace to a part of the world that has never once enjoyed their fruits. But this is the same pride evident in the quotation by Frum and Perle regarding American military might transforming the world. The principle of modesty, by contrast, suggests that politics is the art of the possible and that grand transformations of the type Bush and his advisors promised are the stuff of fairytales, not politics.

What, then, some will ask, should have been done about Iraq?

In retrospect, it seems clear that doing something less than an American invasion to overthrow the regime would have been prudent. Leaving Saadam Hussein in power was likely the wiser path. Taking a modest and far less interventionist path would have required giving up on the dream of transforming the Middle East and the world, but herein lies the point: modesty requires that politics account for the human condition and the ineradicable presence of evil in political life. Moral realism

---

6. George W. Bush, "Remarks by President George W. Bush at the 20th Anniversary of the National Endowment for Democracy," November 2003: http://www.ned.org/remarks-by-president-george-w-bush-at-the-20th-anniversary/.

is the philosophical ground on which modest republicanism stands. It accepts certain truths about the permanence of evil and its place in human nature. Frum and Perle, whose book is titled *An End to Evil*, assume something very different about evil and therefore about human nature.

The difference between modest republicanism on the one hand and both right- and left-wing idealism on the other has its counterpart in a more fundamental difference: the anthropological difference between those who think evil is remediable and those who know it isn't. Consider James Madison's response in *Federalist 10* to the problem of faction. Madison considered factions evil. Their members are more likely to vex and oppress one another than to cooperate for the common good. They are, by definition, adverse to the rights of others. Yet Madison did not talk of eliminating factions in the way that Frum and Perle talk about eliminating the evil of terrorism. Why? Because their causes are part of human nature. The only way to eliminate them is to extinguish liberty, a solution beyond consideration. Consequently, the only path is to control the effects of factions by creating republican political institutions, that is, institutions with representatives that will refine and enlarge the people's will. The second part of the solution is to enlarge the orbit of government in order to multiply the number of factions, thus making it less likely that a majority faction will form and tyrannize the numerical minority. Madison's solution was born of the same moral realism that gave life to the Great Rule. It accepts the permanence of evil and the sober objective of minimizing rather than eliminating it. Frum and Perle, by contrast, argue from an alternative philosophical tradition, a tradition different from the one that undergirds the Constitution, the Great Rule, and Madison's *Federalist* 10.

It may surprise some to learn that supporters of the Republican Party who advocate originalism in judicial politics betray the Framers' political theory in some aspects of their politics. George W. Bush, like Frum and Perle, also argued from a philosophical tradition alien to traditional American constitutionalism. Bush did not disguise his romantic view of America and the world. He stated in his Second Inaugural Address that it is "the policy of the United States to seek and support the growth of democratic movements and institutions in every nation and culture, with the ultimate goal of ending tyranny in our world."[7] You have to wonder how many times Americans will hear from their presidents

---

7. George W. Bush, "Second Inaugural Address."

that we can end war, poverty, fear, drug-use, terrorism, etc., before they begin to see what the costs of democratic idealism really are or before the truth begins to sink in: politics is the art of the possible. Good intentions and humanitarian policies often mask the will to power and the imprudence of actions, actions that will likely lead to disaster.

The first step in restoring American foreign policy to a condition of realism or modest republicanism is to learn from the failed idealism of Woodrow Wilson and George W. Bush; the second is to recognize the incompatibility of such idealism with the political theory of the American Constitution. What we must understand is that something is wrong with how Americans since Wilson have imagined politics. They are deeply imbued with unhealthy and unrealistic views of politics, and the sooner they are disabused of them the better. The philosopher Eric Voegelin used the term "metastatic faith" to refer to an unrealistic belief in the transformative power of political action to change human nature and the very limits of politics. He attributed the widespread presence of metastatic faith to a spiritual crisis in America, and in the West generally, that was the consequence of a gnostic inability to cope with the harsh realities of life.[8] The desire for a transformed world in which specific evils have been eradicated compromises the ability of human beings to see life as it is. Dream replaces reality. To cite just one example of an American thinker who expressed a view of politics inspired by metastatic faith, the early twentieth century progressive Herbert Croly wrote that "Democracy must risk its success on the integrity of human nature."[9] Croly made clear that democracy has the power to improve human nature.[10] He argued that "Democracy must stand or fall on a platform of possible human perfectibility."[11] As human nature is transformed, government "should no longer be subjected to the Law."[12]

Croly's progressive idealism indicated that the moral realism that gave rise to the American Constitution and the modest republicanism on which it was based were losing ground to a competing ideology that

---

8. Eric Voegelin, *Israel and Revelation*, ed. With an Introduction by Maurice P. Hogan (Columbia and London: University of Missouri Press, 2001), 506–508.

9. Herbery Croly, *Progressive Democracy*, With an Introduction by Sidney A. Pearson, Jr. (New Brunswick and London: Transaction Publishers, 1998), 27.

10. Herbert Croly, *The Promise of American Life*, With a Foreword by Michael McGerr (Boston: Northeastern University Press, 1989), 413.

11. Croly, *The Promise of American Life*, 400.

12. Croly, *Progressive Democracy*, 122.

called into question the basic principles and theoretical assumptions of the American Framers. As progressive idealism became increasingly influential in shaping American politics and intellectual life, the Framers' Constitution would have to give ground to democratic idealism. Foreign affairs were not immune from the influences of this idealism, and Woodrow Wilson began the twentieth century with a burst of it. His liberal internationalism was passed on to George W. Bush, who began the twenty-first century with a similar type of progressive idealism, though from the political right.

The problem in restoring American common sense to foreign policy is that sensible approaches to foreign affairs are largely absent from the political landscape. And if Voegelin is correct, the problem requires a spiritual renewal, not a policy change. But this is a spiritual renewal that shows few signs of occurring. The sober views of modest republicanism exist, but you must leave the beaten path of American politics to find them. Imagine a presidential candidate arguing that the United States needs to be less involved in the Middle East, not more involved. Few Americans would support such a candidate as long as idealism is prevalent in American political culture. Even President Obama, who staked his claim in 2008 on ending the war in Iraq, increased American involvement in Afghanistan and returned troops to Iraq. The temptation to fix the Middle East is too great for nation-building presidents to resist because idealism is so ingrained in their imaginations.

In an effort to define modest republicanism as it relates to American foreign policy, I will conclude with a sketch of the principles of modesty on which it is based. Two such principles have been mentioned: that politics is the art of the possible and that the U.S. should mind its own business and avoid meddling in the affairs of other nations. America is not the instrument of God's or history's will. Prudence should be the paramount principle of foreign policy, and this means resisting the temptation to transform the world or act as its policeman. There is a time and place for American intervention. Modest republicanism is not an argument for isolationism, as if such a thing is even possible. But there is a wide gap between democratizing the Middle East and using diplomacy and military force to protect vital American interests. Human nature is part of a fixed structure of reality that cannot be changed by politics, including the implementation of democratic institutions. Our fallen nature is a permanent part of our condition, and it means that politics must contend with the problem of evil. It also means acknowledging that the perfection of human beings and society is impossible. Consequently, there are limits to what politics can accomplish. In foreign affairs it is likely that pride, greed, envy, and the will to power will interfere with efforts to create a peaceful world. Such efforts should be mindful of the limits of politics and align political objectives to the realities of the human condition. This sketch of modest republicanism is a reconstitution of the Great Rule in new circumstances and a call for a new realism in American politics.

The Demise of Virtue in Virtual America[1]

David Bosworth

AFTER THE PUBLICATION OF Thomas Piketty's *Capital in the Twenty-First Century*, a milder version of the fury spurred by our economic system's gross injustices finally migrated from the tents of populist activists into the blogs of the chattering classes. The surge in financial inequality that Piketty enumerated is a truly worrisome phenomenon worthy of debate. But, as Ross Douthat has suggested, the emphasis on a strictly monetary measure of contemporary capitalism's social dangers masks the full range and depth of its destructive impact—both on our civic character and on the local communities and civic associations that have traditionally nourished it.

To a degree that communism never could, consumer capitalism does produce the goods, even if it distributes them unevenly and often unfairly. Yet, contrary to the Pollyanna theory that has justified thirty-five years of economic policy, it in no way naturally produces the Good. As most religions have preached and fairy tales warned, unchecked self-interest—whether in the form of self-liberation for the individual or deregulation for the corporation—is not a plausible route to enlightened behavior. Rather than fidelity to family and community, it leads to dissension, dissolution and addictive consumption; instead of animating a meritocratic marketplace, it produces lobbied loopholes, golden parachutes and stifling monopolies. Disdaining plain speaking in favor of the fog of a profit-seeking expertise, it crafts the fine print of "toxic assets." Fathers fleeing their children for a second bachelorhood and companies deserting their countries for tax-free havens are the unacknowledged ethical twins of our time. As intellectual cult leaders of the 20th century,

---

1. Adapted from *The Demise of Virtue in Virtual America: The Moral Origins of the Great Recession* (Eugene: Front Porch Republic Books, 2014).

Wilhelm Reich, the psychoanalyst who promoted sexual permissiveness, and Ayn Rand, the philosopher who thought individualism so important that she called altruism evil, had a lot in common.

I'm rare among analysts in stressing this, but the financial meltdown of 2008 was, at its core, a moral catastrophe, and one generated by decades of systemic deceit and self-deception. Although our nation's geographical coordinates are essentially the same as they were in 1946, we are now living in a dramatically different place, our days increasingly enclosed within a physical and digital architecture of windowless malls, office cubicles, and online virtual realities. And because control over nearly all the domains of this new Virtual America have been ceded to national and international corporations, the places where we gather to work and play, like the shows we stream, are not only "brought to us by" but also *for* their commercial sponsors.

Today's ideological defenders of *laissez faire* economics insist that it is precisely our full participation in this corporate system that induces desirable ethical traits such as self-reliance and delayed gratification. To a degree, of course, they are right, especially when contrasted with the old communist states, which both stifled initiative and repressed free expression. But in general the development of a robust ethical character is far more dependent on the moral health of families, neighborhoods, schools, and civic and religious associations, all of which possess a richer understanding of human prosperity, and those same smaller institutions are now being overrun by a corporate regime that would monetize and marketize virtually everything.

Such ideologues also conveniently forget that we no longer live in a local economy of independent farmers and shopkeepers, and that most workers today are not entrepreneurs but wage employees necessarily subservient to the moral order enforced inside their corporate offices, factories, sales rooms, and call centers. Nor do they acknowledge the flagrant fact that the spirit of capitalism changed when it aggressively turned to consumer products in the early to mid-twentieth century. As the profit-seeking economy became ever more dependent on inducing mass consumption, the old traits associated with the Protestant ethic, including thrift, self-reliance, prudence, plain speaking, and delayed gratification, became incompatible with the marketing required to boost consumer sales.

So it is today that the virtues narrowly associated with production and consumption—ruthless efficiency in the workplace and seductive salesmanship in the marketplace—have now suffused American life, co-opting alike the themes of our narratives, the planks of our parties, the practice of medicine, the profession of art, and the most intimate aspects of our personal lives, including our beliefs about God, marriage and childcare. Under this moral regime, the civic center has been replaced by the enclosed mall and the Olympics reduced to a global trade fair. The charitable "volunteer" at your door is just another salesman working on commission, taking 30 percent of each donation toward saving the whales, while the shoes, shirts, and hats that we wear have been hijacked to serve as corporate billboards.

Worse, our storehouse of memories is also overstocked with the logos of commerce. Where poems, parables, and patriotic songs once whispered in our ears to steer us through our lives, we now hear and heed the adman's jingles and the banal maxims of management gurus. Following their lead, honesty gives way to salesmanship, generosity is reconceived as productivity, heroes are replaced by celebrities, neighborliness is superseded by networking, and faith is reduced to "prosperity theology."

Our everyday language reflects this widespread conversion to corporate values. These days, people "shop" for a church; universities work at polishing their "brands," and, heeding the demands of corporate philanthropists, school principals are recast as "CEOs." Even those who wish to reform the system are trapped in its tropes, worrying aloud about our rapid depletion of "social capital." As our promiscuous use of the summary cliché "the bottom line" proves, most evaluations these days, sacred or profane, have become a subspecies of financial accounting. But virtues are not "social capital" and, despite the existential delusion recently re-endorsed by our Supreme Court, the modern corporation is not a person. It is instead a highly efficient money machine, self-excused by its charter from most of the duties that natively attend good citizenship.

When designing our democracy, the founders focused on prohibiting the two institutional enemies of freedom that they knew best, a centralized church and a monarchical state. Although uncommonly prudent for revolutionary thinkers, they never fully imagined, and so didn't "check and balance," the potential threat posed by the modern corporation, the character of whose internal governance—strictly rationalized methods serving narrowly materialistic ends—was neither Judeo-Christian nor democratic in nature. Consequently, the primary ethical challenge to the American experiment other than slavery has been whether the obvious productivity of these essentially amoral money machines—unimagined and so unrestrained by our Constitution—can be yoked to serve the same democratic purposes and Judeo-Christian values that they internally refuse.

Not just the subprime scandal that led to the Great Recession but also the broader monetizing of our artistic, scientific, and religious practices highlights our current failure to pass that test. And insomuch as this moral regime enforces two opposing sets of ideal behavior, one for behind the desk and the other for browsing in the mall, it is also deeply incoherent and extremely stressful on a personal level. Each of us is supposed to labor like Sisyphus and consume like Falstaff, the sum of which (as calculated by the fuzzy moral math of free-market ideology) will also produce a naturally virtuous citizenry. But robotic efficiency plus sheer avidity cannot lead to either personal happiness or civic righteousness, and no democracy can long survive a conversion to the service of such dehumanizing lies.

The ongoing submission of our everyday lives to the ways, means, and ruling ideals of radical capitalism is a grievous error, one inherently destructive to the communal associations that nurture the good life. As such, that error cannot be amended by a mere technical fix to our financial system. As a precedent to more substantial reforms, we must begin instead by acknowledging some hard truths about this Virtual America that has become our all-enclosing house even as it sheds the duties and delights of a communal home.

First, a nation cannot license a set of inherently amoral money machines to run its work spaces, public gathering places, and primary media for telecommunications and then expect the behavior of its people to remain morally sound. The core civic contention of the privatization movement—that ethical behavior is a kind of epiphenomenon of rationalized greed; that inside a fully marketized society, self-interest will, routinely, become enlightened—is a disingenuous delusion. As the housing bubble's astonishing scale of fraud and folly proved, it is a con game that we have played on ourselves, the particular way that (to cite Hamlet) "reason panders will" in an American accent.

Second, in a digital age, when messages invade every social niche and private space, a telecommunications system whose ruling intention is to promote acquisition will eventually produce an overly acquisitive population.

Third, when the profit motive prevails, when more money matters most, extreme efficiency at work and consumption at home will be pursued without consideration of the collateral social, psychological, and political damages that may result, for such damages no longer "compute."

Finally, insomuch as human beings are not machines, nor merely the sum of their physical appetites, the unbridled pursuit of efficiency and avidity on behalf of more money is not a ruling purpose worthy of our obedience, nor one conducive to cultural or psychological coherence, and no society (democratic or otherwise) can long survive its conversion to such dehumanizing lies. Charged with justifying the unbidden gift of consciousness in what sometimes seems but a blink of time, a successful life is both richer and harder than the bottom line can ever measure.

Part Three

The Home Economy

We have lost our respect for honest manual labor. We think of "creative" work as a series of abstract mental operations performed in an office, preferably with the aid of computers, not as the production of food, shelter, and other necessities. The thinking classes are fatally removed from the physical side of life—hence their feeble attempt to compensate by embracing a strenuous regimen of gratuitous exercise.

—CHRISTOPHER LASCH, THE REVOLT OF THE ELITES AND THE BETRAYAL OF DEMOCRACY

Work, Death, and the Romantic Agrarian

Mark T. Mitchell

I RECENTLY READ A magazine article describing a problem that some urban and suburban communities are facing. The current enthusiasm for backyard flocks of hens has swept into areas where zoning laws often allow a small flock. However, a hen's peak egg production is in the first several years of life, and after that things steadily decline. On the farm, when a hen stops laying, or even slows down considerably, she becomes soup. The article described an influx of spent hens arriving at the humane society, dropped off by hipsters and other recent chicken enthusiasts who had not fully considered the implications of keeping an animal beyond its productive years. Unwilling to keep a non-productive animal yet unwilling to butcher it, these suburban farmers were taking the easy way out by pushing the problem onto someone else. This points to a more general challenge: people who fancy an agrarian life as a sort of romantic aspiration but are not willing to embrace the full implications of such a life. They are agrarians in theory, but they don't like to get their hands very dirty.

It's not unusual to hear about a person who lives in the city or suburbs but wants to buy a place in the county and carve out a farm. These people want to live closer to the land, to grow at least some of their own food, to do more work with their hands, and to enjoy the many perceived benefits of living in a rural setting. They often speak in terms of a more "authentic" kind of life, one in the company of animals, of work, of an awareness of the natural world.

On the other hand, I sometimes hear people chiding those who express such desires. Why would anyone want to do this? We live in the "modern" world, and to leave any of that behind is foolishness at best and a kind of romantic pathology at worst. We have, in short, the romantic agrarian coming face to face with the sneering modern. This tension has a long history in America, where we can trace certain aspects of the conflict clear back to the debate between Jefferson and Hamilton.

Both the romantic agrarian and the sneering modern traffic in their own particular form of ignorance, and while it is certainly possible to move to the country and build a life near the land, it is important to dispel any romantic notions. At the same time, those who disparage this vision of flourishing are, themselves, often trapped in a myopic mirage of modernity, progress, and globalization. It is necessary to deal with the errors of both positions, and perhaps the best way to begin is to take a realistic look at the agrarian life.

While it would be difficult to claim that there is a movement afoot, it does seem that many people are becoming increasingly frustrated with lives bent on acquisition, consumption, long commutes, and faux communities. There is a perception among many that a return to the land will signal a return to simpler times when the confusions and stresses of the modern world will be pushed back and a better kind of life will be realized. This disposition may be as modest as a home in the country with a large garden and a few chickens. It may be as involved as quitting one's job and attempting to make a living from the land. In more extreme forms this might include eschewing some forms of modern technology and conveniences in favor of animal power and composting toilets.

Some make it happen. For others, however, it remains only a dream to be indulged during the long commute between work and home. However, for the person who actually does move to the country, the romantic patina will soon be replaced with something more gritty, for the "authentic" life in the country consists of plenty of hard work, blood, death, mistakes, and misery. In this respect, the critic of agrarian romanticism is on to something true. At the same time, the potential rewards are great, and the sacrifices and even losses can call forth a view of life that is perhaps uniquely available only in a life lived in close proximity to the land.

As with most things, experience is key. If you have experience growing a garden, butchering animals, or doing hard manual labor of any kind, you will be far better prepared to move to the country than if you have never grown a tomato or cleaned a fish, and if the closest you've been to a cow is reading James Harriot's books.

Several years ago my family and I purchased a few acres, had a house built, and moved to the country. I had, in the preceding years, read a fair number of books by Wendell Berry, and I would be lying if I said his writing had no influence on my thinking. However, we were already living in a semi-rural setting. We had an acre of land with a garden, fruit trees, and a small vineyard. As a kid, my parents kept a large garden, we hunted and fished and did plenty of work with our hands. As a result, I was somewhat prepared for this move to a few more acres with the intent of carving out a small farm. But a little preparation only means the learning curve is not as steep. What everyone needs to know before heading to an idyllic life in the country is that there will be plenty of setbacks. Things will often cost more and take longer than you anticipate. Nevertheless, it can be done. Here's a bit of what I've learned.

Start small. A common temptation, one that is not surprising for any enthusiastic beginner, is to try to do too much too soon. If you have never raised chickens, cows, goats, hogs, bees, or tomatoes, grapes, or apples, don't try to begin doing all of those things in the same year. Develop a multi-year plan that phases in one or two new operations very year or two. Farming is an art, and art requires skill, and skill only comes with time and experience. Each piece you add will involve learning new skills, and even when the skills are in place you will be building a more complex system. So add pieces gradually. If you don't, you will likely become overwhelmed, and animals, plants, land, your confidence and enthusiasm—as well as your pocketbook—will suffer.

Go cheap. Most people don't have money to burn, and many who are heading to the country are not sitting on a pile of extra cash. One of the first things I did was build a chicken coop. My primary building material was pallets I scavenged from various piles of scrap to which I had access. A friend who owns a shipping business delivered a few from his work. I built a frame using 2x6s connecting 4x4 posts that I buried in the ground. I used 2x6s for the floor and then stood up the pallets as walls. Pallets come in a variety of sizes, so I had to make adjustments according to what I had, but the coop's dimensions were built around the frame, which was 12' x 8'. I used 2x4s for ceiling joists and purchased sheets of plywood and corrugated steel roofing for the roof. We had some very large pallets with 8' sides. I had the boys take these pallets apart and used the slats for siding. We caulked the seams, added a door (scavenged) and we had a very large coop for several hundred dollars.

For the three-sided shed for the cows, I got permission from a builder friend to go through piles of used lumber on his property. One of my sons helped me sort the lumber and load it. The biggest task was removing all of the nails, but once that was done we had a pile of very good pressure-treated lumber. I put four posts in the ground forming a 12x12 square. Two posts were 10' long and buried 3' deep; two posts were 8' long and buried 3' deep. This provided a slope for the roof. I added two posts on the sides and several in the back for support, nailed scavenged 2x12s around the base of three sides and along the top and then attached the scavenged boards to form the walls. I then built joists of 2x6s and once again attached plywood and covered it with corrugated roofing. The entire thing cost me less than $400.

Dig deep. One summer we put in fencing in preparation for cows. After some investigation I settled on a high tensile electrified fence. I bought a bunch of eight-foot round posts, and, using a couple of posthole diggers and a digging bar, my three sons and I put in about 150 posts. Fortunately, our soil is deep, and for the most part the holes were rock-free. If we had shallow rocky soil, I would likely have rented an auger for the holes.

Two things everyone should know about fencing: First, set your posts deep. Although it takes longer and is more work, it always pays to dig another foot. Second, pay careful attention your corners. Corners—and this is especially true of a high tension fence—bear a tremendous amount of force. Make sure you don't cut corners here (so to speak) or you will be rebuilding your fence in short order. There is plenty of information on-line (including how-to videos). Research before you build.

Everything is hungry. When you keep animals, you need to feed them. Animals, like your kids, never stop eating. This can be especially difficult in the winter when the cold makes feeding miserable and when the animals need good food just to maintain sufficient body heat. The first year we had cows, I ordered sixteen large round bales. Not having a tractor, the boys and I rolled them off the delivery trailer and lined them up along our driveway. Throughout the winter we rolled a bale into the pasture every week or so. These bales weighed between 800 and 1000 pounds, so it took several of us to move them, especially as the winter wore on and they first froze to the ground and later absorbed moisture and started to flatten out on one side. When the wind was blowing hard and the temperatures dropped to the single digits, this was no pleasant chore. Nor was hauling hot water in five galleon buckets for the waterer that would freeze solid by morning so that you needed a hammer to remove the ice before adding new water. The cows didn't even say thank you.

Things die. Death is a persistent theme in the country. One reason for this relates directly back to the previous point. Hungry critters eat other critters. It's not always pretty, but it's a fact that you will have to live with. However, sometimes things die even if nothing is eating them. The first season on the farm I got two hives of bees. They produced honey that first year, but I didn't take any. I wanted to leave plenty for them during the winter. In the spring they were dead. I tried the next year and lost two more hives. Varro mites. I intend to try again, but needless to say I'm a little gun shy.

Despite my best efforts to protect our chickens, a fox started killing them. Here's the rub. You can keep chickens penned up in a little run that is completely fenced in and covered, but then they can't forage. As a result, most of the food they get comes from the feed store (or kitchen scraps if you have them). On the other hand, a free ranging hen has access to all of the bugs and worms and grubs she can find, but she can also become a pretty easy food source for predators who favor the taste of chicken. One summer our flock of twenty-two hens started diminishing by one every day or two. They were locked in the coop at night, so the attacks were happening during the day. But they happened quickly, and it was with a great deal of frustration that we'd find a pile of feathers in the field and one less chicken on the roost. I sat for a good number of hours at an open upstairs window with a good field of fire. One Sunday afternoon when I was away, my wife heard a commotion among the hens. She ran out of the house yelling, and the startled fox dropped a hen and ran. When I returned home the hens were cowering under the front porch (not where we want them!). I took up my position at the upstairs window thinking that the fox might return to finish his business as the chickens started moving from the front porch across the no-man's land toward the coop. Sure enough he did, and one shot with a rifle put an end to a chicken killing machine. I cut off his tail and nailed it to a fence post as a warning to others of his kind who, I am sure, are lurking about just biding their time.

I could write about the deer whose hind leg got caught in a wire mesh fence belonging to my neighbor. By the time I found her the vultures had begun their grim business without even waiting for her to die. A .45 caliber bullet put her out of her misery, but I hate to think of the time she spent suffering. Or I could write about the infestation of huge black snakes in the chicken coop. I caught the first two and put them in the field across the way, but when a third showed up and started swallowing eggs, I removed his head to save my son's egg business. Killing is never pleasant, but it is sometimes necessary.

Death is a messy business. Perhaps this goes without saying. However, unless you are a vegetarian, a good bit of the food you eat was once a sentient, breathing, and eventually bleeding creature. Cutting a chicken's throat is never fun, but, for better or worse, it does get easier with practice. One year we raised 50 meat chickens, and two of my sons and I butchered them one June morning. Converting a living creature into a piece of meat entails the strange and awful business of taking a vibrant, moving, and sometime frightened animal and reducing it to a carcass to be beheaded, gutted, skinned or plucked. What was only minutes ago a fellow creature is changed to something that can be roasted and eaten. At the very least we should be grateful for the sacrifice. If we ever become numb to the process, if we fail to feel a kinship with the creature and instead see only potential food, then it might be time to stop and become reacquainted with the seriousness of the endeavor.

The same thing happens when, for example, you shoot a deer. What was only minutes before a thing of grace and beauty must be rendered into food with a sharp knife and plenty of tugging, pushing, slicing, cracking, splitting, sawing, and blood. Always the blood.

Work is good. If you don't like hard work, don't move to the country. Or if you insist on moving to the country, better save up to hire someone to do the work for you, for there is work aplenty and, especially if there are animals involved, it is relentless. You can't take a break from feeding your stock. You must keep the fence in repair. You must keep the grass cut. You must weed the garden, pick the basil, fertilize the tomatoes, prune the grape vines, water the cows, gather the eggs, butcher the chickens, shovel the snow, repair the potholes in the driveway, feed the cows, pick the berries, preserve the berries, make pesto from the basil, and the list goes on.

One of my reasons for wanting to start a small farm is that I wanted my sons to learn how to work. I've told them this more than once (and I hope they've paid attention): if a person learns to be a hard worker, he's going to be ahead of most. Caring for other livings things forces you to bear the responsibility of other creatures that depend on you for their lives. The ability to see a job that needs to be done and then doing it is a skill that employers cherish. The ability to solve problems creatively, using resources at hand, is a skill that you can develop on a farm, and again such a skill translates into many contexts beyond the homestead.

Hopefully, the forgoing advice has been sufficient to remove any of the naïve romanticism that sometimes animates prospective farmers. At the same time, I hope that the benefits of this life have not been covered in too much manure and blood, for the benefits are many. This is what the sneering modern simply doesn't grasp or refuses to acknowledge. A life lived close to the land is not to everyone's taste. Some people are, at best, theoretical agrarians who love agrarian ideas and Wendell Berry's novels but prefer to keep their hands clean and to remain in climate-controlled comfort. Others, and I find this a bit strange, seem positively hostile to any suggestion that a good life can be lived in proximity to the soil and to animals. "This is the twenty-first century," they will sputter, as if that in itself provides irrefutable evidence in support of their anti-agrarian position; as if plants and animals no longer constitute our diets; as if our food magically appears in grocery stores and restaurants; as if farming now merely represents an outdated "life-style" choice and not the inescapable and necessary base to our very society. The inability to recognize that a life on the land could be richly satisfying for a sane and non-delusional person is reflective of a mind that despises variety and insists on uniformity. It insists that individuals conform to the patterns set out by a globalizing economy that is driven by the optimism that the latest technology (always the latest) will rescue us from the difficulties of labor and perhaps even the need for thought. Such thinking represents a stunning lack of imagination, for it is first in the imagination that we can see ourselves living in ways that break out of the conformity and complacency that too often characterize our modern "life-style." To question the sanity of anyone longing to return to the land is to be blind to a large swath of the human experience. Innumerable persons, both today and throughout human history, stand as compelling evidence that life on the land, in its many possible forms, is a means to a rich, satisfying, and happy life. That it is not for everyone is not to say that it is not for anyone. And it has to be for *someone*, or else we don't eat.

It is true that some individuals romanticize the life on the land and neglect to see the work involved and the fact that suffering and death lurk around every corner. Nevertheless, a good life is to be found there. But be warned: people should not lightly leave what they know and seek to get back to the land. Start slowly. Make sure you have some of the necessary skills. If all of this is sounds discouraging, remember two things: if you are called to this life, do it. Just don't imagine it will be easy. Will it be rewarding? Yes, it very likely will be. Second, the city needs agrarians as well as the country, for as the Southern Agrarians pointed out, and as Wendell Berry has reiterated, the salient division is not between the country and the city but between two kinds of mind: the industrial mind and the agrarian mind. There are industrial farmers and urban agrarians, and what is needed, in both city and the country, is a renewed concern for stewardship of the land, for human scale endeavors, for family enterprises, and for the neighborly arts. Agrarianism—far from being a romantic dream—is rooted in a thorough-going realism. It is our past and, in one shape or another, it will be our future.

The Productive Home vs. The Consuming Home

Allan Carlson

"A FAMILY IS BUSY in the countryside," writes British anthropologist Hugh Brody in his portrait of family-scale farming:

> Mother is making bread, churning butter, attending hens and ducks, preparing food for everyone. Father is in the fields ploughing the soil, cutting wood, fixing walls, providing sustenance. Children explore and play and help and sit at the family table. Grandma or grandpa sits in a chair by the fire. Every day is long and filled with the activities of this family . . . [all] given purpose and comfort, by a piece of the countryside at the centre of which is home.[1]

Idealized? Perhaps to a degree—certainly this picture leaves out the muscle-aching work and the weather-induced risks facing those living on the small farm. All the same, this is a fairly accurate portrait of life in a pre-industrial economy, centered on the productive home. As late as the 1820s, the great majority of Americans—90 percent—still lived like this on farms or in rural villages. These families raised their own food and preserved their own meat and vegetables. They spun and wove their own cloth and sewed their own clothing. They made the chairs on which they sat, dipped the candles that gave them light, bred the animals that provided them protein, field-power, and transportation, and built and repaired their own shelters.

By contemporary standards, these Americans lived a simpler (but in actuality a more complex) and poorer existence. On the other hand,

---

1. Hugh Brody, "Nomads and Settlers," in *Town and Country,* eds. Anthony Barnett and Roger Scruton (London, Vintage, 1999), 1–2.

this way of life was free from many contemporary problems. There were few quarrels between husbands and wives over "gender roles": the work of both was critical to the survival and success of their small family enterprise. Divorce was unthinkable. They welcomed children in abundance: the average rural family counted eight. Wife and husband, parents and children, were functionally intertwined in these productive homes.

Viewed a certain way, the whole strategy of modern capitalism is to rip productive functions and persons out of the home for reorganization on a more efficient industrial basis. To be sure, dramatic gains can be secured in this way: wealth created, technological innovations encouraged, the productivity of labor enhanced. Yet there are great costs as well; they draw far too little attention. For instance, under the capitalist regime, marriage loses much of its *economic* rationale. As framed by the anthropologists, the standard definition of marriage is "a union of the sexual and the economic." Raw capitalism has no use for marriage of this sort, because such bonds get in the way of the efficient allocation of labor and limit the potential of an industrial consumer economy. Furthermore, children, unless they can be rented out to factories and mines as little workers, also lose their value to parents in a capitalist economy. No longer assets, they become liabilities, and the birth rate plummets.

Moreover, the only theoretical "end" to this process is the elimination of the home. Charlotte Perkins Gilman's *Women and Economics*, written in the 1890s, ably showed how capitalism had already radically altered households. Gone from urban homes were the hundreds of productive tasks that had once defined the family economy: spinning, weaving, sewing, soap-making, laundering, carpentry, gardening, education, and so forth. Gilman claimed that women's tasks in the "modern" home now numbered only three: cooking, cleaning, and early child care. There was no reason, Gilman explained, that these functions could not also be industrialized. Home cleaning could be performed swiftly and efficiently by specialized teams ("Merry Maids"). Meal preparations could take place in industrialized kitchens, and people could collect their warm food in bags at special windows ("fast food"). Meanwhile, mothers—"clumsy amateurs" when it came to baby care—could turn their small children over to trained specialists also organized on an industrial model (the "child care" center). Consequently, women would be liberated from homes that had become "a tangled heap" of degraded tasks in order to move into "the higher specialization of labor" found in the capitalist order.[2]

Indeed, the "Great Transformation" (to use Karl Polanyi's apt phrase) sparked by capitalist industrialism turned economics upside-down. The word had originally come from the ancient Greek: *oeconomia*, which Aristotle defined as tending to the material needs of the family household with the goal of self-sufficiency. Capitalist economics has meant the effective elimination of the self-sufficient home. Our very system of accounting tells the tale. For example, when a mother cares for and breastfeeds her own infant, no "wealth" is created; in economic terms, nothing is counted. However, if that mother pays another woman to care for her baby and feeds the child industrially-produced infant formula, these transactions are counted, the economy grows, and "wealth" is created.

True, capitalism's dismantling of the home has never been wholly complete. Human beings, by nature familial (Aristotle, again), have searched out ways to limit the intrusions of capitalism's incentives into the home. One effort, perhaps the weakest, was to reconfigure marriage into a "companionate" model. The destruction of the productive home would be cheerfully accepted as liberation from wearying tasks; children would be sharply reduced in number, or even renounced altogether; and the purpose of marriage would refocus narrowly on the emotional relationship of the couple as companions and "contracepting" sexual partners. With the children non-existent or being cared for elsewhere, and with the home no longer "a workshop or a museum," the new home—in Gilman's words—became a place of peace and rest, of love and privacy, "where much higher and subtler forms of association" would emerge among "pure, strong, beautiful men and women." Given much less emphasis in this scheme was the need for easy unilateral divorce, because a true "companionate" marriage could last only as long as the intense emotions on which it was created. Of course, divorce would stimulate the capitalist economy by creating two households, each with its own appliances and accoutrements, and very likely snuffing out any residual home production that the couple had achieved.

A second strategy to salvage home life in the capitalist order involved creation of a "family wage" regime. The premise here was that the industrial order could claim one, but *only* one, adult from each family,

---

2. Charlotte Perkins Gilman, *Women and Economics: A Study of the Economic Relation between Man and Women as a Factor in Social Evolution,* ed. Carl N. Degler (New York: Harper and Row, 1966 [1898]), 225–317.

normally the father. In return, the father had a moral claim to a wage that would support not only himself but a wife and children as well. As the Philadelphia Trade Union warned its members in the mid-nineteenth century:

> Oppose [the employment of women] with all your mind and with all your strength for it will prove our ruin. We must strive to obtain sufficient remuneration for our labor to keep the wives and the daughters and sisters of our people at home. . . . That cormorant capital will have every man, woman, and child to toil; but let us exert our families to oppose its design.[3]

Family wage systems took different forms. In Australia "wage courts" fixed compensation so that women would earn only 60 cents for every dollar earned by a man. In France and Belgium, elaborate "child allowance" schemes supplemented the pay of men with children. In the United States, the trade and industrial unions enforced rules that moved women out of the factories. In the mid-twentieth century this was reinforced by cultural conventions that cast high-paying, high-prestige tasks as "men's jobs" (e.g., doctoring, lawyering, and engineering), while low-paying tasks became "women's jobs" (stenography, nursing, and teaching in elementary schools). All such systems rested on some form of discrimination, favoring men as real or potential fathers and women as real or potential mothers.

Meanwhile, industrialists and feminists shared an interest in seeing such systems dismantled The former wanted women—all women—in the labor market, both to cheapen wages and to enhance demand for industrially produced consumer goods; the latter wanted an end to "patriarchy" of any sort. Their collaboration was often quite open: during the 1920s, for example, the National Association of Manufacturers eagerly endorsed the new feminist-inspired Equal Rights Amendment. While this measure was never ratified, the coalition behind it did manage to destroy America's family-wage regime during the 1970s and the 1980s, using instead Title VII of the Civil Rights of 1964, which banned discrimination in employment on the basis of sex.

The most self-conscious attempt to salvage family life in a capitalist environment was the Home Economics Movement. As founder Ellen

---

3. Quoted in Ruth Milkman, "Organizing the Sexual Division of Labor: Historical Perspectives on 'Women's Work' and the American Labor Movement," *Socialist Review* 49 (Jan.-Fe. 1980), 198.

Richards explained, the crisis was real: "The ideal American homestead, that place of busy industry, with occupations for the dozen children, no longer exists.... Gone out of it [too]...are ten of the children." As a result, "in many cities the family if they kept together at all merely sleep under one roof, perhaps with several other families, but have no common life and no common interests."[4]

In effect, the home economists took the three tasks that Gilman said still remained in the home—cooking, cleaning, and child care—and sought to reorganize and revitalize them as a science. As the discipline's founding statement explained:

> Home economics: home meaning the place of shelter and nurture for the children and for those personal qualities of self-sacrifice for others for the gaining of the strength to meet the world; economics meaning the management of this home on economic lines as to time and energy as well as mere money.[5]

Viewed another way, the home economists sought to counter capitalism's social revolution by reorganizing the home on capitalist principles: the quest for efficiency, the enthusiastic embrace of technology, and the celebration of consumerism.

In retrospect, the futility of this effort appears obvious. By bringing the logic and methods of industrial capitalism into the home, the home economics crusaders set in motion processes that could only further erode the family. Beyond the ritual sewing classes, home-economics gave relatively little attention to training girls in productive activities. Instead, the focus was on educated consumption, a complete merger of the home sphere with the industrial sphere, and a retooling of the mother-at-home into a purchasing agent.

With the experimental efficiencies of "Taylorism," the vogue among progressive corporations, home economists worked to apply the principles of time-motion studies and "one best use" to household tasks. In her popular books, *The New Housekeeping* (1919), *Household Engineering: Scientific Management in the Home* (1920), and *Selling Mrs. Consumer* (1929), Christine Frederick created the career of "household engineer," based on a study of factory systems and the use of her own home as an

---

4. Ellen H. Richards, "The Social Significance of the Home Economics Movement," *The Journal of Home Economics* 3 (April 1911), 123–25.

5. Quoted in Earl J. McGrath and Jack T. Johnson, *The Changing Mission of Home Economics: A Report on Home Economics in the Land-Grant Colleges and State Universities* (New York: Teachers College Press, 1968), 11.

"experiment station." The homemaker would become both executive and manual laborer (in practice, a situation wholly at odds with Taylorism), and "the more management" a woman put into housework, "the less friction and the less nervous energy she will have to expend."

When home economics became the favored child of the federal government, the discipline grew rapidly. The Vocational Education Act of 1917 provided federal funds directly to school districts to pay the salaries of home economics teachers. By 1920, six thousand U.S. high schools offered such courses in "scientific" consumerism. In 1945, the U.S. Department of Agriculture launched Future Homemakers of America (FHA) clubs, and "home economics" reached an apogee of sorts during the 1950s. Then along came the new feminism, and the discipline went into its inevitable crisis. In 1972, feminist author Robin Morgan addressed the American Home Economics Association convention and bluntly laid out the new reality. She reminded the delegates that their discipline's purpose was "to reinforce three primary areas: marriage, the family, and . . . consumerism. . . . Now those three areas . . . [are] the primary areas that the radical feminist movement is out to destroy." Her primary recommendation? "You can quit your jobs."[6] And indeed, by the year 2000, "home economics" had largely disappeared: federal subsidies were rescinded, FHA clubs disbanded, and university programs were redirected and relabeled or dissolved.

The mistake of the home economists lay in believing that hyper-consumerism might be a worthy substitute for productive activities in the home as a means of reinforcing family solidarity. But this could not work. Educated women eventually realized the vacuous nature of "household engineering," while the enthusiastic embrace of ever more factory-produced goods could only accelerate capitalism's innate corrosion of pre-capitalist institutions like the family.

Must we accept the effective demise of families as autonomous entities, with hyper-consumerism as the substitute? Or is there an alternative?

There is. It is the obvious one: calling both men and women to restore the productive home, albeit well beyond the tasks of cooking, cleaning, and early child care. How might this be done? The work of Ralph Borsodi suggests a way.

A leader of a "homesteading" movement in the 1920s and 1930s, Borsodi had his quirky side. Yet he also had a keen understanding of the

---

6. "What Robin Morgan said in Denver," *Journal of Home Economics* 65 (Jan. 1973), 13.

situation and he described a clear way forward. He began his working life as a Manhattan-based consulting economist and marketing expert for clients including R.H. Macy and Co. and the National Retail Dry Goods Association. In 1920, his family moved to an abandoned seven-acre homestead in Rockland County, New York. During Borsodi's first summer there, his Iowa-born wife proudly presented him with tomatoes she had canned. The economist in him asked, "Does it really pay?" He did his calculations, including labor costs, and—to his surprise—found that home production of this sort *was* more efficient and cost-effective than factory-canned tomatoes—by a factor of 25 percent. Explaining why led him to write a series of best sellers, including *The Distribution Age*, *This Ugly Civilization*, and *Flight From the City*. Indicting the crony capitalism of his era, Borsodi held the factory in particular scorn:

> It is the factory, not the machine, which is reducing all men and all commodities to a dead level of uniformity because the factory makes it impossible for individual men and individual communities to be self-sufficient… It is the factory, not the machine, which destroys both the natural beauty and the natural wealth of man's environment; which fills country and city with hideous factories and squalid slums.[7]

No Luddite, Borsodi might instead be fairly labeled a creative anarchist. He argued that the internal combustion engine, the electrical grid, and the small electric engine had opened the path to restoration of the productive home. The large factory was "a steam-age relic rendered obsolete by the electrical age," yet it was sustained in the mid-twentieth century by the power of government. Borsodi urged Americans to educate themselves as new homesteaders, combining five to ten acres of productive farm land with home looms, home canning equipment, and home machine shops. Only this would allow them to escape from the tyranny of politicians, advertisers, and industrial engineers. Thousands of Americans responded, becoming part of the Borsodi Homestead Movement.

This creative anarchist should also be given credit for discovering modern homeschooling. He understood that "the factory system [also] dominates modern methods of education." Finding the nearby local school "impossible" for his sons, he looked to his own wife: "[w]hen I compared Mrs. Borsodi to the average school teacher in the

---

7. Ralph Borsodi, *This Ugly Civilization* (New York and London: Harper and Brothers, 1929), 14.

public schools, I saw no reason why she could not teach the children just as well, if not better." Securing an arrangement with the county school superintendent, the Borsodis brought their children home. Once again, this "experiment in domestic production" proved its superiority over a mass system of production. It turned out that two hours a day of course work was all it took for the Bosodi boys to keep up with their public school counterparts. The time so liberated could be used for extra reading and creative activities in the garden, kitchen, or workshop. In addition, home schooling taught the Borsodis that true education "was really reciprocal; in the very effort to educate the boys, we educated ourselves."[8]

"Borsodi homesteads" faded away after 1941, stifled partly by Borsodi's own eccentricities, partly by global war, and partly by new federal preferences for the functionless companionate suburbs. The early twenty-first century, however, has opened up prospects again for restoring the productive home. Most obviously, the home schooling revolution of the past 35 years—anticipated by Borsodi—is already changing the American cultural landscape. Hundreds of thousands of families have successfully brought the educational function back home. Tasting the satisfactions of autonomy and real liberty, most of these families have also found ways to bring other non-commercial functions home as well: gardening, food preservation, and simple animal husbandry (e.g. the chicken coop).

By themselves, the internal combustion engine and the electrical grid were not enough to deliver on Borsodi's vision of a land of small producers for the marketplace. However, the amazing power of the home computer and the remarkable opportunities for marketing provided by the internet now open fresh possibilities for strengthening the productive home within the marketplace. Not all tasks can or should be returned to the homestead. Yet many professional, marketing, and service-sector jobs could easily make the leap, particularly if restrictive zoning laws could give way to a new birth of economic and residential liberty.

We live on the cusp of an era of constructive cultural and economic counter-revolution, resting on the return of vital functions to the home. Its spirit rests on the home-centered economics of Aristotle; its energy comes from the creative anarchy of people who have tasted liberty. The next decade or two will probably determine the revolution's success or failure. Will it merely be a passing historical oddity of brilliant but brief duration, or will it be the catalyst for rebuilding a family-centered nation,

---

8. Ralph Borsodi, *Flight from the City* (New York and London: Harper and Brothers, 1933; 1935), 83–95.

one freed from the curse of consumerism and devoted to the restoration of the productive home?

Killing the Animals We Eat

John Cuddeback

I raise pigs with great attention to their well-being and comfort and then I kill them. Before I kill them we get to know one another, the pigs and I. I'd even be willing to say that we trust one another. They perceive that I'm taking care of them, and I know they recognize me and respond to me differently from how they respond to others. Surely this constitutes a kind of relationship. I know my pigs, and they know me.

One day an earnest student asked, "How can you kill an animal that trusts you?" The question ended up being the occasion for a bit of soul-searching regarding the big picture of man, beast, stewardship, and food. The realization I came to is this: I *should* be concerned about how the animals we eat die, that is, how they are killed. For if people are going to eat meat regularly, someone is going to have to kill animals, and how they are killed matters. And upon closer examination I found that what might seem like a betrayal—namely, killing an animal that trusts me—is in fact not only an acceptable but a good way to kill an animal that is headed for the freezer. I understand that some people do not believe we should eat meat at all, but that is not the question I am addressing, at least not at the moment. I am going to take for granted here that eating meat is a normal and good part of human life. That is a premise. And my contention is that if we are going to eat meat, we must make a better reckoning with the killing of animals for food than we hitherto have made. In any case we should be aware of the killing, and this awareness should affect what and how we eat.

The great philosophers and common human experience alike are unanimous: brute animals experience real passions, among them pain and fear. A proper stewardship—one that sees animals as a gift to be received with gratitude and care—will seek when killing them to minimize this pain and fear. To prolong or intensify pain and fear unnecessarily would be wrong.

Slaughtering an animal means inflicting some kind of physical injury that results in death. This injury is likely to cause pain, perhaps severe pain, if the animal retains consciousness for any length of time after the injury. And because fear is an expectation of something to come, not only will there be pain in the time of consciousness after; there will be fear leading up to it.

So when I slaughter one of my pigs I have to ask myself: a) does the pig anticipate the injury, and for what length of time? and b) how quickly after the injury does unconsciousness set in?

I have had occasion to answer both of these questions in my own experiences of slaughtering animals.

From the start I have felt that I should be the one to pull the trigger. It seems only right that the hand that nurtures the animals be the hand that harvests them. I did not at first realize how many reasons there are for this. What became clear through experience is that the pigs have an almost uncanny sixth sense for perceiving that something is "up." Is it the look, the smell, or just the perception that something is different? I don't know for sure. But I learned early on that the troop of people invited to join in the work of butchering should stay at some distance when it is time for the kill. I want to do all I can to minimize the chances of the pigs' discerning that what is coming is in fact coming.

And then there's the aspect of the quick kill. Everyone with whom I have spoken concurs that a .22 caliber bullet between and a little above the eyes is the way to do it. But placement is very important if the proper stunning effect is to take place, and so here is another reason to keep the pig calm. A moving animal is difficult to stun properly. But if you can do it, you can roll the animal on its back fairly easily and then, using a knife, stuck it through the neck and into the heart. And a good sticking produces a steady flow of blood, which is desirable.

Now what I am about to say is not pleasant, but it needs saying. Even a well-placed bullet, followed by a well-placed stick to the heart, does not cause immediate death. There are always at least a few moments of consciousness between the initial injury and death. The precise state of consciousness in the animal will never be known, but it is appropriate, it seems to me, that we assume that the animal has some level of awareness and thus some capacity for pain. For me the whole process of slaughtering and butchering always comes down to those few moments: how should I think about and handle those moments? For, having attempted to be a salutary and peaceful presence in the pig's life, I strive to maintain that same presence right to the end even though I am killing it.

To some this will seem hypocritical, but I think it is an important part of the most fitting way for a pig to die if it is going to die by my hand. So let me be clear: I would prefer that the pig not have those moments of consciousness at all and that it not feel pain. But if I am going to slaughter the pig, the pig is going to have those moments, and for its sake I want to be in them with it.

Does the pig feel betrayed? My view is that the notion of betrayal is beyond its ken. The pig feels pain, and someone whom it knows is there inflicting that pain, but I do not think this adds up in a pig's consciousness to betrayal. At any rate, I do hope that the pig does not associate my presence with the injury it has just received, which is another reason that the calm preparation period is so important. The shock comes as it were out of nowhere, it is true, but I see no evidence that the appearance of a gun has any associations for the pigs whatsoever.

So I am at peace about killing my pigs—which is far from saying that I enjoy it. As the time for killing approaches I feel a pallor descend upon me and my helpers. It is always the most unpleasant thing I do at my homestead. Then why do it? Because it must be done by somebody, and it is best that I do it. For I have realized that it is precisely *because* my pigs "trust" me that they die in relative peace.

I am well aware that a reader who thinks that the killing of animals for food is unjustified might find my reasoning unconvincing, to say the least. To what mental contortions, this person may wonder, has the desire to eat animals led us? Again, I want to be clear: I am not trying to convince vegetarians of the legitimacy of eating meat. But at the same time I am aware of the legitimate concerns of those who are against eating animals. In fact those concerns, often based in real insights about the welfare of animals, can and should prod all of us to consider many aspects of meat-eating that we would otherwise rather not consider.

I met a man whose objection to eating the flesh of animals was simple, and it has affected how I think about this. Unwilling to kill an animal himself, he is therefore not willing to eat any animals. This position, especially as held by the man I met, is clearly rooted in well-considered premises and reasoning: "I am not willing to kill an animal, for I find such killing repugnant. What I find repugnant I should not expect another to do. Therefore, I should not expect another to kill an animal for the sake of my nourishment."

This position, or perhaps we should say *acting* on this position, can clearly be the fruit of an admirable commitment to moral principles. Yet as regards the specific moral issue at hand, I suggest that we must examine the nature of the repugnance at killing animals. Were it a repugnance at an *unjust* action, then indeed expecting another to perform that action would be morally wrong. I concur that it is fitting to experience a repugnance at the killing of animals—and some people will experience it more than others. But I hold that this is a repugnance not to injustice but to a difficult and painful aspect of human nourishment. If in this I am correct, and again a full defense of this is beyond the scope of this essay, then it would not necessarily be improper to ask another to overcome that repugnance and kill an animal *for me*.

Yet here meat-eaters have the opportunity, moved by the reasoning of the man I met and many others like him, to look more deeply at the issue of killing the animals we eat. The vast majority of meat-eaters do in fact leave the dirty work, if I may put it that way, to others. And even those of us who slaughter some of the animals we eat also consume quantities of meat killed by others. Every hamburger, hot dog, Philly cheese steak, leg of lamb, drum stick, cold cut, and spare rib we've ever eaten was once part of a beautiful living creature. If that creature was stuffed into an overcrowded pen where for the last hours of its life it heard and smelled the death of other animals, this is a problem. Surely, the slaughtering of animals does not have to be done this way.

It is incumbent upon all of us to ask: how are these animals killed? If they are not killed with a reasonable concern for their well-being in the last hours of their lives, then what does this mean for our meat-eating? How animals are killed is a moral issue. We should do all that we reasonably can to avoid eating the meat of animals that are cruelly killed. This of course also raises the parallel issue of the regular living conditions of millions of farm animals. I'm not in the position to write an exposé of these conditions. Nonetheless, I think it is commonly known that a large number of farm animals in our country live in what are objectively appalling conditions. This too is a moral issue.

It is always easier to point out a problem than to solve it. It seems that much progress has been made in the slaughter industry in the last twenty years, through the efforts of such animal welfare activists as Temple Grandin and others. I am not an activist in the normal sense. Perhaps

I should be. But one thing is clear to me: we meat-eaters should be aware, and care, and act.

Wendell Berry has suggested that we become more knowingly connected to the production of our food, in part by participating in that production. Growing a small garden is perhaps the most universally accessible way. I suggest that we also give consideration to participating in the raising of animals for meat, and this especially so that more of us can have first-hand experience of their killing. While there are obvious limitations on the ability of many to raise animals themselves, backyard chickens or rabbits could provide a more widespread experience of raising and slaughtering animals.

Allow me to be clear. My suggestion of broader involvement in slaughtering is precisely to foster a deeper appreciation of animals and the food they provide. Killing an animal should change how we eat that animal. We will eat with more care and more gratitude. We will waste less, and share more, as we become more cognizant of just what we are eating, and what it costs to do so.

For those meat-eaters who are unable to participate in the killing, there is still much that can be done. There are organizations dedicated to promoting good slaughtering practices. We can research these organizations and learn from the labels on meat, some of which give an important indication of what did or did not happen in the life and death of the animals we are eating. We can thus be more selective in what we purchase, and we can seek out local sources of meats, inquiring of producers of meat how their animals were raised and slaughtered.

If more people have occasion to slaughter an animal, either their own or a neighbor's, we would be much more conscious of the realities and issues surrounding the eating of meat. One thing is clear: a consuming public isolated from a producing industry is a formula for problems. Meat-eaters should hold the agricultural industry, as well as themselves, more accountable. We need to be aware of and careful about how the animals we eat both live and die.

In my home the kitchen table is within sight of where our pigs are slaughtered. When it comes to eating bacon and sausage, the life and death of these animals can never be far from our consciousness. This seems fitting, and for it I am grateful.

Part Four

Art and Education

Art, like morality, consists of drawing the line somewhere.
—G.K. CHESTERTON

"A New Magnetic North": 39 Theses on Education

R.J. SNELL

Part I

1. Every pedagogy presupposes an anthropology. That is, every philosophy of education assumes an account of human nature, however well-developed or naïve the account may be.[1]

2. Some pedagogies accord with human nature and thus support flourishing; others are discordant with human nature, either by innocent mistake or ideological revolt. In either error, education tends to interfere with flourishing, sometimes seriously so.

3. This is not to suggest that every pedagogy has an explicit anthropology; often the understanding of human nature is forgotten, buried under layers of custom until so "self-evident" that it is overlooked. When this happens, there is an anthropology by default that controls the meaning and practice of education in its given community. Even those who would reform or resist the model tend to be governed by it, either by an unknown smuggling of its assumptions into their "reforms" or by defining their position against the default, thus allowing the default to shape the boundaries of meaning.

---

1. The basic insights of this argument are developed more fully in R. J. Snell and Steven D. Cone, *Authentic Cosmopolitanism: Love, Sin, and Grace in the Christian University* (Eugene, OR: Pickwick, 2013). We learned much from James K. A. Smith, *Desiring the Kingdom: Worship, Worldview, and Cultural Formation* (Grand Rapids: Baker, 2009), esp. 17–34.

4. In the West, the default anthropology is "the thinking thing." While the tradition admits of nuances and different emphases, we've tended to consider ourselves primarily as minds or intellects, as thinking things or rational animals.

5. Envisioning the human as intellect fosters education predominately concerned with persons-as-minds, on the creation and transmission of ideas, concepts, analyses, worldviews: "directed almost exclusively at the intellects of students; that it is the communication of truths and skills and habits and qualities of intellect—as though keenness and method in knowing and voluminousness in one's learning constitutes one liberally educated."[2]

6. So dominant is the "thinking thing" default that challengers are viewed as strange, even illegitimate—we *are* mind, as everyone knows, and so education is for, of, and about *minds*:

> to set the purpose of education outside of knowledge, would we not be abandoning an insight shared by all of Western culture since Aristotle—that knowledge is a good in itself, worth pursuing for its own sake? Would we not be abandoning the intellectualist view of man that came from Aristotle through Aquinas, to shape centuries of intellectualist humanism: that the highest good for man is truthful knowledge because, as Aristotle put it, "Man is *nous*—man is mind"?[3]

The domination of mind is virtually total in education, perhaps especially in the university, determining the goals, methodologies, structures, content, and assessment. "It would be difficult to overestimate the educational consequences of this simple expression of the philosophic nature of the human person and the identification of his highest good."[4] (This is not to suggest the university is dominated by reasonableness, I hasten to add.)

7. Since the human is not entirely, not even primarily, a thinking thing, the "educational consequences" of this model include a truncated education, one forgetful of its task to form and care for the whole person—*cura*

---

2. J. Donald Monan, "Value Proposition," *Boston College Magazine,* Summer 2009, http://bcm.bc.edu/issues/summer_2009/features/value-proposition.html.

3. *Ibid.*

4. *Ibid.*

personalis. Consequently, such truncated education tends to over-emphasize some aspects of human flourishing while forgetting others.

8. Not only truncated and forgetful, the default model also distorts and interferes with flourishing—it is detrimental to well-being in four fundamental ways.

9. First, in its truncated reduction of the human to mind, the default model is dualistic, separating care of mind from care of body, thus separating the individual from the community of embodiment—family, neighborhood, civic life, religious congregation, place, creation. It is an education that alienates, fostering in its deracinated pupils a profound homelessness, a Gnostic hovering "above" the entanglements of embodied life. Always visitors to the campus and never residents, students are trained for intellectual work to be done here or there or nowhere, wherever is convenient. The best faculty are *not there* but en route to some other place; so too their disciples. The default model encourages *alienation*.

10. Second, in its detachment, the default model privileges *autonomy*, the relative lack of hindrances on one's self-determination and poetic construction of purpose. Freedom is governed not by relation to *being*—from which the pupil is alienated—or to *truth*—which is shaped by the autonomous agent—but by choice.

11. Third, as loci of disembedded choice not beholden to concrete places and people, the products of default education are also prone to view creation—personal or non-personal, animate or inanimate—as raw resource, as thin and weightless factual reality to be bent, subdued, dissected, or manipulated to serve their own interests, guarantee their own comforts, and offer security against the chaos of nature, will, and death. No longer is reality to be understood and valued, but rather to be changed. Oddly, then, by turning to disincarnate mind, the default model returns with fury to the embodied, but now as *dominator*: "the possibility of a limitless and unchallenged dominion seemed to unfold; more and more, the good of man's journey would be determined by science and technology. . . . Man is the master of his own destiny."[5]

12. Fourth, having rendered "man himself" the "*Dominus* who had the right to determine life and the cosmos . . . through the use of reason,"

---

5. Luigi Giussani, "Religious Awareness in Modern Man," *Communio* 25 (1998), 113.

Promethean man discovered not reason but unreason, and is given over, almost entirely, to *pointlessness*: "Condemned to a certain conception of freedom, man comes to realize that freedom is estrangement. And thus, he is free for nothing. . . . If man is so free as to be the measure of reality, he is condemned to an abysmal loneliness."[6] Rendered impotent by his power, man is no longer reason, but will; no longer mind, but choice, but anxious, frantic, fearful, having "the power to throw temper tantrums in the face of being."[7]

13. The default model both depends upon and causes (in a malevolent feedback loop) alienation, misguided autonomy, domination, and pointlessness; further, the "thinking thing" model fails to provide the objectivity or peace it promised, instead entrenching itself in the war of will against created order.

14. However strange it may appear to those whose imagination is the default, "[w]hat is sorely needed to break out of this vicious circle is to establish a reference point outside of knowledge itself, to serve as magnetic 'north.'"[8] To our good fortune, a substantial counter-tradition already exists, one for which "the measure of a man or a woman was never to be found in the magnitude of one's intellectual attainments. That measure was to be found rather in how sensitively, how responsively, one exercised his or her freedom. The great Commandment is this: Thou shall love the Lord thy God with thy whole heart and mind and soul, and thy neighbor as thyself."[9]

15. The compass needs reorienting. We are primarily lovers, not thinking things, and a worthy pedagogy teaches the *ordo amoris*, the order of love.

16. Still, while the tradition contains the resources necessary to reorient ourselves, and while it is true that ideas have consequences, it would be largely futile to respond to disorientation with ideas alone. When loves are disordered, analysis and argument are insufficient, for ideas and concepts, however thoroughly deconstructed, will be placed within the horizon of the default model, and thereby tamed. Reorientation will not occur through ideas about the order of love but through the ordering of

---

6. *Ibid.*, 125.
7. *Ibid.*, 127.
8. Monan, "Value Proposition."
9. *Ibid.*

the loves of concrete persons in actual communities. Not worldviews, but practices.

Part II

17. In his *Republic*, Plato outlines practices of education, the creative retrieval of which provides a corrective to the default model and its pathologies.

18. The form of the *Republic*—dialogue—is itself a practice of resistance against the Sophists' model of "knowledge-accumulation."

> Philosophy no longer meant, as the Sophists had it, acquiring knowledge, know-how, or *Sophia*; it meant questioning ourselves, because we have the feeling that we are not what we ought to be. . . . [T]his feeling comes from the fact that, in the person of Socrates, we have encountered a personality which, by its mere presence, obliges those who approach it to question themselves. . . . Socrates acts upon his listeners in an irrational way, by the emotions he provokes and the love he inspires.[10]

Education as *practiced* by Plato is dialogical, communal, and centered on conversation as the means by which loves are re-formed. Given his practice, it is unsurprising that the *Republic's* "teaching" on education involves a similar embodied dialogical model. Education is not merely cognitive, but includes a form of life, a way of living, and such a form requires the ordering of persons within an ordered polis.

19. Consequently, the text begins not with the dialectical education of the philosopher but with the cultivation or *paideia* of the Guardians. They present a unique problem, for they must be warlike enough to attack enemies while placid and docile enough to avoid harming their fellow citizens and instituting military rule. Like dogs, they must be willing to attack what is unknown while preserving, defending, and loving their own household. Cultivating souls with such a unique tension of desire requires more than passing on the proper ideas; Guardians need souls of a certain timbre, with virtuous desires and loves.

---

10. Pierre Hadot, *What is Ancient Philosophy?* (Cambridge: Harvard University Press, 2002), 29–30; cf. Snell and Cone, *Authentic Cosmopolitanism*, 16–23.

20. Prior to acquiring knowledge, the Guardians are formed in right opinion about pleasures and pains through an education of music and gymnastic: first, music, including stories of gods and heroes (poetry) as well as rhythm, and then, subsequently, physical training (the body—no pure minds here!). Stories are given to the young when most malleable, forming in them a taste or love for the noble and a repugnance or distaste for the base. They are taught that the gods do not lie or change, do not cause evil, do not seek their own satisfaction; so, too, heroes are little prone to extremes of emotion; they willingly suffer for the common good and view injustice as shameful. The purpose of rhythm and gymnastic is similarly virtue, prompting an orderly and courageous soul and a connatural ability to recognize order and disorder. Guardians cannot explain or analyze order; they feel it in their gut, sniffing the odious by a kind of habitual disposition.

21. Tellingly, Plato defines the cardinal virtues—wisdom, courage, moderation, and justice—based not on the knowledge of philosophers but on the good character possessed by the Guardians. Virtue is not analyzed so much as recognized in the practices of the virtuous. *Wisdom*, the good counsel possessed by the rulers, is not specialized knowledge, but, rather, the good sense to preserve and continue the lawful system of education. *Courage*, too, is the "preserving of the opinion produced by law through education about what . . . is terrible."[11] *Moderation*, likewise, is "a kind of order and mastery of certain kinds of pleasure and desires."[12] And *Justice* is steadfastness, a pious regard for harmonious order.

22. Given philosophy's proclivity to dissolve customary order, students must pass tests of capacity and character before admission to dialectic. Only those of intelligence, strong memory, and those who are "friend and kinsman of truth, justice, courage and moderation" are accepted. Those latter qualities constitute the character of well-formed Guardians, those already formed through music and gymnastic; philosophy is permissible only for those with a firm love of right opinion: "Don't think we devised all that for any other purpose than that . . . they should receive the laws from us in the finest possible ways like a dye, so that their opinion about what's terrible and about everything else would be colorfast."[13]

---

11. Plato, *The Republic*, trans. Allan Bloom (Basic Books, 1968), 429c,d.
12. Ibid., 430c.
13. Ibid., 429e-430b.

23. Philosophers, like everyone else, begin in the cave, knowing no other reality than immediate sensory satisfaction, explaining their violent reaction against those who liberate and lead them into the heights of air and light. It hurts to be liberated; it is unpleasant, and pleasure is a gaoler. But how are they freed from their want of education? Socrates is a savior of sorts, one who descends to free prisoners, but the text insists that "education is not what the professions of certain men [Sophists] assert . . . that they put into the soul knowledge that isn't in it, as though they were putting sight into blind eyes."[14] Instead, "power is in the soul of each"—the prisoner already has sight—but he "must be turned around."[15] Education, "an art of this turning around," is "not an art of producing sight," nor is it accomplished first by dialectic.[16]

24. Education, philosophic or otherwise, does not impart sight; it merely turns the gaze of the prisoner from the dark to the light. Dialectics, or the philosophical education, is presented *after* the analogy of the cave, and, moreover, the philosophical education in varieties of math and dialectics intends realities *outside* of the cave, not the images and things *inside* the cave. So the philosophic education is not the art of turning. *Periagoge*, turning, conversion, is the work of the right opinion of the Guardians, those who are freed from base pleasures and towards a love of the permanent, unchanging, and good, even though they access the permanent, unchanging, and good only through opinion. Still, it was *right* opinion, *true* opinion, and thus moving already towards the realm of Being and Good. Opinion is not sufficient to escape the cave, but it is *necessary*. It develops a love of the good; it develops the moral qualities without which the dialectician becomes vicious; it leads to moderation and an inner life of justice necessary for inquiry.

25. *Paideia* is the art of turning and forming virtuous loves. *Paideia* is formation in the right opinions given by the received heritage of the community, a heritage which is to be preserved. *Paideia*, as an art of turning, points the soul and its loves in the right direction, and if ordered love is needed to reorient our alienated and pointless age, then *paideia* accords with a new magnetic north.

---

14. *Ibid.*, 518c.
15. *Ibid.*
16. *Ibid.*, 518d.

Part III

26. All education forms moral imagination and opinion concerning the pleasant and painful. Even silence about such aims teaches and forms opinion about them, albeit generally in keeping with the default model, but there is no choice educating loves or not, for all teaching is the art of turning; the question is whether the loves are ordered in keeping with human nature and human well-being or not. The default model forms love, too—alienation, autonomy, domination, and pointlessness. In avoiding a truncated reduction of education and anthropology, *paideia* resists these errors.

27. Of course, it is one thing to claim this by *fiat* and quite another to actualize it; moreover, attempts at *paideia* encounter the existing deformations of the default model as well as the vicious disorder of love endemic to human character. An education of love not only requires coherent practices and structures to actualize itself, but must create those structures from within an already disordered system, with already disordered persons. Mere technique seems insufficient to the task. But avoiding the rationalistic optimism of technique's sufficiency is a mark of wisdom consistent with a coherent anthropology. As persons, we *ought* not to be manipulated like instruments through some technique; further, as bearers of freedom, we always outstrip any reductive attempts of merely technical control. Rationalistic techniques of formation are, generally, both useless and wrong.

28. Still, prudence gained from long experience allows certain practices to be judged as particularly in keeping with human flourishing. While not exhaustive, a list of six practices suggests itself as particularly helpful.

29. First, moral formation ought to be acknowledged explicitly and clearly as a goal of education. Education cannot not form, and the pretense of value-neutrality ought to be rejected as just another instance of value-commitment. Schools, thus, ought to know the type of women and men they wish to form—good citizens, or productive workers, or gentlewomen and gentlemen, or orthodox believers, or cultural elites. Some goals may be out of step with human flourishing, but if they are acknowledged, they may subsequently be critiqued. All schools operate *in loco parentis*, and this should be clear.

30. Second, Plato is correct in thinking that the appetites are ruled by reason through spirit—the head rules the stomach through the chest—and thus *paideia* seeks to form both reason and spirit. Doing so in our current context may require colleges within the university, something like Cardinal Newman's prescription.[17] For Newman, both academy and university were distinct from the college; the academy created knowledge while the university diffused knowledge, primarily through teachers, through the exchange of culture from teacher and student. *Cura personalis*, the formation of the entire person, required the residential college, which for him was a permanent and necessary element of the university. The residential college within the university is *home*, providing moral and perhaps religious training, guidance, care, formation, maturation. As he puts it, the "the College is for the formation of character, intellectual and moral, for the cultivation of the mind, for the improvement of the individual."[18] Perhaps a single institution could perform all these tasks, but what no *paideia* may permit is the forgoing of any of these tasks.

31. Third, creating knowledge, teaching, and forming character require, perhaps, a differentiation of faculty or instructors. Again, some faculty may be able to perform all three tasks, but no *paideia* can overlook the necessity of instructors for each task. There may be pure scholars, but there must also be faculty who when asked "What do you teach?" reply, "I teach men and women."[19] But then there must be faculty not only of gifted minds, but also mentors of ordered loves.

32. Fourth, whatever their majors, all students ought to be provided with education in music and gymnastic, that is, with the sources of moral imagination, especially poetry, literature, history, and rhetoric. *Belles-lettres* should be central, with ample attention to the acts and actors of statecraft, including the context of law, political economy, and religion in which those acts occur. But models of rightly ordered persons performing great acts are central to *paideia*.

33. Fifth, *paideia* inherits and bequeaths a heritage, passing on the texts, music, institutions, laws, values, religious insights, heroes, and discoveries

---

17. See *The Idea of a University* (Garden City: Image Books, 1959) and "Rise and Progress of Universities," *The Newman Reader*, http://www.newmanreader.org/works/historical/volume3/universities/.

18. "Rise and Progress of Universities."

19. Josiah Bunting, III, *An Education for our Time* (Washington, D.C.: Regnery, 1998), 205.

of the past. Still, heritage is not bequeathed in a thoughtless or jingoistic manner, for the Guardians do become philosophers capable of critical investigation and judicious deliberation even about their own form of life. Heritage is not something to be passed on as mindless repetition or thoughtless traditionalism, but rather as creative retrieval or creative fidelity. We turn to the sources—*ad fontes*—to be capable of acting differently, as is required, which we learn to do from imitating what was done, and why. But we also examine those actions in light of how the tradition develops in its understanding and capacity.

34. Sixth, *paideia* is placed. It studies heritage, but not heritage only of that which is large—the West, say. It also studies that which is near, like the local town; not only religion, but the churches within a neighborhood; not only biology, but also the trees on campus. Students should be able to identify the flora and fauna on campus, know the history of the locale, understand the local economy, know the people who live and work and worship there even after graduation.

35. *Paideia* is embodied, communal, dialogical, inherited, and placed—it is not alienated.

36. *Paideia* presents a normative vision of human life—it is not free-floating in its autonomy.

37. *Paideia* involves a formation of responsibility for oneself and others, including love of the other—it does not dominate or view the world as resource for satisfaction.

38. *Paideia* forms the *ordo amoris*, including a profound sense of gratitude for the many gifts provided by others in the tradition, and the duty to pass on those gifts, and more, to others. It is not pointless, nor does it throw tantrums.

39. *Paideia* knows that the life well-lived is a life of deep, abiding, creatively faithful, self-transcending love. *Paideia* seeks the magnetic north of love.

Reimagining the University with Wendell Berry[1]

Jack R. Baker and Jeffrey Bilbro

HIGHER EDUCATION CATERS TO our most selfish tendencies: American universities promise to deliver lucrative employment and "upward mobility," and for these sought-after commodities they can demand ever-higher tuition. As Wendell Berry has been arguing for decades, however, an education founded upon such a reductive economic exchange should not expect to form healthy, virtuous community members. Yet as the ecological and human costs of our hollowed-out rural communities and destructive agricultural practices mount, the need for graduates who have been educated for "responsible membership in a family, a community, or a polity" becomes ever more pressing.[2]

The health of communities depends on members educated "to renew, to make / whole, what ill use had broken."[3] Our ability to imagine wholeness even in the midst of brokenness is central to this task of renewal. Unfortunately, though, contemporary universities often fail to form students' imaginations in any holistic manner, choosing instead to focus on narrow, specialized training. Berry suggests an alternative model of education, one that begins by establishing a standard of health and training students to judge their work and lives against this standard.

---

1. Adapted from *Wendell Berry and Higher Education: Cultivating Virtues of Place* (University Press of Kentucky, 2017). Used by arrangement with the publisher.

2. Wendell Berry, "Bellarmine Commencement Address," 2007, http://christianstudycenter.org/wp-content/uploads/2009/10/WendellBerry-BellarmineCommencement.pdf.

3. Wendell Berry, *This Day: New and Collected Sabbath Poems 1979–2012* (Berkeley: Counterpoint, 2013), 355.

Berry's novella *Remembering* poignantly depicts the importance of the imagination in healing the dismemberment and displacement that contemporary education causes. Early in his life Andy Catlett had given up his place by succumbing to the narrative of upward and lateral mobility that he had learned from his college education. After graduating from college, Andy "resigned himself to living in cities. That was what his education was for, as his teachers all advised and he believed. Its purpose was to get him away from home, out of the country, to someplace where he could live up to his abilities. He needed an education, and the purpose of an education was to take him away."[4] Andy, following these expectations, got a job as a journalist in San Francisco and then got a better job writing for a magazine based in Chicago. He was moving up in the world. But then Andy was assigned to write a story about a "successful" farmer who grew corn on two thousand acres. As Andy interviewed the farmer, Meikelberger, he came to realize the emptiness of this life: Meikelberger was permanently in debt, he and his wife worked constantly to keep solvent, and the stress had given Meikelberger a stomach ulcer. By following the "get big or get out" logic of industrial agriculture, "Meikelberger's ambition had made common cause with a technical power that proposed no limit to itself, that was, in fact, destroying Meikelberger, as it had already destroyed nearly all that was natural or human around him."[5]

This destruction left Andy uneasy with Meikelberger's version of success, but he didn't have an alternative way of imagining success until the next day when, on his way to a meeting in Pittsburgh, he drove by an Amish farm. The farmer was plowing his field with horses when Andy drove by, and Andy pulled off the road, drawn by the beauty of the horses working the land. The man, Isaac Troyer, stopped his team and offered to let Andy take the reins. As Andy plowed a few furrows, his memories of farming as a boy returned, and he began to remember a vision of success quite different from Meikelberger's. Andy spent most of the day on the Troyer place, meeting the family, sharing a meal, and hearing about the neighborly economy in which the Troyers lived, an economy that didn't require them to go into debt or to attempt to buy up the surrounding farms. His day with the Troyers enabled Andy to imagine that he and his family could leave Chicago and return home. So as he walked over an old farm for sale near where he grew up, Andy realized that he "had begun

---

4. *Remembering: A Novel* (Berkeley: Counterpoint, 2008), 59.
5. Ibid., 63.

to dream his life" in this place, in this community. When he shares his dream of returning home and buying this rundown farm with his wife Flora, she responds, "'Well, it's about time.'"[6]

Andy's father Wheeler took a parallel journey away from home before dreaming of a more settled life. Wheeler went to college and then worked in Washington for a congressman while attending law school. When he graduated, his boss advised him to accept a good job Wheeler had been offered in Chicago. After all, this would enable Wheeler to fulfill his "destiny," which was "that of thousands of gifted country boys since the dawn of the republic, and before: college and then a profession and then a job in the city. This was the path of victory, already trodden out and plain."[7] But it wasn't that easy for Wheeler; he was torn by conflicting desires. Finally, he asked himself,

> "Do I want to spend my life looking out a window onto tarred roofs, or do I want to see good pastures, and the cattle coming to the spring in the evening to drink?"
>
> Elation filling him, he answered, "I want to see good pastures and the cattle coming to the spring to drink." For suddenly he did imagine what he could be. He saw it all. A man with a law degree did not have to go to Chicago to practice. He could practice wherever in the whole nation there was a courthouse. He could practice in Hargrave. He could be with his own. . . .
>
> Andy knows how firmly ruled and how unendingly fascinated his father has been by that imagining of cattle on good grass. It was a vision, finally, given the terrain and nature of their place, of a community well founded and long lasting. Wheeler held himself answerable to that.[8]

So like his father who came home to be faithful to his imagined vision of wholeness, Andy returns home to be restored to his place in the community.

The crucial parallel between Andy and Wheeler is that both return home when they can imagine a healthy, flourishing, placed life. Wheeler's vision of cattle on good grass includes by implication the health of his whole place; such a vision is possible only if small farmers maintain healthy pastures with small herd sizes, which is possible only if they are not under financial duress. As Andy knows, it is a vision "of a community

6. Ibid., 75–6.
7. Ibid., 56.
8. Ibid., 57.

well founded and long lasting." But these are also particular visions. Andy doesn't read about the Amish in the abstract; he gets to know an Amish family. Wheeler doesn't have a desire for some generic rural community defined by its statistics; he sees cattle grazing on good grass.

An education, then, that hopes to form students to serve the health of their communities must offer students particular, complex images of health that they can desire and work toward. In Andy's case that particular complex image is the Troyer farm, in Wheeler's case cattle grazing on good grass. For both, the images represent that "responsible membership in a family, a community, or a polity" upon which health depends. Without the ability to imagine what such a healthy, placed life would look like, students will be at the mercy of the standard American narrative of success; they will be drawn by the vision of an upwardly mobile life, always on the lookout for better opportunities in better places and, as a result, always contributing to the destruction of the places they never live in long enough to care about.[9]

It is important to note that for both Andy and Wheeler this imagined wholeness comes in opposition to the formation they received in college. And this isn't surprising given Berry's rather dim view of universities. Our schools, and particularly our universities, are structured to prepare students for mobile careers, careers that take place away from the home and that, in all likelihood, reduce the possibility of achieving Wheeler's vision of healthy cattle grazing on the hill. This stems, in large part, from the fact that contemporary American universities are fragmented institutions and are fundamentally confused about their purpose. This has led to increasing specialization at the expense of any sort of unified whole; as Berry argues, "the rule of specialization" leads modern society to become "more and more organized, but less and less orderly."[10] Universities have little coherent sense of what they are educating students for, even while their academic bureaucracy grows ever more intricate. Berry's diagnosis that the "modern university . . . more and more resembles a loose collection of lopped branches waving about randomly in the air" suggests to us that the first step toward educating for place must be to imagine organic

---

9. Richard Gamble, in his essay on Berry and education, offers a complementary reading of *Remembering*, although he emphasizes different features of Andy's journey home. Richard Gamble, "An Education for Membership," in *The Humane Vision of Wendell Berry*, ed. Mark T. Mitchell and Nathan W. Schlueter (Wilmington: ISI Books, 2011), 28–39.

10. *Unsettling*, 21.

wholeness.[11] Our current fragmented way of organizing knowledge—a furniture warehouse is one of Berry's images for it—cannot hope to provide such a vision, but a university organized more like a tree, its branches issuing from a common trunk, can. If, like Wheeler Catlett, we are guided by a vision of health, then it is at least possible that education can serve this health rather than contribute to its destruction. Therefore, one of the essential tasks of a placed university must be to cultivate this vision of health and teach students to judge their lives against this standard: this is the work of imagination.

Currently, many universities are much too fragmented to guide their students coherently. In keeping with the fragmented nature of our age, different parts of these institutions serve different ends: student development helps students find their social place, academic departments provide career training in whatever area a student wishes, and a smattering of required courses may suggest a cultural, national, or possibly religious tradition. As likely as not, however, these various divisions of the university will lead students in different, conflicting, directions. This is the consequence of an institution that has succumbed to competing pressures so that it is no longer a university, but what Clark Kerr has aptly termed a "multiversity."[12]

The only thing that the multiversity can agree on is the need to train students to get good jobs, which means the university now serves the private interests of students conceived not as citizens but as consumers "participating" in the economy. This can be seen most clearly in the rise of technical or vocational schools and for-profit schools that promise their students greater marketability. Yet even agricultural institutions that were ostensibly founded to serve farming communities actually function either to train rural children to get jobs elsewhere, or to train farmers to turn their land into factories for industrial agriculture. Serving the health of their communities is not one of their goals. Even purportedly liberal arts schools often follow suit, justifying their high cost by promising remunerative employment for their students. This leads to their inability to justify any sort of moral formation, and too often these schools also focus on specialization and career training. Clark Kerr's assessment is grim: "The ivory tower of old has become an arm of the state and an arm of

---

11. "The Loss of the University," in *Home Economics: Fourteen Essays* (Berkeley, CA: Counterpoint, 1987), 82.

12. Clark Kerr, *The Uses of the University*, 5th ed. (Cambridge: Harvard UP, 2001), 103.

industry, and the students inside reach out toward the labor market and toward political influence."[13] Berry perceived this problem in the early 1970s, when he stated flatly that in America "the purpose of education is the mass production of producers and consumers."[14] The institution which began with the purpose of leading students out of ignorance to serve their communities now primarily serves the nation-state's industrial complex. In the absence of any higher purpose, the multiversity defaults to serving the economy, to training students to be effective cogs in a capitalistic machine.

But an education for health, one that forms students to serve their homes, will have to begin by reforming students' imaginations so that they begin to ask better questions. For, as Berry explains, boomers and stickers—terms Berry derives from Wallace Stegner to contrast those who are always on the lookout for better opportunities with those who desire to serve the health of their places—ask different kinds of questions and operate in different economies because of their contrasting affections. Whereas the boomer or "exploiter asks of a piece of land only how much and how quickly it can be made to produce, the nurturer [or sticker] asks a question that is much more complex and difficult: What is its carrying capacity? (That is: How much can be taken from it without diminishing it?)"[15] Berry expresses this contrast even more simply in an interview with Bill Moyers: "The answers will come not from walking up to your farm and saying this is what I want and this is what I expect from you. You walk up and you say 'What do you need?'"[16] These different questions stem from differently orientated desires—one desires quick profit and the other health—and from the different complexities of their accounting—one values only profit and externalizes costs and damages, whereas the other seeks to give an account for all things. These distinctions mark the contrast that Berry draws in "Two Economies" be-

13. *Uses of the University*, 214.

14. "In Defense of Literacy," in *A Continuous Harmony: Essays Cultural and Agricultural* (San Diego: Harcourt Brace & Co, 1972), 169–70.

15. *Unsettling*, 7. Berry also expands on this line of questioning in his two commencement addresses, urging graduates to ask questions about where they are and how they can serve these places. "Bellarmine"; "Major in Homecoming: For Commencement, Northern Kentucky University," in *What Matters? Economics for a Renewed Commonwealth* (Washington, D.C.: Counterpoint, 2010), 34–35.

16. Wendell Berry on His Hopes for Humanity, interview by Bill Moyers, Television, November 29, 2013, http://billmoyers.com/segment/wendell-berry-on-his-hopes-for-humanity/.

tween our industrial economy, which "tends to destroy what it does not comprehend," and the "Great Economy" or the "Kingdom of God," which "includes everything" in its comprehensive "pattern or order."[17]

This fundamental difference between teaching students to get what they want from their places and teaching them to ask of the place "what do you need?" marks not only the difference between boomers and stickers but also the difference between a more medieval way of organizing knowledge and the organization (or lack thereof) in modern universities.[18] Asking "what do I want?" simply leads to education in techniques of extraction for personal appetite, but the question "what do you need?" leads to an education in charity and health. C. S. Lewis describes this difference in terms of the contrast between medieval learning and the mere technical training increasingly offered today: "For the wise men of old the cardinal problem had been how to conform the soul to reality, and the solution had been knowledge, self-discipline, and virtue. For ... applied science ... the problem is how to subdue reality to the wishes of men: the solution is a technique."[19] The work of conforming our souls to reality via knowledge, self-discipline, and virtue is long and arduous, but if universities hope to educate students to inhabit their places responsibly, this is the work they will have to take up.

The contrast between boomers and stickers—the different desires they have, the different stories they tell, the different questions they ask, the different economies they participate in, and the contrasting models of the university that they propose—should now be clear: the boomer wants to isolate knowledge from its origins in order to maximize its utility and profitability, but the sticker values a medieval, rooted kind of learning whose branches connect as much as possible. Thus, the way we organize and order knowledge stems from the kinds of questions we ask, which in turn rise from the orientation of our desires.

A rooted education, then, should begin by teaching students how to trace the interconnections of wisdom and health through an emphasis on imagination; such an education might begin to form the affections of students so that they desire the health of their place. While boomers

---

17. "Two Economies," in *Home Economics* (New York: North Point P, 1987), 54–55.

18. For a helpful description of the medieval curriculum, see Jim Halverson, "Restored through Learning: Hugh of St. Victor's Vision for Higher Education," *Christian Scholar's Review* XLI, no. 1 (2011).

19. *The Abolition of Man, Or, Reflections on Education with Special Reference to the Teaching of English in the Upper Forms of Schools* (San Francisco: Harper, 2001), 83.

tend to allow their desires to form their questions, Berry argues that a mature, nurturing person will shape his desires and questions to the limits of his place: "We have, in fact, no right to ask the world to conform to our desires. Sooner or later, if we hope to grow up, we have to confront the opposite imperative: that our rights and the realization of our desires are limited by human nature, by human community, and by the nature of the places in which we live."[20] Teaching our students to be stickers, to be nurturers, thus involves teaching them patiently and faithfully to ask their neighbors and places, "What do you need?"

In order to foster such questions, universities need to educate students' imaginations so that they are capable of judging whether or not our knowledge and work are serving the health of our places. For the standard by which we need to judge all our learning and work is found outside of the university, in the ground in which the tree of knowledge is rooted. This rootedness is not only metaphorical but also literal; as Berry explains, the standard to which we must ultimately remain faithful is "the life and health of the world."[21] Of course the task of making our knowledge and work faithful and responsible to everything is a task that is never complete. It requires the ongoing work of judging and correcting our visions, and it ultimately requires a healthy imagination, one that like Wheeler's envisions the health of the land—perhaps in the form of cattle grazing on good grass—and sees the complex needs of the community that lie behind this vision. Difficult though this task may be, it is a necessary one, for if the learning that universities foster fails to stem from and contribute to the health of the "Great Economy," then the university and the communities it exists to serve will wither and die.

And so we are left where we began, with the importance of cultivating healthy, vibrant imaginations, ones capable of relating disparate disciplines to each other and to their likely effects on the world. And our imaginations, Berry argues, should always remain open to further growth and correction:

> The imagination is in the world, is at work in it, is necessary to it, and is correctable by it. This correcting of imagination by experience is inescapable, necessary, and endless, as is the correcting of experience by imagination. This is the great general work of

---

20. "The Conservation of Nature and the Preservation of Humanity," in *Another Turn of the Crank: Essays* (Washington, D.C.: Counterpoint, 1995), 83–84.

21. "Discipline and Hope," in *A Continuous Harmony: Essays Cultural and Agricultural* (San Diego: Harcourt Brace & Co, 1972), 164.

criticism to which we all are called. . . . One of the most profound of human needs is for the truth of imagination to prove itself in every life and place in the world, and for the truth of the world's lives and places to be proved in imagination.[22]

Universities, then, need to pay more careful attention to forming rooted imaginations, ones that can guide graduates as they attempt to make their language and work serve the health of their places.

We've implicitly modeled the role of the imagination by offering a reading from *Remembering*. This novel emphasizes our need to tell better stories and to follow more beautiful, robust images of flourishing places. These stories and images act as standards by which we can judge our education and indeed our lives. Such stories are particularly important in a time when many universities are moving toward professionalization and over-specialization. Instead, we propose a curriculum that values the power of narrative to shape students and their communities; the trunk of the curricular tree must include the humanities, and in particular literature. Too often when literature is present in the curriculum, it is taught as a specialty. When literature becomes only another specialty, it loses its ability to critique stories of upward and lateral mobility, of success gained only in leaving our homes behind. Our imaginations are shaped by figures like Abe Lincoln, the farm boy who became president, or Horatio Algiers Jr.'s heroes, who go from rags to riches often by leaving their homes for the bustling city. Through these stories we have imbibed Huck Finn's attitude and like him plan to "light out for the territories" if things get rough.[23]

Berry's response to our deracinated and impoverished vision of the good has been to write compelling stories about Port William in which he imagines what a healthy place, with its community and economy, might look like. Berry's contributions are nowhere more needed or more valuable than in his fiction, where he portrays a rich, vibrant vision of health, a vision that includes all the members of creation as they seek to live in accordance with the Kingdom of God. One of the primary tasks of a rooted education, then, is to tell better stories and provide students with a healthier imagination of the good by which they can judge their lives. Consider, for example, Wheeler's vision of healthy cows grazing

---

22. "The Loss of the University," 96.

23. In "Writer and Region," Berry offers an extended reading of the conclusion of *Huckleberry Finn*.

in a green pasture, or the memory of the shire that guides the hobbits on their journey to Mount Doom, or the flourishing Eden that anchors *Paradise Lost* and *The Divine Comedy*, or the olive tree bed and the house and community that extend from it in *The Odyssey*, or the pentangle emblazoned upon Sir Gawain's shield to which all his affections tend. We desperately need these visions of rich health, of *shalom*, to guide and motivate us in much the same way that Wheeler's vision of grazing cattle guides his work as a lawyer. Providing students with this vision of health should be the foundation of a well-rooted education: it enables students to have some common standard when they ask, "what are the effects of my work?" and "does my work tend toward health?" and "what is my education for?"

While such stories of journeying and return were once common—the archetypal example is *The Odyssey*—these stories have largely fallen out of favor in the past two centuries. Berry dates this shift to Wordsworth's *Michael*, and he mourns the loss of this narrative of return.[24] Yet the book you are holding in your hands forms part of an effort to renarrate homecoming, thus shaping the imaginations of students so that they will want their education to serve the health of their places. Young people rooted in an imagined vision of health will be prepared to put their knowledge in the service of their places. For as they proceed up the tree of wisdom, such students will remember the standard of health that is the judge of their work and their lives. Only if their studies are rooted in their desire to make a place home, to see cattle grazing on good grass, will they perceive knowledge to be like a tree. Only then will they understand "responsible membership in a family, a community, or a polity." And it is these desires and this tree of wisdom that will enable students to put their learning in the service of their places.

---

24. Wendell Berry, "The Work of Local Culture," in *What Are People For? Essays* (New York: North Point Press, 1990), 161–163.

Art, Beauty, and Communal Life

James Matthew Wilson

ONE OF THE CONTENTIONS that contemporary advocates of human-scale economies, local agriculture, decentralized governance, and rooted, small communities must routinely overcome is that their ideas amount to little more than a charming aesthetic miasma that has overflowed onto the rockier, sturdier banks of real public policy. Though claiming to be concerned with quality produce, better nutrition, and responsible stewardship of the earth in an age that suffers from a dearth of such things, promoters of local agriculture find themselves dismissed as privileged aesthetes, as if they had somehow confused the apples on Cézanne's painted table with the apples they would pay a connoisseur's price to have on theirs. Such dismissals persist, even after all sides acknowledge that terms often thrown at localists, such as "crunchy" and "granola," are themselves ugly and refer to a rustic homeliness that speaks more of careless, antisocial neglect than aestheticized preciosity.

That charges of aestheticism do not obviously suit many contemporary advocates of localism does not settle the matter, however. For it was indeed once the case that the most powerful voices in favor of economic, political, and communal localization were chiefly literary men whose positions on these matters were patently extensions of their larger philosophical notions of the central role art and beauty ought to play in human life. I spy in this a double irony.

Not only would I observe that arguments for localization in our age are more frequently grounded on concrete, often quantitative, evidence than they are on aesthetic "tastes." But, I propose, precisely to the extent that such public-policy-advocating quantitative analysis has displaced—rather than complemented—arguments rooted in the beautiful, arguments for localism in our age are inferior to those so easily—and wrongly—dismissed in decades past.

Convictions about the shape of our culture, economy, and body politic are fundamentally rooted in our understanding of aesthetic form, that is to say, in beauty. I suggest that we need to recover a sense of beauty as having a binding claim on our perception of these various bodies, these organic wholes, just as truth has a binding claim on our intellects and goodness on our desires. If this can convincingly be shown to be the case, then it will become much clearer why earlier advocates of localism hoped for the cultivation of communities that would find their highest expression in shared delight in the arts of the beautiful. Further, it will become clear that we need to strive for such expression in our age. To misquote Burke and Cicero, a good community like a good poem ought to be beautiful. And a beautiful community will always have at its center the fine and the literary arts. But, to accept such a claim, we have first to understand our own present circumstances and what beauty truly is.

Two of the great early-twentieth-century voices of localism best remembered in our day are the Distributists, as represented by G.K. Chesterton, and the Southern Agrarians, whose early leader was John Crowe Ransom. Basing their thought expressly on early Catholic social doctrine, the Distributists sought a third way between *laissez-faire* capitalism and collectivist socialism, setting as the highest political good not the efficiencies of the market nor the centralized management of all goods, but the widest possible distribution of private, property-owning households. Such an arrangement would make each household a good little order unto itself. Critics incessantly derided the schemes as backward, to which Chesterton replied that it was far more reasonable to propose a solution that has worked in the past than to bet on utopian programs as yet untried. The Distributists were also accused of nostalgia—something to which Chesterton, in a sense, readily assented. He indeed longed for a rebirth of "jolly old" England, whose delight in the minutiae and misadventures of an essentially comic and Christian society struck him as a sure sign of health. That Chesterton was more successful at conveying a vivid and persuasive description of what a good society looks like than he was plotting the course to realize it is clear enough, but his task was above all to clarify perceptions so that human beings would seek consciously what they already wanted instinctively. England would in a sense realize the *Canterbury Tales*, comic art would provide the model for the form of a happy community, and much story-telling and beer-drinking would ensue.

The case of Ransom more directly answers to the description of aestheticism. In his contributions to the Southern Agrarian symposium, *I'll Take My Stand* (1930), Ransom appears as a friendly critic of the South, tracing the etiology of the Old South's failure and of the New South's reconstructed servility before northern industrialism. Ransom's contributions to the symposium and his book, *God Without Thunder* (also 1930), propose that religion, society, and art are deeply interdependent. Religion itself manifested our justified fear of the forces of nature, the thunder of God. In his brief, old-time southern Christian fundamentalists—the same people derided by the press in the Scopes-Monkey trial in 1924—more truly understood the human condition than did modern, demythologized liberal Protestants or arrogant secular humanists (both of whom were the natural allies of Ransom's *bête noire*, the southern Chambers of Commerce). Ransom held an at-best-tenuous and generalized theism: he believed in a god of nature whom we should fear. And he believed religion constituted the assent to myths crafted by poets and intended to serve as a check on an otherwise ceaselessly ambitious human nature. For Ransom, the authentic South was a place where, if it could recover its properly religious roots (which were not located on the plantation but in the clapboard chapels of the Tennessee hills), a shared life of joy and fear in the arts—a prayerful rehearsal of poetic myths—would be realized.

It is worth noting that alongside Distributists and Agrarians thrived more practically minded, if less provocatively eloquent, movements. But I wish merely to suggest that these groups drew essential inspiration from the evocative accounts of the beauty of small ownership and stable communities that such writers as Ransom and Chesterton sketched. And they did so with good reason, for they could recognize the goodness of the form such Arcadian sketches left in the mind and promised to the community. They saw that there is a real, indeed an essential, good that finds its adequate image in a community joined together in taking delight in beautiful words, music, dance, and sculpture. And they saw that this delight could not simply be manufactured by our work, but had to be inspired: given to us from above, from the God who made all things, or at least the "heavenly muses." For, while one may desire small-scale agriculture to ensure a wider distribution of ownership of productive property and a stable, locally self-sufficient source of food and other goods, one ultimately desires such things because the activities they involve lead to the formation of communities with deep attachments, communities that thoroughly interweave the necessities of human life with the discipline of sociability and responsibility to one's neighbors, and with a joyful consent to the source and sustainer of these good things.

At the heart of all localizing movements lies the—sometimes inarticulate—conviction that human beings want to hold truths in common that have been given to them in trust. They wish to belong to a community of knowledge about the reality that transcends each one of us as individuals, as becomes all the more obvious every time the volume in our ever-more-vocal but increasingly inattentive society increases. Furthermore, they want to hold goods in common, within their family and across generations, and between families, in the life of a neighborhood, or town, or city. As I shall consider in a moment, this also becomes more obvious the more parents become possessed with the prepping of their one or two children for admission into an elite university, or the more the already outrageous hours many Americans work increase for the sake of ensuring they have capital sufficient for serious long-term investments. We defer gratification in order to secure practical goods on a scale few civilizations have attempted before us, but the huge scale of these activities seems largely driven by their failure to find direction to their proper end. What Chesterton and Ransom saw that few of us do today is that the desire to share truths and goods with others like us finds its realization in the communal contemplation of art. For there, beauty, which some philosophers call the synthesis of truth and goodness, or truth-experienced-as-good, becomes an object around which we all gather in a moment not only of stillness or silence but of stasis. Such literary localists provided an image of what peace may look like in this world; only a society that finds its fulfillment gathered into communities of delight over something properly delightful can be a happy one. And, as St. Thomas says, it is the beautiful that delights when seen.

In our day, we tend to recognize this positive claim largely in terms of absences and anxieties. It is no novel observation to highlight the loneliness typical to modern life. The restless and fidgety use of communications technology seems only to intensify our experience of being part of a lonely crowd, ever surrounded by sounds and sights, new information we must hear, and new persons we must meet, and yet all of it eerily distant from ourselves. We search the internet for the latest college football recruiting news, and if there is none to be found, we feel an ache that has nothing to do with sports but that merely propels us on to the next distracting object of curiosity. Married couples become obsessed with protecting their children from harm, because even the neighbors they know well have only been their neighbors for a short span.

Human beings have always pursued their small share of glory in work, or in participation in one political or charitable activity or another, and well they should. But the hungry diligence typical to our age speaks of needs and desires that the workplace and the public square cannot slake. And yet almost nothing in our culture suggests there is anything outside of work—besides, of course, the reprieve of play—that might be more satisfying. Similarly, parents are markedly terrified that their children are being perverted by their saturation in the information technology that actually constitutes most of our "play" nowadays. However fearful they may be, they have no compelling vision of the norm from which their children might be deviating. And so parents in our age seek to "balance" the exposure of their children to these things, but this in practice means simply limiting it, because they have no alternative, higher set of goods in mind to set in the scales against such troubling and entrancing indulgences. To the extent that we are unhappy, we are unhappy in consequence not of specific evils in our lives but of a sense of absence. And while it is not at all my intent to suggest that works of art will somehow fill the void, or allay our restlessness, in themselves, I propose that the image of a community delighting in beauty provides us a good guide to the form our actual communities ought to take if we are to live well.

As others have compellingly stated, we have an abundance of reasons other than the shared experience of beauty to work toward the reform of our society in a more localized, decentralized, and rooted direction. And, thanks to the unhappy contingencies of our political culture, we tend to divide the desire for, say, strong local agriculture and strong religious families into competing, even antagonistic, programs. We thus lose sight of their true end and in the process untether them from its image in a community joined together in the contemplation of a beauty its own members have helped to fashion.

In comparison with the vision of times past, in other words, the aesthetic vision that gives a larger purpose to many localist movements has been muted. Wendell Berry and Scott Russell Sanders, along with a handful of other writers and artists, have provided us compelling visions and arguments in favor of a re-localization of human culture in fiction, poetry, and essay. And their individual achievements would constitute any literary period as a rich, if not a flush, one. But the forces that have been pulling us apart at the seams for decades have only grown louder and stronger the more dire the condition into which they lead us has become. If the localist response to global markets and distant, technocratic rule has become more adept in its arguing, it has also become surprisingly "wonkish": more beholden to the instrumental reason of the regime it would reform and to its blaring "sound bite" tactics of persuasion than to a coherent and comprehensive vision of human happiness. Whatever else it requires, our age sorely calls for moral and spiritual solutions to its material, technological, and political problems.

The image, if not the fullness, of such solutions must come in a renewal of a shared life in the arts—the arts of good homes, furniture, cooking, beer, and building, but above all, the *fine* arts whose beauty stands out above any useful aim. We need a vision of the beauty that binds us to itself and to what is most permanently true and most wholly good. To unpack such a claim, we ought to examine the role that the arts—or things much like the arts—presently play in our society. For, it is true, much of the delight that has traditionally been associated with the arts of the beautiful is nourished, if not satisfied, by the ever-novel and vertiginously saturating role information technology and the mass media now play in our lives. We may often be bored, but we are never idle; our eyes dart about the surfaces of the world and find brief enchantments everywhere. This damages us to the extent that it causes us to associate the satisfactions of the aesthetic broadly conceived as answering superficial, if inveterate, appetites. Additionally, much of it tends to draw us away from serious thought and from the kind of sociality in which such thought can find expression. We seldom feel we are encountering truth in what we see or hear, and what we do encounter seldom requires being shared with another in the way one normally desires to share what is good.

But let us consider a partial exception to this furtive and restless condition. The same media that generally isolate us also provide occasions for our rare moments of feeling raised into community. We do frequently cherish the watching of a certain few films together, or the conversations that the separate viewing of television programs makes possible, when we are arrayed around a table for lunch at work. However inadequate the communal contemplation such things afford, and however much our saturation in information technology blunts our understanding of how to delight in the beautiful as a community, it also provides some small space for that deep human need to subsist.

This hardly means most of our lives are void of art. In wealthy parts of the country, and especially on the coasts, a huge infrastructure supporting the arts thrives and grows. Unfortunately, it does so in a highly instrumentalized form; the rearing of children for elite colleges makes essential the having of some creative ability to note on one's application, and music, as the ancient Greeks knew, is a great aid to "math skills." Children are trained in music, and to a lesser extent in the other fine arts, in impressive numbers. All those children learning strings entails a great number of concerts and recitals. But the music falls silent after the acceptance letter arrives in the mail. Even so, and once again, what in some way seems a sign of a deadening utilitarian spirit nonetheless bears within it a fertilized seed.

The case is similarly ambiguous in those centers where the fine arts most flourish. High art has nearly reached the end of a long process of cutting itself off from human life and humane audiences. Where, once, Immanuel Kant sequestered the beautiful in subjective disinterested judgment, now, the wealthy patrons of the arts and artists themselves do not believe in beauty. They believe rather in the peeling away of the scales of complacency and credulousness they attribute to the anonymous masses. Because those masses seldom know of such art's existence, most high art would seem to afford a curious satisfaction: a small audience is willing to pretend to a vicarious shock at a work's "transgressive" theme or character, and to experience that shock in the name of persons it does not really know but holds in contempt. If one can take any consolation in such spectacle it is that, despite our elites' having lost all conception of the fine arts as committed to beauty or the lasting expression of human experience, the habit of treating art as something privileged and valuable has nonetheless persisted.

The salutary but instrumentalized arts of youth and the scandal-seeking nihilism of contemporary high art converges with the banalities of the mass media in only two places in our age: in public monuments and on college campuses. But we have become so suspicious of the monumental as classically understood—as the giving of enduring form to some passing instance of heroic virtue—that such monuments as now get built are usually monstrosities consecrated to the remembrance of collective victimhood. The notion of a community gathering about some sublime statue has been replaced by the vicarious experience of social guilt. Those who come to view such works experience a kind of dual consciousness not quite identifiable with repentance, congratulating themselves for condemning their racist, sexist, or imperialist ancestors even as they sense that the sin of the fathers demands their own therapeutic "confrontation" of privilege. No wonder so many of the most recently constructed monuments are low, even subterranean, and extensive, so that everyone who visits them must submit to something like a long walk among the faceless dead.

One may say something similar about college campuses. University orchestras, college art museums, and student theater remain for the most part deferential to older notions of what constitutes real art, and, to the extent that the arts have a respectable public life in our time, it is to be found in arts centers on college campuses more than in the major cities. But, when the directors of such centers get ambitious, it is usually to confront students and communities alike with some dreadful didactic work of the "transgressive" and liberating. The raw masses are invited in to hear their manners derided as the source of oppression and "victimhood." No community could center its gaze on such spectacles for very long or to any good. The experience itself works like a solvent further to isolate us in our individuality, shame, and loneliness.

If the experience of beauty really is distinct from but related to that of truth and goodness, then we ought to feel obliged to undertake the project of building communities that gather to delight in the arts of the beautiful, even if we must begin with such inauspicious fragments as I have described. For beauty is the perception of form; the beauty of the individual arts provides us models and criteria for what a well-formed community ought to look like. And so we find the end of our argument in arriving at a sort of circular first principle: the encountering of great art helps us to form good communities, but a good community will always be one capable of finding its internal fulfillment in its members gathering in delighted stasis to contemplate beautiful artwork. There, a community will find its own earthly life made available for grateful reflection, its failings summoned for dramatic reckoning, and its ultimate destiny in religious life gestured toward, however fumbling the gesture.

How, then, shall we build? Arts education should probably play a larger role in children's lives, and it should be justified less in terms of its possible benefit for standardized tests in mathematics and more in terms of the public celebrations that musical performances and artistic exhibits might highlight. Most communities ought, also, to increase the number of public feast days that would occasion such performances, so that music escapes the school recital hall, crowded with bored parents, and becomes more fully integrated with town life. Musical performances by students seem the most obvious and easy species of art to reintegrate with and elevate public life. But we should also consider the rebirth of Shakespearean and popular theater and of poetry recitation that have taken place during the last decade, mostly through National Endowment for the Arts initiatives. Building up a local culture of youth performance—one independent of federal funding—would prepare an environment in which those children, grown to adulthood, would likely seek to continue performing, to continue providing music and other art to enrich the public celebrations of their communities. It would reduce the sad instances of those with serious musical or artistic interests feeling obliged to head to major cities as supposed centers of culture in order to find an audience. Similarly, the continued promotion of poetry-recitation contests in schools would prepare the ground for a more expressly public, more popular and yet more sophisticated, literary culture than we have at present.

More challenging would be the recovery of a sense of the monumental and sacred in our public arts, for present patrons of the arts chiefly view such notions with contempt. A rebirth of good architecture and sculpture does not want for visionary architects and artists, but for commissions, from those with a genuine sense of the heroic and noble. Similarly, a desire for a greater sense of the beautiful in sacred art is not wanting in Catholic parishes and Protestant congregations, but at present the means and sensibility necessary to fulfill it largely is. A renewed public commitment to celebrating the heroic virtues of the past and our capacities for the divine life in the future would be only a first step in a difficult process of rediscovering why, when human beings want to know the truth about themselves and to anticipate the goods they most deeply desire, they have always gathered together for story, spectacle, and song.

The drive for upward mobility and the largess of federal bureaucracy have, for some time, been lifelines of the arts as mass culture eroded their traditional audiences, utilitarianism relegated them to juvenilia, and a sensibility of scorn and nihilism encouraged the most prestigious art to become savage and elitist. But if we appreciate how deeply we require an encounter with real beauty in order to form and to find happiness in good communities, we will also appreciate that any renewal of the arts, if it is to serve any great purpose, will have to emerge from the initiative of good people in their own localities seeking to share with their neighbors a keen delight in what they have made.

Part Five

Civic Life

A community is the mental and spiritual condition of knowing that the place is shared, and that the people who share the place define and limit the possibilities of each other's lives. It is the knowledge that people have of each other, their concern for each other, their trust in each other, the freedom with which they come and go among themselves.

—WENDELL BERRY, *THE LONG-LEGGED HOUSE*

A Land Like No Other: American Exceptionalism and the Problem of Scale

Richard Gamble

Just before national holidays, my town's local Kiwanis chapter places American flags at the homes of residents who make a small donation. A lot of these flags fly in our rural community in southern Michigan. At the end of August, 2012, club members put a flag in my front yard to mark Labor Day and the approaching anniversary of 9/11. Sometime before 9:30 p.m. the following Saturday, person or persons unknown (as legal-types say, at least on TV) cut down Old Glory, leaving a ragged strip of cloth attached to the bent pole. My neighbor, a Navy veteran, was the first to notice it. I assumed the vandalism was a random act of unkindness committed by juvenile delinquents. We have a handful of those. I did not consider it an act of domestic terrorism. I did not call the FBI. But I did report it to the local police, and they found me down at the ice cream shop one evening, interviewed me, and kindly followed up on the incident. Without saying a word, the Kiwanis Club replaced the flag a few days later.

This minor incident left me a bit shaken—more than I would have expected. It troubled me to know that someone in our small town would impulsively destroy a flag. The red, white, and blue sliver of cloth hanging from the pole also started me thinking about patriotism and our national banner. I was raised to respect the flag. I remember as a kid reading an illustrated entry in the 1960 World Book encyclopedia about how to treat the American flag. It seemed as though there were customs and laws to cover every contingency—whether it should stand on a speaker's left or right, how it should be displayed on a casket, how it ought to be folded. Until his death at the age of 86, my father, though not a veteran, put out the flag every morning and brought it in every evening. He and my mother would never have thought of leaving it out in the rain or in the dark. They did not worship the flag; they respected it. And by their example they taught me to do the same.

I am just old enough to remember the counterculture's abuse of the flag in the late '60s. Displaying it on the rear pocket of a pair of jeans or wearing it as a bandana signaled anything but an act of patriotic devotion in those days. Maybe that lingering impression accounts for my reaction to seeing so many flags appear after 9/11. While the media on the Left and Right gushed over the number of flags on display—probably the most in American history—I was struck instead by how many dirty, wet, shredded remnants of flags were attached to the roofs of passing cars a few weeks later. Was this patriotism, I wondered? Or was it a sign of an exhausted, mindless nationalism? Had 9/11 mobilized American resolve and revealed the enduring vitality of America's moral health? Or had it provided more evidence of our loss of manners, our growing cluelessness about how to act in public and how to treat a flag with simple decency? I suspect the latter. We can take our veneration of the flag too far, of course. And I wouldn't mind seeing a few more Michigan flags on display in my town along with the Stars and Stripes. (Our modest state motto, translated from the Latin, is "If you seek a pleasant peninsula, look around you"—not exactly the stuff of crusades to make the world safe for democracy.) But the extremes of carelessness and worship both point to the same cultural problem.

I am a patriot, not a nationalist. Because I am a patriot, I am also a localist, or at least a localist-in-training who is trying to learn how to become native to my place, in the words of Wes Jackson quoted so often by Wendell Berry. I'm a bit nostalgic for the old federal republic that didn't need the "city on a hill," the "American Idea," the Battle Hymn of the Republic, or the Pledge of Allegiance to tell it what it was and what it stood for and what it was willing to fight and die for. At one time Americans managed to be honorable citizens without these slogans and creedal affirmations. I think it ought to be possible even in modern America for us to love our country without falling for political Gnosticism, heresy, or idolatry. In fact, true patriots have well-ordered loves. They know the difference between family, community, God, church, and nation. True patriots respect genuine diversity—a localist conservative principle. The misnamed Antifederalists in the 1780s pointed to America's economic, geographic, and even cultural diversity as compelling reasons why a consolidated nation-state would never work—or, rather, why it would "work" only too well at the expense of self-governing communities with their own notions of the good life and how to get there.

Local communities are not perfect, but it never occurs to them to try to be so. Communities rooted in places, ancestors, history, and a way of life do not need the modern exceptionalist narrative to tell them how to think and live. But nationalist consolidation thrives on such a story. Localists are proud of their homes and flower gardens and Fourth of July parades. My Michigan neighborhood has community pride, but it doesn't think of itself as heaven on earth or the answer to the world's problems. It doesn't want to be an Idea. It is content to be a place, a place like no other. We leave it to Home Depot and Applebee's to aspire to uniformity. Who has ever said, "I really like the way they do Big Macs in Portland, Oregon"? (If you can say this, you have sampled way too much fast food.) Distinctiveness is the very thing these big boxes and generic eateries shun. They succeed on standardized predictability, and so does creedal nationalism. But my modest town is content to be a town like no other—for good and bad.

Nationalist "exceptionalism" knows nothing of this modesty. There was once a way of boasting about America that took pride in inheritances, character traits, political, civic, and economic associations, and cultural achievements that made it unique. It talked like a larger version of home pride, school pride, and team pride. Today, politicians, speechwriters, journalists, and public intellectuals insist that America is a land like no other but they do so in ways that have little to do with America as a place. Instead, Americans are asked to subscribe to an abstract ideology cut loose from history, human scale, and the ordinary experience of real people. The exceptionalist orthodoxy, policed and enforced as the test of what counts as authentically American and what does not, imposes a single story onto a massive homogeneous community. The current nationalist, exceptionalist creed stands for things too big for human habitation. Exceptionalists like to tell us that America is a creedal nation, and they appear to have G. K. Chesterton on their side. "America," he wrote in 1922, "is the only nation in the world that is founded on a creed."[1] But exceptionalists miss Chesterton's irony by their selective quotations (in the same way they miss Tocqueville's criticisms and warnings in their

---

1. G. K. Chesterton, *What I Saw in America* (New York: Dodd, Mead, 1922), 7.

eagerness to proof-text their way through American history). Chesterton found this "nation with the soul of church" admirable in many ways, but with creeds can come Inquisitions to enforce the boundaries of the faith. Before we participate in the national liturgy, then, we ought at least to know the statement of faith to which we are expected to subscribe in order to be welcomed into the true church of Americanism.

Americanism is all around us. It is often felt more than defined. It also changes with the times and with the expediencies of shifting political coalitions. Yesterday's heretics can become today's saints, yesterday's saints today's heretics. One spirited defense of the exceptionalist creed, deployed against Democrats by Republican opinion-makers, appeared in *National Review* in March 2010. In "An Exceptional Debate: The Obama administration's assault on American identity," editors Rich Lowry and Ramesh Ponnuru lay out what they claimed has always defined Americans.[2] The authors work hard to defend the current version of movement conservatism, and they do so by defining America in such a way that it can be used as a weapon in their partisan battles. The real conservatives are "advocates of the dynamism of an open society." They say, in fact, that if these future-oriented Americans lived in any other society they would be "the opposite of conservative"—a telling concession.

To their credit, Lowry and Ponnuru highlight the legacies of political, religious, and economic liberty, written constitutions, and limited government as accomplishments in which we can all take pride. But their exceptionalist, nationalist creed claims much more. Several key doctrines run through this editorial:

First, America is a "striving," "hustling," "fluid" place. This is no doubt true, but the editors present these traits as if they were unambiguously positive characteristics that make us who we are as a people. There is no hint that anyone, such as Tocqueville, feared the consequences of this restlessness.

Second, America "is freer, more individualistic, more democratic, and more open and dynamic than any other nation on earth." The implication here is that the really orthodox exceptionalists need to keep America this way. Lost here is any recognition that eighteenth- and nineteenth-century Americans worried about unconstrained individualism

---

2. Rich Lowry and Ramesh Ponnuru, "An Exceptional Debate: The Obama administration's assault on American identity," National Review Digital, March 8, 2010 https://www.nationalreview.com/nrd/articles/339276/exceptional-debate.

and even thought of democracy in ways that still sounded like the ancient fears of the Greeks and Romans.

Third, America is "special," a "model," an "exemplar." Depending on just what ideas, institutions, and character traits Americans are meant to model to the world, this doctrine could restrain national hubris. We could be an example to the world of decentralization, federalism, and a foreign policy based on national self-interest narrowly circumscribed. In the context of the other doctrines, however, this self-understanding becomes a potent force for ideological nationalism and even imperialism, as the next point makes clear.

Fourth, America has "a unique role and mission in the world." The qualification the authors add to this principle warrants scrutiny. Every word counts: America is a "vindicator of [freedom], through persuasion when possible and force of arms when absolutely necessary." Not her own freedom, mind you, but freedom in general. This is an abstract, open-ended commitment. Such a role in the world has been controversial throughout American history, but you would never know it from the creed. Dissenters from interventionism get written out of the story. Nevertheless, the authors claim that "throughout our history, we have sought not just to secure our interests abroad, but to export our model of liberty." True, Woodrow Wilson and other global democrats have claimed that exporting liberty was what "we dreamed of at our birth." But this hope has hardly been the shared, uncontroverted aspiration of the American people. Nevertheless . . .

Fifth, these traits have always been true of America. The historical reality, as I have noted along the way, has been quite different. The authors promote a unified story that cannot hold up, unless of course anyone who disagrees with the creed is by definition un-American. If we begin with the presupposition that only one set of ideas has ever marked "real" Americans (and that set just happens to be the current political message of one party or another), then the resulting creed shouldn't surprise anyone.

Sixth, America was "blessedly unencumbered by an *ancien regime*." The reference here of course is to medieval Europe, the kind of aristocratic, monarchical, traditional society that the French Revolution tried to wipe off the continent. There is some truth to this, but the presupposition here is that America was a blank slate, or enough of a blank slate that a highly ideological way of thinking and living could be imposed upon it at will. "It was as close as you could get to John Locke's state of nature," the authors claim. But, again, history is against them. American settlers did not come to the New World stripped of their ties to king and country. But even when the authors concede that American colonists brought something with them from the Old World, they claim that it was the "most individualistic" and the "most liberal fringe" who left England. They then revolutionize the implications even of this atomistic inheritance, as the next point shows.

Seventh, America took "English liberties," turned them into a "creed," and "universalized them" in obedience to its "missionary impulse" and in repeatedly deploying "the maximum plausible effort to spread our democratic system."

Taken as a whole, this version of the national creed affirms that America is revolutionary; more forward-looking than any other nation; a model to others; on a mission to export that model; confident that this identity has always been so; free from Europe's history; and what it did retain from the past it turned into a universal creed. No mention is made, however, that anything called Christianity, or communities, or the South, or a fear of populism and nationalism were ever part of American history. And the greatest act of faith here is the proposition that this creed counts as "conservative" and that it is therefore the duty of the Republican Party to defend the creed against all enemies foreign and domestic.

Perhaps this creed wouldn't matter too much if it remained confined to partisan opinion magazines. But it appears in campaign politics as well. One example will show its prominence. The disjointed closing paragraph from a speech Mitt Romney gave on August 12, 2012, soon after announcing his running mate, borrows heavily from the creed. These words are best read as if they comprised a slideshow of evocative images: "We love this country," Romney pledged.

> We know it's an exceptional land. We understand that when the Founders wrote those words that said the Creator endowed us with our rights that they were right. That among those rights are life and liberty and the pursuit of happiness. We're a nation given those freedoms. We share them with people around the world. This is the greatest nation the world has seen in part because of that extraordinary beginning, that idea, as Paul [Ryan] said. We are not going to change America into something we don't recognize. We're going to restore to America the principles

that made America the hope of the earth. We're going to do everything in our power to keep America strong—in our homes, in our economy, in our military, second to none. This nation has a mission to perform. We're going to make it happen. We're going to keep America the shining city on the hill.[3]

In a mere 157 words, Romney managed to fuse together exceptionalism, the opening of the Declaration of Independence, universalism, America as the "hope of the earth," the nation's "mission," and the "shining city on a hill."

Americans who would rather not live inside an ideology need to be alert to these stock phrases and images that fill the dominant exceptionalist narrative. Making them visible is the first step to containing them and hopefully replacing them with something compatible with America as a place, a people, a history, and a way of life and not as a perpetually revolutionary abstract Idea armed with a mission statement.

Does this mean that localists should intentionally melt down the exceptionalist narrative and subvert the civil religion of the American creed? Nietzsche, along with some of his modern disciples, worried about the consequences of modern historians going around dissolving the horizon of meaning. Supposedly this is what historicists do and why they are dangerous to the moral health of a people. If you teach people the Socialist origins of the Pledge of Allegiance, the political Gnosticism embedded in the Battle Hymn of the Republic, and the blasphemy of the city on a hill, then what will they possibly believe in? What will be left to motivate them to die for their country when the time comes? If we debunk the civil religion, what survives but a corrosive agnosticism? Some intellectuals in the 1930s said that the United States needed a national "Grand Opera" if it was ever going to stand up to Fascism and Communism. We had to fight ideology with ideology, spectacle with spectacle, we were told. These diabolical regimes offered a powerful narrative, a sense of belonging, and the capacity to mobilize their peoples for heroic outpourings of energy and wealth and life. But this is precisely what the modest republican fears. And finds insulting. Is defending hearth and home not enough? Is it really nobler to fight for wooly abstractions than for a place and a people? The Grand Opera metaphor suggests that Americans need staged extravaganzas with rousing choruses in order to fight and die for

---

3. See, for example, http://www.weeklystandard.com/romney-in-waukesha/article/649904.

the things they hold dear. Nationalists certainly do, but ordinary patriots don't. They can't even imagine wanting to think and feel such things.

What if localists debunk in order to bring that "horizon of meaning" closer to home? What if we restore a smaller place by dismantling the bloated non-place? What if the nationalist narrative, the aggressive imposition of "one story" onto something that can never be one story, destroys human scale? What if nationalists and their bedfellows the internationalists have always wanted to use big stories to melt down diverse communities as so many obstacles to big ideas and big plans? If so, then Front Porchers and their sympathizers ought not to hesitate to dissolve the myths and symbols of creedal nationalism.

America is indeed a land like no other, but not for the reasons the exceptionalists claim. It is a land like no other because it is our home, the place of our birth or adoption, and we love it because it is home. We fear for it because it is home. A feet-on-the-ground exceptionalism, suited to a human scale, should respond patiently and persistently to a head-in-the-clouds exceptionalism. Generations must be reared that know the difference between nationalism and patriotism.

I often wonder why what is bizarre at one scale can appear normal at another—in this case, why the exceptionalist creed that would be so strange, absurd, or frightening at lower levels becomes acceptable, ordinary, or even praiseworthy at higher levels. If you affirmed the dogmas of the nationalists' creed about yourself, or your family, or neighborhood, city, or state, and if you sounded like you really meant it and talked loudly about it all the time, people would begin to worry. If you announced to your neighbors that you were a light to the nations, they would keep an eye on you. But suddenly, when we leap up to the level of the nation-state, all of this otherwise offensive behavior becomes (allegedly) patriotic. Can we really believe that this is so? Can vanity, vulgarity, delusion, and heresy at one level become virtuous when we ratchet it up a notch? Can you be a "respectable nation"—something the generation of the 1780s said repeatedly it aspired to be—if you clothe yourself with such pretense? A respectable nation would talk and act a lot like a respectable man, or family, or town, no matter how proud it was being a land like no other.

Do-It-Ourselves Citizenship

PETE PETERSON

Remember, for this is the kernel of the matter, that the theory of democracy assumes a far higher level of good sense, judgment, honest purpose, devotion to the public welfare in the citizen of a free country, than is either looked for or needed in the subject of a despotic monarchy or of an oligarchy. Thus the deficiencies which free governments show reduce themselves to the failure of the citizens to reach the needed standard of civic excellence.

—Lord James Bryce, *The Hindrances to Good Citizenship*

CHINA MAY SEEM LIKE an odd place to begin a discussion on the changing citizen-government relationship in the United States. But all political change is based on cultural change, and the recent news about the fate of an American company in China is revealing. Home Depot, the extremely successful home improvement chain, announced that it would close the remainder of 19 stores it had opened in China. It turns out this economic decision has a societal cause. As a Home Depot spokeswoman described Chinese consumers to the *Wall Street Journal*, "the market trend says this is more of a do-it-for-me culture."

But her implication that Americans are "do-it-yourself" people is not quite right either. We have always been more "do-it-*ourselves*" folk— people who work together with family, friends, and community members to solve common problems. It is a quality we have long been known for. Alexis De Tocqueville famously commented, "Everywhere that, at the head of a new undertaking, you see the government in France and a great lord in England, count on it that you will perceive an association in the United States." He penned these words in 1833 as he marveled at Americans' ingenuity and "associativeness" in constructing infrastructure such as roads and schools, as well as civic structures to take on many of society's challenges, from public safety to caring for the poor. It is worth noting that many of these people would have been first- and second-generation Americans.

Even today, the image of the barn-raising—that coming together of a community in sweat-drenched support of one member—evokes a knowing smile even among Americans who have never participated in one. Television advertising for American hardware stores draws on this accepted premise, and entire cable channels from the "DiY Network" to "HGTV" are devoted to it. These programs never portray a solitary person; instead, they always show a couple or a group of friends painting the rooms, building the decks, or replacing the fixtures. We now understand that such pictures do not appeal to the Chinese.

Some argue that the longing for things like "community" and "self-governance" is a nostalgic, if understandable, response to a "flat world" of instant communication and rapid transportation, where barriers, boundaries, and customs appear to be collapsing all around. However, this response is not a retreat into a nostalgic myth but a thoroughly relevant revitalization of that uniquely American capacity to unite with others in solving problems.

There *is* a quiet revolution occurring in local and state governments across the country. In particular, we are witnessing the faltering of the "service state" and the rise of new platforms for civic engagement, which are rooted in the deeply American practice of association.

But this transition is not without obstacles. Any local government official can tell you about the "vending machine" metaphor. Rick Cole, the city manager for the city of Santa Monica, California, popularized the term in local government circles to describe a particular relationship between citizens and their governing institutions. Residents often see government leaders as mere service providers (the vending machine), and view taxes/fees as the "cost of doing business." In phrases and examples that echo the aforementioned description of the Chinese, many Americans have taken consumerist tendencies from the private sector into the public sector. For many, government has become a deliverer of services, not a place of convening for civic participation and defining what living "here" (wherever that is) means.

Bringing the Public Back into Public Policy

For those of us who work in and with local government, the NBC sitcom *Parks and Rec* (now in reruns) is a bittersweet pleasure—bitter because there is a moment in every episode when the humor hits a little too close to home. In one episode that included an attempt to engage the public in a "Public Forum," the Parks Department Director Ron Swanson laments, "You go to some sweaty rec center to get yelled at by the public." He then deadpans to the camera: "I hate the public." Play that video for any public official (as I do in the public engagement training programs I lead around the country), and you'll get wry smiles—and not without reason. Even when trying their best to make decisions for the common good, these public officials have been the victims of public engagement—usually in three-minute segments of what is politely called "public comment" during a council or commission meeting. But this confrontational, non-deliberative view of public participation in policy-making is changing.

If you attend local government conferences and read the major "industry" magazines, you could be forgiven for thinking it is all just a fad: talk of how local governments can improve their "public engagement" or "citizen participation" is everywhere. At a recent National League of Cities (NLC) Conference, which brings together thousands of local elected officials from around the country, over one-third of the "Leadership Training" seminars covered the subject. At an International City/County Management (ICMA) Conference, the premier gathering for local administrative officials, "Engaging Citizens" was an entire "education track," and over a third of the pre-conference "University Workshops" related to different aspects of citizen participation—from using online tools to running better public meetings.

ICMA's Public Management magazine, *PM*, once ran the cover story, "Harnessing the Power of Your Community," about new methods to engage residents not only in decision-making but in service-delivery. And *Governing* magazine regularly runs stories on the changing relationship between municipal governments and the citizens they serve.

Public engagement is not just popular among current public sector officials; schools of public policy and administration—the educators of tomorrow's administrators—are training their students to lead city halls in ways that are much more participatory. Six or seven years ago, the course I teach at Pepperdine's School of Public Policy, "Leadership through Public Engagement," was one of the first of its kind. Today dozens of programs offer coursework on the subject. The title of an American Society for Public Administration (ASPA) Annual Conference—the meeting of most of the country's major graduate policy/administration programs—was "Redefining Public Service through Civic Engagement," and its quarterly journal, *Public Administration Review*, regularly runs such academic pieces as "Designing Public Participation Processes," "In Search of the Public Participation Recipe," and the alliterative "Public Engagers and the Political Craft of Participatory Policy Making."

What is happening?

In a 2010 study titled "Aligning the Work of Government to Strengthen the Role of Citizens," several long-time municipal officials described this changing relationship between local governments and citizens. Dave Knapp, city manager of Highland Park, Illinois, put it this way:

> It used to be that if you did something, you had to tell the public about it. And then it became, if you are planning to do something, you have to tell them about it. And then it became, if you are planning to do something, you have to offer them an opportunity to come in and say what they want to say. You don't have to do anything about it, but you have to give them the opportunity to come and have input. The model now is when you have an issue, you are better off to have the community weigh in on the definition of the problem, the possible solutions of the problem, and to actually affect the outcome of the decisions process.[1]

In the same report, Daly City's (California) city manager, Pat Martel, noted, "We got trained back in the day to do things differently than we have to do them today. We all have to learn and develop new skills to be responsive to the communities of today as opposed to 30 years ago when I started.... There is a different mindset today, a need to be responsive to the public in a different way than in the past."

In a comprehensive 2013 statewide study of 900 California municipal officials, 85 percent of respondents said that their views on engaging residents had changed since their own public sector careers began, with 42 percent answering that their views had "changed a lot." In focus groups, experienced local government officials said things like, "The old

---

1. Pearce, Barnett and Kim Pearce. "Aligning the Work of Government to Strengthen the Role of Citizens," 2010, Kettering Foundation, February, 2010.

style of decision-making just doesn't allow for good community participation," and "I have a greater appreciation of the value for public input. It provides a greater range of problem-solving ideas and creates better consensus for decisions."

The issues on which citizens are weighing in can range almost as widely as the methodologies by which they're engaged. In Anchorage, Alaska, the midtown district is being planned through a Charettes process in which residents draw and label their opinions on satellite map images of the area. In Chesapeake, Virginia, citizens are invited into a "Priority-Based Budgeting" process in which they're provided with a virtual $500 to be apportioned across a variety of city services. In Philadelphia, Pennsylvania, the Upper Darby School District asked the Penn Project for Civic Engagement at the University of Pennsylvania to lead a series of facilitated community forums about budget priorities. The State of Oregon has used a "Citizens' Jury" of 24 citizens to evaluate statewide ballot measures in a process called the "Citizens' Initiative Review." The results of the jury's five-day deliberations are featured in the ballot information packet that goes out to all Oregon voters.

There has been an explosion of online public engagement platforms with such names as "Balancing Act," "Open Town Hall," "Crowdbrite," "Budget Challenge," and "MetroQuest," hosted by municipalities to gain public feedback on issues ranging from general city improvement ideas in Omaha to park planning suggestions in San Francisco to transportation policy in Lake Oswego, New York.

The most rewarding part of my work at the Davenport Institute is witnessing the benefits from practicing this "participatory governance": from better solutions to policy challenges to fundamentally changing the perception of a city. Our institute consulted on a yearlong public process with the Humboldt Bay Municipal Water District in Northern California. The District faced a unique challenge for California: after two local pulp mills closed, it had too much water and didn't know what to do with it.

There were no easy answers. Even allowing the water to run to the ocean carried environmental and economic impacts. But when the municipality attempted (with minimal public input) to make a deal with another water district to sell the water, the community fractured. After several years of battles between the District and area residents, including the recall of a board member and numerous lawsuit threats, leaders were ready for a new approach. They sought to engage citizens in a well-planned process with an independent facilitator to get a clearer picture of the "common sense" of the community.

Over the thirteen months of the "Frank Language about Our Water" (or "FLOW") series, hundreds of residents met in Elks Club halls, library meeting spaces, and recreation centers throughout the region to deliberate over proposed policy solutions to a very complex issue. At one meeting I attended in the city of Arcata, two local residents—who happened to be environmental scientists—proposed water uses that the District had never considered, and at all of the gatherings attendees learned that there would be no "silver bullet" answers; they also gained a new appreciation for the hard choices facing the District. At the end of the process, a report was issued to the District, and decisions have now been made based on public input. Importantly, no board members have been recalled, and many broken relationships have been healed.

A more surprising success story comes from the city of Bell, California. Just ten miles south and west of downtown Los Angeles, Bell is one of America's ten smallest cities geographically, so it was understandable that up until 2010 even most Californians had never heard of it. But when the headline, "Is a City Manager Worth $800,000?" splashed across the front page of the *Los Angeles Times*, people from around the world suddenly learned of the tiny town rife with what was dubbed "corruption on steroids." The *Times* revealed that for several years after the hiring of a new city manager and accompanying staff, the connection between city hall and Bell's 30,000 citizens was a damaging enabling relationship in which city staff and council kept the public in the dark about their dealings while most residents disengaged from the community's political life. The results, once uncovered, were devastating. The overwhelming damage done to the city's finances by the malfeasance of elected and administrative leaders left it teetering on the brink of collapse.

But when long-time city manager Ken Hampian volunteered to step in as Bell's first interim city manager after the scandal broke, I knew there was hope. One of Ken's first tasks after landing was attempting to change the identity of a local government known to many of its citizens as "the Kremlin." He assembled a group of advisors from the area (myself included) to devise a public budgeting process that would both inform Bellians about the dire state of the city's finances and also allow them to prioritize city services for the upcoming budget cycle. This budget process would be unlike anything the city had ever undertaken.

On a rainy Saturday morning in Bell's Community Center, dozens of residents turned out for a "Community Budget Priorities Forum"—the first in a series of opportunities the city's new council and staff were providing so that residents could participate in the budget process. Providing easy-to-understand materials along with translation services for the city's many Spanish-speaking residents, the Forum asked attendees to help set priorities on city services from public safety to business fees to capital improvements. "We did some hard work today," Bell resident Marco told me at the table I facilitated that morning. This was the hard work of citizenship. Those first public budget meetings have become a part of an overall turnaround for the city in how it engages its residents, and how those same residents engage the city. From livestreaming council meetings on its new website to posting officials' salaries online, Bell recently earned an A- grade for transparency from the Sunshine Review—an amazing turnaround.

Citizens Building When Government "Unbuilds"

In a 2013 study titled "Beyond Citizen Engagement: Involving the Public in Co-Delivering Government Services," researchers found dozens of efforts in which citizens either worked with government in new ways to provide services (called "co-production") or actually took over the full provision of a public service ("co-delivery"). In short, due to a variety of factors, from fiscal to generational to technological, citizens are moving beyond simply advising the government to taking on roles in service-delivery.

The Internet eases some of these relationships, but most are being forced by an enduring fiscal crisis. This is a significant paradigm shift in how both citizens and public officials see their roles. Rather than lamenting or gloating over the loss of these services, creative citizens are responding with an amazing mix of civic partnership arrangements (with and without government involvement) in order to maintain programs communities want. As long-time California city manager Rod Gould recently told me: "By stepping out of the lead service delivery role and acting as facilitator and convener, local government can expand services and increase their legitimacy. . . . By involving more people and organizations in dealing with vexatious problems, local governments can gain greater citizen satisfaction. All this runs against the grain but is the next great frontier of civic engagement and government reorientation."

The fiscal crisis that began with the bursting of the housing bubble continues for thousands of municipalities across America. And while there is some hope that a sense of normalcy will soon return, most government finance experts understand that, especially at the local level, we are entering a "new normalcy" in which ongoing fiscal malaise is matched with ratcheting obligations to public sector pensions and benefits: an economic calamity extended by a demographic one in the retirement of "baby boomers." As Harvard's local government expert (and former Indianapolis mayor) Stephen Goldsmith described, "The current fiscal crisis isn't just a passing phase; it's a new enduring reality that must be confronted. Crisis is now the new norm."

In recent years, cities and counties have gone bankrupt through the death spiral of decreasing revenues and increasing expenditures. In a 2012 study, the State Budget Crisis Task Force, a bi-partisan panel of economists and finance experts, found that "unfunded liabilities for health care benefits for state and local government retirees amount to more than $1 trillion." At one point in the report, the group's Democratic Co-chair, Richard Ravitch, warned that "the ability of the states to meet their obligations to public employees, to creditors and most critically to the education and well-being of their citizens is threatened."

The study goes on to remark that, in response to dire fiscal choices, state and city governments are beginning to actually pull back from service commitments that have been moving in an upward trajectory for decades. As the Task Force writes, "This is a fundamental shift in the way governments have responded to recessions and appears to signal a willingness to 'unbuild' state government in a way that has not been done before."

"Unbuild" is a unique word to describe a unique period in the government-citizen relationship. For someone who works with local governments, the evidence is hard to miss. From libraries to parks to public safety commitments to education, municipal governments are indeed withdrawing from the service levels they have provided for years.

The city of San Bernardino (pop. 213,000) is one of the latest municipalities to seek bankruptcy protection. During a city council meeting on the possibility of slashing the city's police force by a third, city attorney James F. Penman begged councilmembers to make the tough decisions now that might stave off even more difficult decisions later: "The people of San Bernardino are appealing to your patriotism," Penman is reported to have said, "not to country but to city." This city-based "patriotism" is emerging across the country, as new collaborations form to maintain public services, even if they're not being delivered by the "public sector."

When Central Falls, Rhode Island, was forced to declare bankruptcy, its library was one of the first things cut. To keep it open, retired library director Thomas Shanahan stepped into the lurch, recruiting volunteers to shelve books and mop the floors. Shanahan told a reporter that managing volunteers is tougher than managing paid staff, but the rewards have been greater: "I have a core group that has stayed with me from the beginning, and if it wasn't for them, it would be a nightmare."

When Stockton, California, sought bankruptcy protection, the number of city policemen assigned to school patrols had to be cut. Chaplains from the community have stepped in to oversee about 20 city schools. As retired pastor and volunteer Jim Reid accedes, "they all know we're not cops," but "we have a close connection and obviously a lot quicker connection than the average person would have to a police department, so, if we ever have any crisis situations, we can get help very quickly."

When California Governor Jerry Brown closed a multi-billion dollar state budget deficit, 70 of the state's 280 parks were placed on the chopping block. Rather than concede their fate, Marin County assemblyman Jared Huffman wrote and passed AB 42, which cut the red tape, allowing interested local governments and non-profits to take over management responsibilities for these facilities. Within a year, almost every single fated park had been saved through the efforts of local organizations. The resulting relationships have created intriguing community-building opportunities, such as keeping some parks open into the evening to host local concerts and theatrical productions.

Additionally, community-based philanthropy has also responded. One of the repercussions from a bankruptcy filing in Harrisburg, Pennsylvania, was the dimming of lights across the city's historic Walnut Street Bridge. Springing to action, local attorney Matthew Krupp founded "Lighten Up, Harrisburg," which raised funds to keep the lights on. What began as an effort to keep the Walnut Street Bridge alight has now expanded to take on other municipal lighting projects throughout the cash-strapped city in what has become a network of community organizations.

The University of California-Berkeley's 120-year old baseball program may not seem like a government program, but when recent state-wide budget cuts reached the state's public university system, the team's $1 million annual budget became another line-item to be cut. Responding to the sword of Damocles held by the school's chancellor, the Cal's coach, David Esquer, devised a plan. Through an effort that included everything from having baseball players cold-call for financial support to hosting a three-day tournament at the home of the San Francisco Giants (AT&T Park), what began as the team's last season ended with a 10-year/$10 million funded strategic plan, taking the program off the chopping block. Even fans of Cal's archrival, Stanford, helped out. In a *Wall Street Journal* piece on the events, former Stanford Cardinal and pro player Ed Sprague remarked that "Everyone needs a rival to hate—I guess now you have to help pay for it."

Cal's Athletic Director, Sandy Barbour, described what transpired in terms broader than baseball: "I absolutely think that in this new financial reality for higher education, we will need to look more to philanthropy and business development." But it was former Cal player (current New York Yankees' outfielder) Brennan Boesch who framed the story in a way that could be applied to the entire citizen-government relationship: "It may have enough people that are passionate enough; you can take power away from the university and put it in the hands of people that care more about the program."

Gov2.0 Brings Citizen 2.0?

When online social networks like Facebook, LinkedIn, Twitter and Flickr moved the Internet from a uni-directional mode of communication to a multi-directional one, the term "Web 2.0" was created to describe the difference. When some of these technologies—and many others—began to infiltrate the public sector, that nomenclature was borrowed. There is now an exploding "Gov 2.0" world of public officials and technologists who are forcing this change in the government/citizen relationship.

Technology is also having a real impact in how citizens engage with one another. Ask for your town's annual budget and you are likely to be greeted with a three-ring binder at least two inches thick with printed Excel spreadsheets. But, increasingly, governments are making this and other data available in formats that can be both downloaded and manipulated. This is the "open data" movement, and it is opening numerous opportunities for civic participation.

Palo Alto is often regarded as the "capital of Silicon Valley," so when the planning department wanted to develop a map-based web page to show construction projects throughout the city, there was a good chance someone working outside the offices of city hall might know how to do it. To create this internally would have cost tens of thousands of dollars and taken weeks, if not months. When the City made the raw building permit data available digitally, and issued an invitation to build the website, staff was greeted a couple weeks later with an emailed link to exactly what they wanted. The link came from a private citizen. The cost? Free.

Of course, there was some "self interest rightly understood here," as the creator could now market this to other cities, but many of these new applications built from public sector data are built simply for the common good.

The city of San Ramon's Fire Department knows that when one of its residents has a heart attack, the closest helper is often a fellow citizen with CPR training. But how to find him or her? The city developed a CPR app for smartphones so that residents with CPR training can register online. The application's geo-locator is activated by the Fire Department whenever a heart attack occurs, alerting someone nearby.

In Boston, an engineer for the group "Code for America" developed an "Adopt a Fire Hydrant" application that invites residents to take responsibility for shoveling out fire hydrants after a blizzard. The same technology has been used for "Adopt a Storm Drain" in Oakland to clear drains after rain showers and for "Adopt a Tsunami Siren" in Hawaii to monitor batteries, which are often stolen. In each of these and more, technology is being used to connect citizens to services previously conducted by the public sector.

Evangelists of Gov 2.0 appeal to civic participation. Jen Pahlka, the executive director of Code for America (also known as "Peace Corps for Geeks"), declared that "the people of America need to start thinking of themselves as citizens again," adding, "and if you're a citizen, it's not just about the benefits you get, but also about the responsibilities."

But along with citizens working with government more collaboratively through technology, a growing crop of online platforms is helping to engage them with one another outside government. These micro-networks may only target a few hundred people living within a geographic area of a few blocks. Their purpose is not to keep relationships online, but to facilitate face-to-face community building.

One of the first of these networks was developed quietly back in 2006 by Valerie and Michael Wood-Lewis in Burlington, Vermont, when the couple, upon moving to town, found it hard to meet their new neighbors. They named their platform the "Front Porch Forum" (FPF), and what began as a personal effort has now been multiplied across dozens of towns in Vermont.

While the term "online communities" gets thrown around blithely, the Front Porch Forums are truly communities in that they are particularly geographic in focus. Not everyone can join an FPF; you have to be identified as living in a particular geographic area to be a part of that neighborhood's Forum. As the testimonials illustrate, FPFs (and others like it) are more than micro-craigslists. Marianne Eaton writes, "FPF connects me to my community, makes the bond between us stronger, and personal conversations continue due to FPF postings. I look forward to reading it every night. I'm not a Facebook fan but I LOVE Front Porch Forum." And Bruce Duncan adds, "just wanted to give thanks to all the quick replies to my request last week for a sump pump to help with our flooded basement. I got several calls and emails. It's nice to know we live in sump pump rich community."

Front Porch Forum is now one of a couple dozen community-based platforms. One of the major new players in this space is Nextdoor.com, which has over 11,000 platforms in place nationwide. Adam Tratt in the Sand Point neighborhood of Seattle gushes, "we're making new neighborhood traditions through Nextdoor, like the first-ever pumpkin carving contest. Staying in-touch during our long wet Seattle winters makes the community feel closer, more welcoming and fun!" And Anne Clauss of Nextdoor/Hamilton, NY, offers, "our neighborhood dynamics have improved significantly since we launched Nextdoor—the collaboration between neighbors has showered an unprecedented feeling of community upon us."

This "associativeness" of Americans—even those who were relative newcomers—bewildered foreign observers, and though Tocqueville is the best-known painter of the American, hundreds, if not thousands, of others wondered at it. Sandor Farkas came from Transylvania at the same time as Tocqueville (actually meeting him at one point while visiting the Charlestown, Massachusetts, State Prison), later penning his experiences in *Journey to North America*. Walking the streets of New York in 1831, Farkas said that

New York has many such associations whose purpose is to encourage and advance human enterprise. Coming from that part of Europe where the government acts and thinks for the people, a traveler can hardly comprehend how these associations can exist without public money and without governmental supervision and meddling. But in America the people govern, look after their own welfare, and make sacrifices, neither by borrowed power nor by catering to the privileged few, but through the free exercise of self-government—the greatest pleasure of citizenship.

The "pleasure of citizenship": this is what we're seeing across America in response to a fiscal crisis and the increasing presence of technology. This is what a republic looks like.

Luxury and Buying Local

David Cloutier

One of my great pleasures is an early-morning run through downtown Frederick, Maryland. It is an especially well-preserved pre-WWII urban landscape—a landscape to which I'm partial, I suppose, since I grew up in one like it on the northwest side of Chicago. I run along the marvelous 1920s urban oasis of Baker Park, with its tidy white-pillared schoolhouse perched above the creek. I run past the WPA-built fountain and skating house (winters are too warm to skate now). And I run up Market Street, filled with small shops and restaurants, looking probably better than it did 40 years ago. With the exception of a Starbucks and a Ben & Jerry's (and some of the banks, but not mine), almost everything downtown is local.

And almost everything is expensive. Truth be told, I don't shop down there a lot. Frederick's downtown, like many older towns, has not been revived by the return of hardware stores, grocery stores, and everyday greasy-spoon diners. Mostly, it is upscale restaurants and specialty boutiques, with a smattering of artists' galleries and antique stores. The entire city of Frederick has no locally-owned hardware store, but its 65,000 people now have two Lowes and two Home Depots. True, I use my food co-op and farmers' markets for my groceries, but even these are located on the edge of town, because downtown is both too expensive for rents and too difficult to access by car. So our "main street economy" is really one founded on catering to the whims of the wealthy. Supporting local economies is often understood as a *sine qua non* of localist, place-based thinking. But are local economies a luxury? Are they built today on *encouraging* superfluous spending by the wealthy?

Despite Thorstein Veblen's classic take on "conspicuous consumption," David Riesman was already pointing out in the early 1950s how "inconspicuous consumption" is taking over in many of the "educated classes" as a kind of reverse-snobbery.[1] Not infrequently today, people criticize local foodies as elitists who are out of touch with the economic realities that drive people to big-box stores. Is local a luxury? And if so, should localist thinking encourage luxury, rather than critique it? I want to review briefly the traditional critique of luxury, say a bit about why it disappeared, and then offer some discussion of where the critique might land today. I want to argue that we need to reimagine the critique of luxury, but recognize that it might be better applied, in the spirit of the concerns of the ancients, to the commercial life among big-box stores and discount centers.

The traditional critique of luxury is exemplified in Plato's *Republic*, where Socrates consistently identifies the desire for luxury as a root cause of disharmony in the city. Socrates maintains three grounds for this critique: one, luxury promotes disharmony in the individual, which harms fitness and health; two, luxury promotes disharmony among citizens, since it gives birth to competition over resources made unnecessarily scarce by overextended desires; and, three, luxury ultimately promotes expansionist warfare, since more and more resources are needed to sustain the "quality of life" expected by the luxurious city. In each case, resources are diverted from uses that would be more beneficial. Socrates' vision of the non-luxury city is not "Spartan": poverty, he says, "leads to meanness and incompetence." Instead, citizens of the republic have "bread, wine, clothes, shoes, and houses," desserts of "figs, chickpeas, and beans," of which they partake while wearing "garlands, and singing hymns to the gods and enjoying one another's company ... all the while drinking in moderation."[2] Critics of luxury need not condemn the material world

---

1. David Riesman, "New Standards for Old: From Conspicuous Consumption to Conspicuous Production," in *Individualism Reconsidered* (Garden City, NY: Doubleday, 1954), 148–163, at 155.

2. Plato, *The Republic*, tr. Richard W. Sterling and William C. Scott (New York: W.W. Norton, 1985), 372c.

in toto—they criticize excessive attachment and use. The counterpart to luxury in the realm of sexuality might be "promiscuity" or "lust."[3]

After centuries of consensus, eighteenth century England witnessed the breakdown of this suspicion of luxury. Bernard Mandeville's *The Fable of the Bees* argued for the "public benefits" of "private vices," especially luxury. While Adam Smith critiqued this "licentious system," which encouraged "vice . . . to appear with more effrontery and to avow the corruption of its motives with a profligate audaciousness which had never been heard of before,"[4] Mandeville's work paved the way for the more thorough work of David Hume. Hume argued that the classical critique of luxury is exactly backwards. Plato equated luxury with "indolence," but Hume said the arrival of luxury, especially through trade, "arouses men from their indolence and, presenting the gayer and more opulent part of the nation with objects of luxury which they never before dreamed of, raises in them a desire of a more splendid way of life than what their ancestor enjoyed."[5] Even further, Hume suggested that luxury leads to moral elevation, for these pursuits lead to "an increase of humanity from the very habit of conversing together and contributing to each other's pleasure and entertainment."[6] Luxury is not state-destroying; it is the mark of the truly civilized state.

Though Adam Smith retained some skepticism about luxury—he called the glamour of it a "useful deception"—Hume eventually won the day. This victory may give localists pause: are we likely to give up "luxuries" like indoor plumbing, central heating, and even a "personal chariot" on call? Don't we live like kings and queens of old? And aren't all these things brought to us by an expanding economy that enables more and more people to have them? After all, the problem for localists, economists will tell us, is that the basic goods of life are now delivered

---

3. The Latin term *luxuria* witnesses a transformation in late antiquity and the early Middle Ages, such that the English word first appears in terms of excessive sex. But the more ancient meaning in relation to excessive material goods is found in all the literature of the Italian Renaissance, and becomes prominent in England especially in the late 17th and 18th centuries. For more detail, see David Cloutier, *The Vice of Luxury: Economic Excess in a Consumer Age* (Washington: Georgetown University Press, 2015), chapter 1.

4. Adam Smith, *The Theory of Moral Sentiments* (Oxford: Clarendon, 1976), 318, 313.

5. David Hume, "Of Commerce," in *Political Essays*, ed. Charles W. Hendel (Indianapolis: Library of Liberal Arts/Bobbs-Merrill, 1953), 130–141; here, 138.

6. Hume, "Of Refinement in the Arts," in *Political Essays*, 123–129; here, 124.

through extremely sophisticated yet efficient systems by low-skill labor, assisted by ingenious machines of increasing complexity that reduce human labor. Such an economic system makes available a wide variety of merchandise, even with some artful design, at the lowest possible cost. With the advent of computer point-of-sale and inventory systems, an immense network can be managed with efficiency in order to deliver our cheap soap and cheap socks.

And cheap flat-screens, and cheap "faux designer" fashion lines, and cheap throw rugs for every season, and so on. The difficulties with this system are not that it can't deliver lots of cheap goods cheaply. It can. The problem is, I contend, that the system promotes luxury—cheap luxury at that—and it does so by introducing disorder into both the agent and into social relations. I think localists can respond to the critique of nostalgic escapism by naming this disorder, and its name is luxury—reconceptualized for our situation.

How do we identify this disorder? Naming luxury as a vice involves a rejection of the idea that developing and satisfying complex desires for material goods is a *part* of the good life, rather than a *hindrance* to it. The constant development and gratification of needs ends up demanding more complex systems of manufacturing and distribution. A contemporary critique of luxury, therefore, will focus first not on specific goods themselves but on the desiring self and the social relations required to support such a person. For Wendell Berry, a disordered economy is an outgrowth of disordered, undisciplined people: "there are not enough rich and powerful people to consume the whole world."[7] These people do not understand how to provide for themselves, but, most importantly, they have multiplied their "needs" (often at the feet of clever merchandisers) so that they can no longer be satisfied by their local communities. The problem, as Berry tirelessly repeats from his work in the 1970s to some of his most recent essays, is that we do not want to recognize any *limits* on these desires. Christopher Marlowe's devil points out "hell hath no limits," thus indicating the direction of our economy: "the fantastical possibility of limitless growth, limitless wants, limitless wealth, limitless natural resources, limitless energy and limitless debt. The idea of a limitless economy implies and requires a doctrine of general human limitless."[8]

---

7. Wendell Berry, "Conservation is Good Work," in *Sex, Economy, Freedom, and Community* (New York: Pantheon, 1993), 32.

8. Berry, "Faustian Economics," in *What Matters?* (Berkeley: Counterpoint, 2010), 43. See also *The Unsettling of America* (San Francisco: Sierra Club Books, 1977), where

Most notably, Berry does not simply indict big capitalist bankers, for the problem is ultimately "our unrestrained consumptiveness," which, he writes in an essay simply entitled "Waste," "is the fault of an economy that is wasteful from top to bottom—a symbiosis of an unlimited greed at the top and a lazy, passive, and self-indulgent consumptiveness at the bottom."[9]

When we identify the workings of this "self-indulgent consumptiveness at the bottom," we can offer a description of the disorder of luxury for our day. The luxury-enamored self is disordered, I would contend, in three key ways that we should learn to see as "luxurious," and regard with the scorn of the ancients. Unlike the ancient economy, the modern economy suffers from the fact that it is capable of producing far more than we really need. Dealing with this problem of excess means getting people to consume more than they need. How does this happen?

First, the system gives us too many choices that are plainly trivial but that we too often regard as important. Barry Schwartz has pointed out that one way to deal with this prodigious production is to multiply choices beyond measure, like "85 different varieties and brands of crackers" and "285 varieties of cookies."[10] I joke to my students about the breakfast cereal aisle, but equally indicative is the toothpaste aisle. Didn't we just have Colgate, Aim, and Crest—one kind of Crest—in the 1970s? This new, expanded choice is demanded by the self whose identity is devoted to consumer choice as the way to a better life, who obeys the command of "new and improved." Schwartz contends that this sort of situation not only privileges the luxurious self, but results in unhappiness for others, who do not care about choice, since it makes consumption time-consuming and frustrating.

Because it's all "so cheap," if you don't like what you bought, well, just throw it away and buy something else. Not surprisingly, there is a lot of waste. Amy Frykholm recently wrote in *Christian Century* about her local Safeway's new corporate policy against donating fresh food.[11] Such availability promotes *carelessness* in use, a second hallmark of the luxurious life. We can now waste tremendous amounts of food because

---

restraint and limits already play a big role.

9. Berry, "Waste," in *What Are People For?* (San Francisco: North Point, 1990), 127.

10. Barry Schwartz, *The Paradox of Choice* (New York: HarperCollins, 2004), 9.

11. Amy Frykholm, "Gone to Waste: Why is Safeway Throwing Out Good Produce," *Christian Century* (August 10, 2011), http://www.christiancentury.org/article/2011-08/gone-waste.

it is so cheap.[12] The same is true for many non-food items. Carelessness with material goods means that we no longer hire people to fix things. Cheap socks mean no darning of socks. The wanton waste of food and dishes and clothing (i.e. by discarding disposable dishes, or by serving enormous amounts of foods, especially meats)—these are now the habits of the masses. What is lacking in the luxurious life is a conserving care for basic goods. This carelessness is *luxuria*.

Third and finally, like the rich of old, we depend on a rather large coterie of "servants" in order to enjoy this whimsical choice and irresponsible carelessness. Vegetables from our Tuscarora Growers Food Co-op cost more because the co-op guarantees a sustainable living to their farmers and a high-quality product to their customers. These fair prices for quality goods—prices that support good land practices and small family farms, not commodity pseudo-family farms—mean that we treat these suppliers as *people*, not as slaves. Unfortunately, this is not the way it works in the world of cheap goods. Whether through exploited immigrant labor harvesting raw material or sweatshop conditions in manufacturing or retail workers forced to do overtime off the clock, we must save 50 cents on our soaps, our socks, and our steaks. It is no coincidence that the single most-watched number by Wal-Mart management is store labor costs as percent of sales, a number that they drive down further than any other company in America, to an astonishing 10% of store sales.[13] The only major retailer whose full-time retail wage would support a person at poverty level is Costco. Every other company more or less relies on the Earned Income Tax Credit to "supplement" the wages they pay.[14] Moreover, much of this we simply do not see. It happens "out back," like the work done by servants of old. Berry reminds us that "most people aren't using or destroying what they can see," and the invisibility of the effects of our choices is perhaps our greatest luxury. Jonah Lehrer, in reviewing

---

12. Estimates range from a quarter to 40% of all food produced is wasted. See, for example, Brian Fung, "How 40% of Our Food Goes to Waste," *The Atlantic* (August 23, 2012); http://www.theatlantic.com/health/archive/2012/08/how-40-of-our-food-goes-to-waste/261498/.

13. See Nelson Liechtenstein, *The Retail Revolution: How Wal-Mart Created a Brave New World of Business* (New York: Metropolitan/Henry Holt, 2009).

14. See Ellen Ruppert Shell, *Cheap: The High Cost of Discount Culture* (New York: Penguin, 2009), 228–229. Costco is an interesting case, for they also do not privilege unlimited choice; but, in a different way, the enormous quantities (surely with much waste?), bought because they are "so cheap," also conjure up images of the storehouses of kings of old!

the neuroscience of altruism, writes of experiments that show a great deal of what one might call "natural reciprocity" with others until the point at which the person with greater power in the arrangement *cannot see* the person with whom he is dealing. At that point, the person in power tends to become a tyrant and seeks to get as much as he possibly can.[15] That's surely an aspect of the luxurious life, now made possible for many of the rest of us.

By contrast, a more reasonable system that sought not maximal goods at minimal cost would produce a different, better order in the self and in society. It would not put a premium on choice; indeed, it might privilege knowledgeable retailers who seek to *select* their goods well and provide knowledge to their customers. One would make do with what is reasonably available. Because goods would be more expensive, we would be more careful with the goods we purchase and perhaps more interested in knowing how to repair them. Finally, such a system could support reasonable wages, more skilled labor (at a smaller level retailers will be more interested in laborers who are versatile, who can learn the business, and who can thus be paid more), and, just as important, more humane relationships.

Such a system would be attractive to agents who had learned to resist the siren songs of luxury—infinite choice, convenience, and cheap, disposable labor. Most importantly, as I emphasized earlier, the agent would have to recognize that the good life, in economic terms, does not consist in complex and constantly changing elaborations of consumption desires. This is the thread that ties ancient critiques to our current situation. A local economy, far from a luxury, would require people to recognize that this is a disorder of the self (which produces social disorders in its wake), a vice, that requires reordering.

If we follow Socrates, we will properly understand that while such an economy does require change and sacrifice, it need not be "Spartan." Stories abound of the creative energy animating developments in local economies today,[16] and, from a Christian perspective, such initiatives should be understood as adding what Benedict XVI calls "quotas of

---

15. Jonah Lehrer, *How We Decide* (Boston: Houghton Mifflin Harcourt, 2009), 180–188.

16. See Lyle Estill, *Small is Possible: Life in a Local Economy* (Gabriola Island, BC: New Society Publishers, 2008) and Bill McKibben, *Deep Economy* (New York: Henry Holt, 2007).

gratuitousness and communion" to economic exchanges themselves.[17] The richness might be found in better (though fewer) goods, but even more, they are found in the human relationships forged through and around the goods. As Bill Cavanaugh has written, our present consumer economy is actually based on an almost Gnostic detachment from things, since goods are radically ephemeral and not context-bound.[18] A local economy promotes the proper enjoyment of goods, even the "basic" goods of food and hardware, in a kind of sacramental context where goods end up "meaning more" even as we have fewer of them. Such a context promotes moral agents and communities who understand that there are more important necessities in life that should not be traded for cheap luxuries.

---

17. *Caritas in Veritate*, no. 39.

18. William Cavanaugh, "Consumer Society," in *Gathered for the Journey: Moral Theology in Catholic Perspective*, eds. David Matzko McCarthy and M. Therese Lysaught (Grand Rapids: Eerdmans, 2007), 241-259.

Part Six

The Urban Challenge

These and all else were to me the same as they are to you,
I loved well those cities, loved well the stately and rapid river,
The men and women I saw were all near to me.
—WALT WHITMAN, "CROSSING BROOKLYN FERRY"

Chicago 2109: The Metropolitan Region as Agrarian-Urban Unit[1]

Philip Bess

THE FRONT PORCH REPUBLIC (FPR) is perceived by many as an agrarian movement and without doubt bears within itself an ideal of communities of self-governing yeoman proprietors of small farms, businesses, and manufacturing operations. Among its intellectual heroes—Wendell Berry, Alasdair MacIntyre, Jane Jacobs, E.F. Schumacher, Flannery O'Connor, Walker Percy, Dorothy Day, The Southern Agrarians, G.K. Chesterton, Henry George, Alexis de Tocqueville, Thomas Jefferson, Thomas Aquinas, Augustine, ultimately and inevitably Aristotle—many do argue that normative human flourishing is essentially small, agrarian, and rural. Nevertheless, many FPR thinkers contend that *place, limits, and liberty* are not *necessarily* anti-urban ideals and that such ideals both can and should be characteristic of larger and denser urban environments. So can human flourishing—understood per Aristotle as a life of moral and intellectual excellence lived in community with others—occur in a modern metropolitan environment? Can a modern metropolis be (re)conceived as a *range* of less-dense-rural-to-more-dense-urban settlements that cumulatively, at the scale of a metropolitan region, attain the local intimacy, beauty, formal legibility, and densities of human capital that have historically made cities both central to the dynamics of human achievement, discovery and excellence, *and* as beautiful places that feel like and anticipate home?

---

1. The author acknowledges financial support for *The Notre Dame Plan of Chicago 2109* from The Historical Society, as part of its two-year multi-disciplinary research project *Religion and Innovation*, and also from the James Madison Program in American Ideals and Institutions, Princeton University.

I want to address these questions by way of an exercise that imagines the future of a specific place. The exercise operates with two foundational premises. One is that almost all human beings view individual freedom—the ability to be an agent of one's own life—as a genuine human good. The second, equally important, is that almost all human beings experience communal belonging—the pursuit with others of a shared goal, with attendant obligations and pleasures—as a genuine human good. Understanding these as constitutive elements of human nature (axioms of human being, as it were), and understanding as well the inherent tensions these two goods necessarily engender, goes far toward explaining differences of political opinion even among persons of good will; and this is because different people (whether by temperament, or simply at different points in their lives) are disposed to emphasize freedom over belonging and vice versa. Nevertheless, if both premises are true, two conclusions seem to follow: a) it is essential to both individual and communal human flourishing that people discover some kind of nexus, however temporal or imperfect, between these two great goods; and b) the very boundaries of just and humane civil discourse are defined by a common acknowledgement that both of these great human goods require political recognition.

To the aforementioned premises add a third: *beautiful and durable places that we love and in which we feel at home provide the best context for human life, and best support the inventiveness and daring that human flourishing in any age demands.* Mindful of these premises, and mindful also of a certain mid-western sensibility characteristic of the Front Porch Republic, let us ponder the mid-west's aspiring but probably doomed-to-fail global city: Chicago. Understand that I do not think Chicago is doomed to fail *as a city*, only rather as a post-humanist *global city*; and this is because, by the criteria of humanist urbanism, it is possible that most if not all global cities will fail.

William Cronon's *Nature's Metropolis: Chicago and the Great West* is a landmark in the long-term cultural project to recover from and move beyond ruthless 20th century applications of Cartesian rationality to human occupation of the landscape. Cronon's book occasions 'a-ha' moments for many readers about several important realities: that cities and landscapes are not independent and competing entities but rather mutually defining and mutually dependent entities; that the city itself is best understood as part of an agrarian–urban unit; that human beings are not independent of nature but rather part of nature; and that it is part of *human* nature to make a variety of human settlement types,

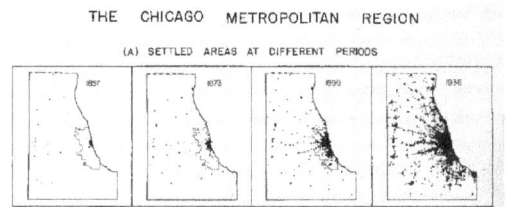

FIGURE 1: The Growth of Chicago Regional Population

Left to Right, 1857: 271,000 / 1873: 506,000 / 1899: 2,146,000 / 1936: 4,581,000 from Homer Hoyt, *The Structure and Growth of Residential Neighborhoods in American Cities* (FHA, 1939)

including cities—which means that cities, though artifacts, are also *natural*. Nineteenth-century Chicago was both a milestone and a paradigm of the industrial era [FIG.1], a modern mega-city that arose virtually overnight in the theretofore pre-modern center of a continent, that harnessed (uneasily and incompletely) the forces of modernity to transform its aboriginal western landscape at a historically unprecedented scale and speed. Chicago in the nineteenth century became an inland economic giant, a continental nation's center for the sale and distribution of grain, lumber, and meat by virtue of its geographical location, its dominance as a railroad hub, and the entrepreneurial genius of its residents.

Cronon's concluding chapter alludes to Chicago's efforts early in the 20th century to figure out what to do with the wealth nineteenth-century Chicagoans had created, how to contain if not repair the environmental damage they had caused, how best to govern themselves, and how best to live; that is, Cronon's work raises philosophical and existential questions about nature, human nature, and human settlements that historians *qua* historians cannot answer. *Nature's Metropolis* correctly identifies human beings as part of nature but addresses neither human exceptionalism nor questions about obligation and stewardship (and their further implications) that necessarily arise from considering our collective human powers and capacities. Likewise, *Nature's Metropolis* does not address directly the meaning of human flourishing, or the relationship of human flourishing to environmental and economic sustainability. Nor does it address questions about urban teleology, i.e., the nature and purpose of cities. And finally, though it alludes to the subject in its final chapter, *Nature's Metropolis* does not address directly the issue of urban form and how urban form is related to ideas of both the city and human flourishing.

Happily, however, there is a long intellectual and artistic tradition of classical humanist urbanism that addresses each of these issues: an intellectual tradition as old as Aristotle's *Nicomachean Ethics* and *Politics*, and an artistic tradition theorized by Vitruvius in the oldest remaining architectural treatise from classical antiquity, the *De architectura* (or *Ten Books on Architecture*). And especially happily for my purposes here, it is a tradition once brought to bear upon Chicago by Daniel Burnham in the 1909 *Plan of Chicago* that Burnham designed and co-authored with Edward Bennett.

The *Plan of Chicago* is noteworthy for many reasons. It was exemplary in the regional environmental scope of its ambitions [FIG.2] and in its proposal to preserve metropolitan Chicago's lakefront and forests as public places. It was also exemplary in its desire for a civic realm of beautiful buildings and spaces formed to engage an urban population gathered from all over the world and to foster in them affection for a

FIGURE 2: Plate 1 from the *Plan of Chicago* (1909): Chicago in regional context with surrounding landscape and towns

FIGURE 3: Plate 107 from the *Plan of Chicago*, showing the meeting of the north and south branches of the Chicago River

place where they, their fellow citizens, *and their descendants* could flourish [FIG.3]. Although the *Plan of Chicago* was sponsored by Chicago businessmen, Burnham envisioned Chicago not simply as a place of commerce but rather as both quotidian and sacramental *home*. Over the course of the twentieth century, Burnham's plan succeeded more in its conservation and lakefront park ambitions than in its civic and regional ambitions. But the *Plan of Chicago* is noteworthy not least because it was arguably the last great planning proposal of the modern era to attempt to bring classical humanist moral and aesthetic sensibilities—the concern for beauty, the concern for home—to bear upon the practical problems of a modern metropolitan region.

The twentieth century successor to classical humanist traditions of architecture and urban design was modernist architecture and city planning, which in Europe began in earnest in the early 1920s immediately after World War I and in America after 1945. Thereafter, modernism quickly became the dominant architecture-and-planning theory throughout the so-called 'first world'; and, with missionary fervor, it came to establish itself globally as a new occupying colonial and imperial power, though the modernists lacked both the self-knowledge and the humane aesthetic ambitions of their antecedent culture. In the United States modernism's most conspicuous fruits were 'urban renewal' and automobile-centered suburban sprawl. But perhaps modernism's most insidious legacy has been its success in establishing, as a culture-wide habit of both thinking and practice, today's (hyper) modern / utilitarian / emotivist approach to the built environment. As a result, architects today are encouraged to imagine every building as a *sui generis* monument the aesthetic merit of which is determined by the novelty of its form, and the cumulative symbolic effect of which is to represent in city skylines throughout the world the power and extent of global crony capitalism. In spite of a prophetic *cri de coeur* against modernist planning as early as 1961 in Jane Jacobs' *The Death and Life of Great American Cities*, modernism remains to this day modernity's default form of human settlement-making, notwithstanding organized opposition that began in earnest with the founding of The Congress for the New Urbanism in the early 1990s—a counterattack joined more recently by the Front Porch Republic, not on the CNU battlefields of real estate development, transportation policy and climate change, but rather on the fronts of environmental stewardship, human nature, and human flourishing. Let me return therefore to the questions with which I began: Can human flourishing—the life of moral and intellectual excellence lived in community with others—occur in a modern metropolitan environment [FIG.4]? And can a modern metropolis be (re)conceived as a range of less-dense-rural-to-more-dense-urban settlements that cumulatively, at the scale of a metropolitan region, attain the local intimacy, formal legibility, and densities of human capital that have historically made cities both central to the dynamics of human achievement, discovery, and excellence, *and* as beautiful places that feel like and anticipate home?

To these questions *The Notre Dame Plan of Chicago 2109* (hereafter *Chicago 2109*) offers a confident affirmative answer. *Chicago 2109* is both a critique of contemporary Chicago and a proposal to further develop ideas and forms already deeply embedded in both the history of Chicago and a larger history of which Chicago is part. It employs classical humanist urbanism and Catholic social teaching generally, and the 1909 *Plan of Chicago* specifically, as reference points for imagining Chicago a century forward and reconceiving it as an example of a humanist alternative to today's allegedly inevitable hyper-modern high-rise post-humanist global urbanism. *Chicago 2109* envisions a metropolitan Chicago population 3.5 times denser, and a city of Chicago population about 35% denser, than they are today (while still being only 43% as dense as present-day Brooklyn and only 28% as dense as present-day Paris). Among the benefits of Chicago's increased density would be a more active and intentional

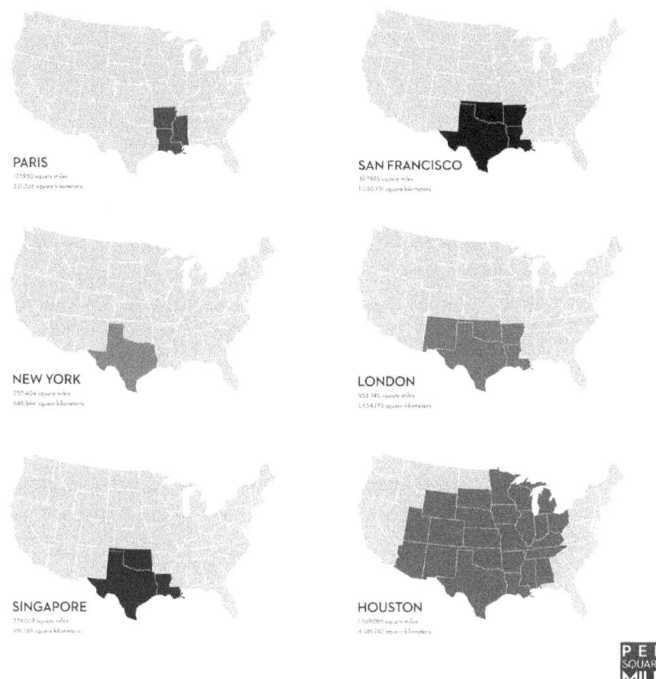

FIGURE 4:

World population and the amount of land it would occupy at the density of various international cities, from persquaremile.com (n.b. this does not illustrate the amount of additional land necessary to sustain a world population at these densities)

relationship to metropolitan Chicago's immediate landscape [FIG.5]: the recovery in metropolitan Chicago of more than 70% of currently developed land and its reversion to water-permeable agricultural land, forests, prairie, and wetlands; as well as a tripling of the amount of open land in the city of Chicago itself. Moreover, this imagined increase in population and building density can be accomplished by taking advantage of Chicago's existing public transportation infrastructure, in a range of densities and residential building types, and without the need for high-rises.

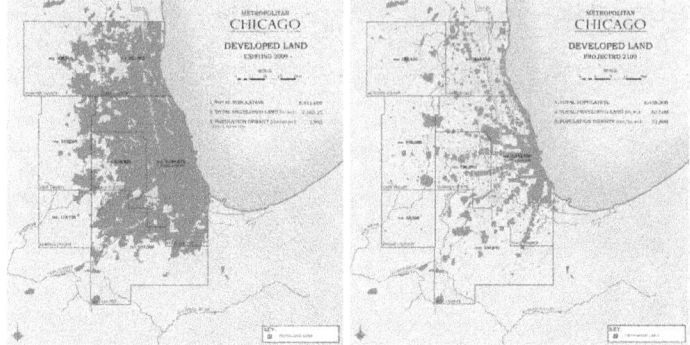

FIGURE 5: *Left*: Existing Metro Chicago 2009: 8.5M people occupying 2100+ square miles at 3900 / sq. mile (11500 / sq. mile in Chicago)
Right: Proposed Metro Chicago 2109: 8.5M people occupying 600+ sq. miles at 13800 / sq. mile (15500 / sq. mile in Chicago)

Central to *Chicago 2109* is the designation of four identifiable less-dense-to-more-dense settlement types defined according to both density and area [FIGS.6 & 7]. These are the more rural settlements of the Hamlet and the Village, and the more urban settlements of the Town and the City—the latter comprised of neighborhoods, themselves defined in *Chicago 2109* in part by their proximity to public transit stops. Each of these settlement types is compact and includes a mix of commercial, residential and civic uses. In *Chicago 2109*, hamlets and villages exist

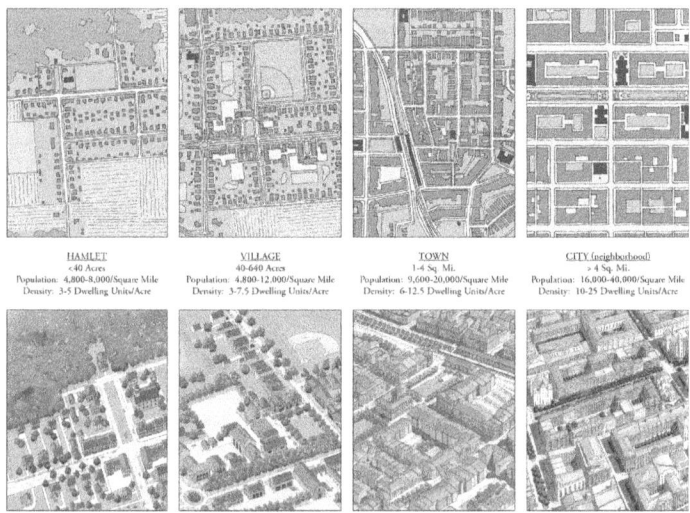

FIGURE 6: Hamlet / Village / Town / City as rural-to-urban settlement types defined by population density and land area

THE METROPOLITAN REGION AS AGRARIAN-URBAN UNIT   203

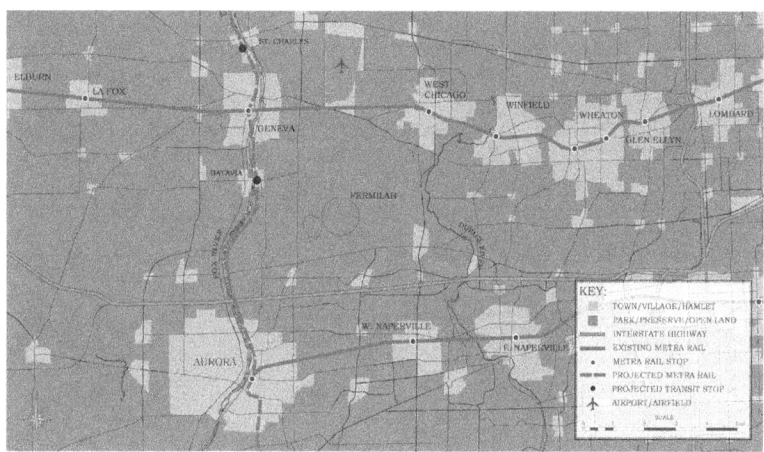

FIGURE 7: Western Metropolitan Chicago, with City of Aurora and various Towns located around commuter rail lines. Villages and Hamlets are located at intersections of major state and regional roads, surrounded by natural or agrarian landscape

at the edge or crossing of state and/or county roads, and are *surrounded* by either a natural or agricultural landscape, with which they presumably have some working relationship [FIG.8], whereas towns—larger and denser settlements organized in relationship to rail transit—have a natural or agricultural landscape *at their edge*.

In order to work in a metropolitan context (and in contrast to post-1945 suburbs), each rural and urban settlement type requires—in proximity to commercial, religious, and civic buildings and spaces—a

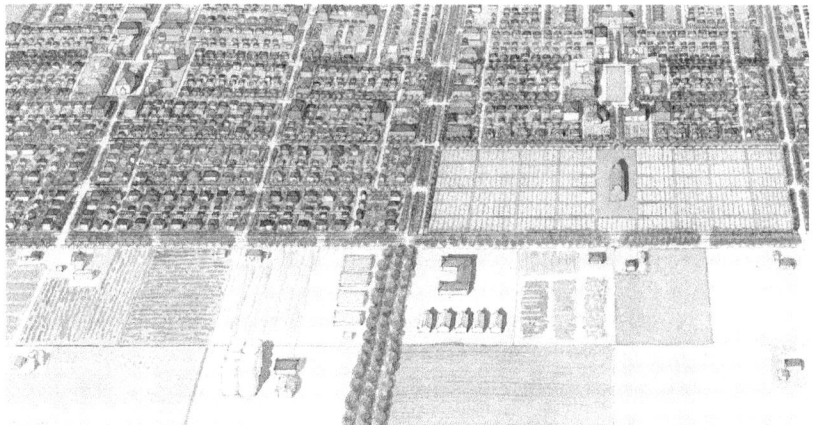

FIGURE 8: Town settlement meets agricultural landscape in metropolitan Chicago

FIGURE 9: Chicago's historic center viewed from the southwest, 2109

variety of residential building types suited for persons in different stages of life: young children, teen-agers, young adults, working families, and retirees. This was the pre-1945 historical norm, and it can work again if Chicagoans will study, learn from, and improve the unusually good mix

FIGURE 10: Proposed new high-rise city hall and boulevard fronted by sacred buildings, a crossing of civic and sacred axes to replace the freeway interchange in Chicago's historic center

of neighborhood housing types developed locally prior to 1930: detached single-family houses large and small (some with front porches), owner-occupied two- and three-flat buildings, six-flat buildings, twelve-unit corner apartment buildings, the three story U-court walk-up, and the mid-rise apartment / condominium building. The highest residential densities envisioned in *Chicago 2109* can be accomplished humanely in buildings of six stories or fewer [FIG.9], allowing for taller residential buildings on Chicago's lakefront, but leaving it to individual neighborhoods to regulate building heights in a regional Land Value Tax regime (see below).

But what of Chicago as a historic city of high-rise buildings? *Chicago 2109* proposes no high-rise demolition, but does envision an economy and cultural sensibility in which tall buildings will be preserved and maintained to the degree they are *well built* and, above all, *loved*. New tall buildings may even be built, most likely for important civic structures [FIG.10]. However, in Chicago imagined as a classical humanist city—both by Daniel Burnham in 1909, and in *Chicago 2109*—high-rise buildings are not normative. What of the alleged environmental benefits of high-rise buildings, and the need for higher urban population densities to affect better stewardship of land? It is true that higher-than-present densities have environmental benefits, but not true that density can only be satisfied by high-rises. Paris, a city of six-story buildings, is almost four times denser than the city depicted in *Chicago 2109*, and Paris does not have the lower-density, predominantly single-family residential building-types that would be most characteristic of the metropolitan regional settlement pattern of hamlets, villages, towns, and city neighborhoods envisioned in *Chicago 2109*—which *also* means, n.b., that if and when the time comes, metropolitan Chicago has the capacity for substantial population growth within the patterns of land use shown in *Chicago 2109*.

Like the anticipated decline and demise of unloved and poorly built high-rise housing and office buildings, the anticipated decline and demise of Chicago's post-1945 suburbs and their restoration as rural land is *not* an active policy proposal to shut down suburbs. Rather, the decline of suburbia seems the likely unfolding of fixed near-term demographic events—specifically, aging Boomers and late-procreating Millennials—and their slow-growth or contracting economic consequences.

In tandem with increasing awareness of both the economic and environmental costs of low-density suburbs, *Chicago 2109* depicts a future in which both small-town and big-city urbanism *and* landscape recovery and restoration have become pro-active public policy. Similarly, although *Chicago 2109* indicates that driving will be less common than it now is because the high infrastructure maintenance costs of low-density suburbs will ultimately render their form economically obsolete, the elimination of automobiles as conveniences is neither presumed by nor essential to *Chicago 2109*. What *is* essential is intelligent land-use coordinated with *existing* but improved public transportation and, probably, a revision of current land taxation policy. The latter especially is easier said than done; but insofar as justice is an element of human flourishing, and even though a revised tax policy is insufficient to secure human flourishing in metropolitan Chicago, such revision does seem necessary. The failure of metropolitan Chicago's current city and regional political institutions to live within their means parallels similar failures at the state and national levels; and the growing inequalities of opportunity that these failures foster, and their economic unsustainability as policy, make land tax reform at the regional level a potent political issue. There is not space here to explore the subject in depth, but one possible solution—in the best traditions of American federalist experiments in self-government, and arguably best employed at the level of the local metropolitan region—is a Land Value Tax that eliminates all other regional taxes in favor of a tax on land *regardless of its improvements or lack thereof*. This theory of taxation (most often associated with nineteenth-century social theorist Henry George, and endorsed by modern economists ranging from Paul Krugman to Milton Friedman) has appeal across the political spectrum because on the one hand it "socializes" land (a finite common good) and on the other hand removes disincentives to for-profit private development. Employed on a regional metropolitan basis, a Land Value Tax has the potential simultaneously to discourage private sector land-banking, encourage development, and spread more equally both the benefits and the costs of externalities associated with human settlement.

What kind of governmental structure is implied by *Chicago 2109*? In recognizing the social principles of the dignity of the individual person, communal solidarity, and subsidiarity, and in keeping with American traditions of democratic self-governance, *Chicago 2109* presumes two levels of political organization below (and, in the event of some crisis or emergency, perhaps independent of) state and national government. One is the *metropolitan region* (in this case the existing seven counties of northeastern Illinois); the other is *local political communities of place* as found in hamlets, villages, towns, and city neighborhoods. All of these would be funded by the same metropolis-wide Land Value Tax. Local governments would bear responsibility for developing their own local design development guidelines (including local zoning and street design codes), providing public safety, street and sanitation services, maintaining public parks, and articulating and enforcing (as required) communal norms within some larger constitutional framework of individual rights. Metropolitan government would be responsible for overseeing regional land use (including nature preserves and ag-land), water treatment, watershed protection, waste management, public transportation, major road (not federal interstate highway) infrastructure, and funding for elementary and secondary education (however defined and delivered). All of these issues are important to the well-being of the entire metropolitan region, and are both manageable and most equitably addressed *at a regional scale*, whereas in contemporary metropolitan Chicago they are now overseen by multiple agencies in multiple uncoordinated jurisdictions that operate in no small part as sources of patronage and fiefdoms of entrenched economic and political power.

What is the likelihood of this political reorganization of metropolitan Chicago? Only time will tell. Some problems cannot be solved by politics, and for such a reorganization to prevail the battles ahead will be both political and cultural. Its most likely alternative—what is in fact now happening—is almost certainly a two-tiered metropolitan Chicago of elite privilege coexisting with increasing poverty. (In the absence of a revived marriage and family ideal and discipline and their positive ripple effects, this circumstance will be cruelly exacerbated among the poor by ongoing modern technological innovations and their effects upon work). In contrast, the twenty-first-century history imagined by and depicted in *Chicago 2109* is one of productive self-governing communities of place anchored in a local landscape. Given present-day metropolitan Chicago's aging population and unfunded pension liabilities, the loss of its households with two biological parents, the pressure on its family structures, its below-replacement-level regional birth-rates and in-migration, general state-wide economic stagnation, and the breakdown of a shared and functional civic and political culture, the metropolis envisioned by *Chicago 2109* represents a cultural and economic revival on the far side of the cultural and economic decline likely to be Chicago's actual immediate future. Nevertheless, its near-term pessimism notwithstanding, *Chicago 2109* has been conceived in hope grounded in Christian anthropology, classical humanism, and American traditions of religious pluralism, local associations, and strong but limited government. Simply and succinctly: if Chicago gets better, it will get better as a consequence of disciplined love exercised by many persons in and for many places—and of disciplined love's hard demands.

Port City Confidential

Susannah Black

I

I have often observed that extremely violent noise and activity go with good-fellowship and heightened spirits.

— Patrick O'Brian, *The Letter of Marque*

Here's where we are: the localist movement has dug itself in against a set of tropes that we all recognize. It is agrarian rather than urban; it values rootedness and suspects mobility; it sees the beauty in strong local cultures, strong families. It sees trade as suspect, at least as a way to make a living. It loves the land.

These are good things. But what do we do in a world that is more than half urban, and what do we do if we find ourselves happy in a city with all its ebb and flow? What do we do if we love the sidewalks—or the sea?

We need to learn to see the beauty of the urban and (even) the cosmopolitan. Seeing the beauty of strong traditional cultures, the localist movement needs to see the beauty of the place where those cultures mix. I appreciate the work of every Kentucky homesteader. But if one of them could somehow be persuaded to come visit me in New York, I would make my case. The first thing I'd do is take him down to the waterfront.

Go to a new city and feel your way down to the waterfront, following the gravity that pulls at your body and the clues of the light in the sky that looks different over water from how it looks over land. You'll find yourself somewhere familiar—if, that is, you know other waterfronts.

My island—Manhattan—disguised itself, in my childhood, as a placeless place, not built on bedrock (and landfill) but on clever ideas and good graphic design and symbolic cash transactions. My discovery of the waterfront was a discovery of the physicality of my city, and of its historical identity: it's a port city, something that New York has in common with Odessa and Mumbai. That means something specific.

II

We'll rant and we'll roar like true British sailors ...

—Anonymous, "Spanish Ladies"

The crew of Clipper City, the schooner I sailed on for two summers (one year part-time, the other year very part-time) was made up of—among others—a Hawaiian, a Ghanian, a kid from Long Island, a compact highly muscled first mate from Vancouver who looked like Popeye, a guy from Bushwick whose family came from Puerto Rico, a black kid from, I think, downtown Brooklyn, and, on and off, me, an Upper West Side half-Jew.

Such crews have been characteristic of the maritime industry throughout its history. They're united by skill, by an unfortunate intimacy with bilgewater, and by a proprioceptive awareness of the weather. They're not united by blood or birth. Sailors, and waterfront people generally, come from somewhere else—from another ship, or another waterfront. And it's far easier to come from another waterfront than it is to come from an inland area of that same city. It's easier, in other words, to get from the marinas of the Colaba district in Mumbai to the artificial harbor of Atlantic Basin, in Brooklyn, than it is to get there from the Upper East Side.

This has been true for centuries: Paul du Noyer writes in his cultural history of Liverpool that it is "deeply insular, yet essentially outward-looking: it faces the sea but has its back turned on England. There were local men for whom Sierra Leone was a fact but London only a rumour. They knew every dive in Buenos Aires, but had no idea of the Cotswolds. And Liverpudlians speak with merry contempt for their Lancashire neighbours, displaying all the high indifference of a New Yorker for Kansas."

This attitude is not spread evenly over a port city but concentrates on the waterfront: on what in Liverpool was called "Sailortown," which

John Belcham of the University of Liverpool described as "a distinctive space and culture . . . replicated in major port cities across the globe."

In a paper presented at an English Heritage conference in 2008, Belcham describes Liverpool's "seafaring cosmopolitanism"; he describes as well the role that such sailor towns played in the British Empire:

> When they landed in foreign ports visiting mariners . . . seldom penetrated beyond the familiar cultural and spatial boundaries of this 'sailor town' area. In ports where Europeans were recent arrivals, sailor town remained a European or inter-colonial enclave. Bars, lodging houses and shops were run by expatriates from all parts of the maritime world.[1]

These sailor towns were a perpetual blend of the strange and the familiar, and the people who inhabited them were the vanguard of the national and ethnic hodgepodge of modern cities: "In the early twentieth century," Belcham writes,

> Valparaiso's worst waterfront bar was managed in succession by an Irishman and a West Indian; Kobe's China Dog tearoom was run by a Malay; and Singapore had cafés run by Italian women. Names cloistered visiting mariners from anything alien or unfamiliar: Antwerp, Amsterdam and Hamburg each had a bar called "Channel for Orders," while Marseille and Liverpool both had a "Flags of all Nations."[2]

The interpenetration of port city cultures did not run only one way: du Noyer characterizes Liverpool as "a sort of sunless Marseilles," and foreignness crept into English cities via their waterfronts just as Englishness crept into foreign cities. Here's the thing to be noticed: port cities, and especially their waterfronts, are distinct kinds of communities, which operate according to a set of traditions and a particular ethos that sets them apart from other places. Trade can destabilize some communities, but it is constitutive of port cities. Inland, yes, let's stipulate that, per standard Burke-and-Kirk analysis, trade spins people off the stable atomic structures of their families and communities, sends them through the mall like free electrons, their gaping need like a negative charge that picks up a cruft of discount mascara and Tory Burch shoes and pants

---

1. Belcham, John, "Shock City: Sailortown Liverpool" in *On the Waterfront: Culture, Heritage and Regeneration of Port Cities* (http://content.historicengland.org.uk/images-books/publications/on-the-waterfront/waterfront-part2.pdf/).

2. *Ibid.*

engineered to a kind of perfection by designers working somewhere in the infospace and manufactured by slaves in China.

But on the waterfront trade does something different: it gives jobs to a group of people, primarily men, who deal with the shipping containers that are stuffed with these pants and that mascara. It gives jobs to the Harbor pilots—in New York, that elite group is the Sandy Hook pilots—who won't take as an apprentice anyone out of his or her early twenties, because to learn the peculiarities of the Harbor bottom and all the channels is the work of more than one lifetime. It gives structure to the lives of the boys who get their TWIC cards (that's Transportation Worker Identification Credential) and start accumulating days at sea and find themselves—kids from Brooklyn—as officers, having worked their way up from deckhands, dodging pirates in the Gulf of Aden.

The stability of the waterfront is based on a respect for hierarchy, tradition, and skill. It's a culture that survives even the powerful solvent of ideology. A friend of mine, a 70-something Hungarian man who hangs out in my coffeehouse, once spent a summer during his university career as a deckhand on a cargo ship. Things were different on board. "Socialism," he explained to me, "did not make it so far."

It's true that at some points, in order to get along on the waterfront, you had to be Irish or Italian; but along with this story of ethnically homogenous waterfront work there was a set of parallel stories, of ships with radically multiethnic crews, of waterfront areas that were disreputable in the eyes of the larger city precisely because they were the sites of racial mixing. Madison Grant, in The Passing of the Great Race, goes on about how "the coastal and seafaring populations of northern Europe are everywhere Nordic[,] . . . and among Europeans this race is preeminently fitted for maritime pursuits," but the picture we get from other sources is far different. And these sources are varied. There are ships' logs, of course. There is the disapproving 1928 proto-social-scientific report of the eugenicist fellow traveller Muriel Fletcher, who decried the miscegenation of the British waterfront, despairing of the use that the "half-caste" children of British women and West African sailors could be to themselves or to society.

There's also the journalism of Dickens, who in *The Uncommercial Traveller* described slumming it in Sailortown one evening. He had finagled what would now be called a "ride-around": he joined a police superintendent on his nightly rounds. The "Jacks" that Dickens and his police guide see are of all colors and nationalities:

> There was British Jack, a little maudlin and sleepy, lolling over his empty glass.... Loafing Jack of the Stars and Stripes, rather an unpromising customer, with his long nose, lank cheek, high cheek-bones, and nothing soft about him but his cabbage-leaf hat ... Spanish Jack, with curls of black hair, rings in his ears, and a knife not far from his hand, if you got into trouble with him; there were Maltese Jack, and Jack of Sweden, and Jack the Finn, looming through the smoke of their pipes, and turning faces that looked as if they were carved out of dark wood, towards the young lady dancing the hornpipe.[3]

There was even, much to Dickens' distress, "Dark Jack," hanging out in a tavern with "Dark Jack's delight, his WHITE unlovely Nan." This evidence of miscegenation is troubling to him—the more so because the girl in that tavern was the "least unlovely Nan, both morally and physically, that I saw that night."

The commonality of these men, which persists despite their differences in race and nationality, is evident to Dickens. They are a tribe, united by their exploitation, by their residence in Sailortown and—he can see from a distance—by their work.

And of course the multiracial nature of ships' crews can be seen nowhere so well as aboard the Pequod, where not only do Danish, Lascar, Manx, Spanish, Native American, Sicilian, Maltese, Chinese, French, Azorean, Dutch, English, and Irish sailors work shoulder to shoulder, along with freedmen and Native Americans, but hands from Nantucket even manage to get along with those from Long Island.

III

> *We came ashore in Carbonear*
> *with nothing but our rights*
> *and I wondered if I e'er again*
> *would see my London lights...*
>
> —Great Big Sea, "England"

This sounds like everything that traditionalism is against: troubling to the branch of the traditionalist movement that values local cultures, and the

---

3. Charles Dickens, *The Uncommercial Traveller* (London: Chapman & Hall, 1866), 31.

fever nightmare of those embarrassing-uncle conservatives who have a particular horror of the mixing of races to produce a presumed polyglot population of racially indeterminate, placeless people.

Further, the mobility of British sailors was arguably one of the things that spread the idea of individual human rights disconnected from one's community and from duties. The worldview that includes such rights is far closer to the truth than a worldview that sees no objective universal moral truths and no stable human nature. It can, of course, just as obviously lead to a corrosive individualism that many seventeenth- and eighteenth-century natural-rights theorists would have been quick to disavow.

These Sailortowns, these mixed crews, are clearly the result of globalization and capitalism. Jack is, after all, Mercantile Jack: he is a merchant marine, not one of the men with a heart of oak who fought under Nelson. His lifestyle is one of perpetual temptation: of corruption, drunkenness, improvidence, and prostitution. He famously leaves behind his sweetheart, who waits for years, a potential mother, the mistress of a potential household, worse off than Penelope because she has no Telemachus to comfort her. How is this situation in any way reclaimable by a conservatism that values stable families, place, and the countryside over singleness, placelessness, and the city?

There's nothing to be said in favor of the exploitation of sailors or of their corruption. But that's a distinct issue, separable from the vitality and culture-making that goes on in these places: the abuse of a thing does not take away its use. And what we see is that the result of this racial and cultural promiscuity is not a dull blandness but rather the formation of a very particular new tribe: the tribe of the waterfront-dweller. The waterfront is a distinctive place, with those good qualities that distinctive places have, and just as a woman who'd grown up in San Francisco's Chinatown might find comfort and familiarity in New York's Chinatown, so a man who'd grown up on the waterfront in Chelsea might find comfort, familiarity—and skilled work—on the waterfront in London or Liverpool or even, if worse came to worst, Hoboken.

If the mixing I've described is constitutive of both port cities and of ships' crews, several conclusions can be drawn, and one of them is that those who are too particular about cultural and ethnic mixing may be sailors, in the sense of buying a yacht and taking lessons on how to operate it; but they will never be shipmates. They may be Americans, or may through naturalization, as in the case of John Derbyshire, become

Americans. But if New York is a port city, they will never, until their hearts are changed, be New Yorkers.

IV

Christ works on a certain pier...
—Father John Corridan, "Christ in the Shape-up"

Every now and then, throughout the history of New York, one of the inland people will notice the existence of the waterfront. Daniel Bell did, and Dorothy Day. Budd Schulberg marveled at the willingness of the *New York Times* obliviously to "live in blissful co-existence only a few blocks apart" from the Hell's Kitchen ILA (International Longshoreman's Association) Local 824—the "pistol" local. Jane Jacobs did too, and articulated a vision of leisure and consumer-commercial use of the waterfront, which was what in fact eventually happened:

> Part of the district's waterfront should become a great marine museum—the permanent anchorage of specimen and curiosity ships. . . . [I]n summertime it should be a great thing for the evening. Other features of the shoreline should be the embarkation points for pleasure voyages. . . . [T]hese . . . should be as glamorous and salty as art can make them. If new sea-food restaurants and much else would not start up nearby, I will eat my lobster shell.[4]

When, fifty years after she wrote, I found myself down at the waterfront, the boat I was crewing on leveraged precisely this waterfront kitsch to bring tourists and hedge-fund office parties and school kids out for a two hour cruise around the Statue of Liberty, feed them rum-based cocktails (not the school kids) and potato chips, and disgorge them onto Pier 17—the old Fulton Fish Market pier, with the fish market building itself converted into a three-story mall; there were restaurants all through the building, heavily maritime-themed. It was not the world of the longshoremen of the '40s—fewer handguns, for one thing; the first mate, who slept aboard, made himself a defensive weapon out of a batch of bamboo sticks duct-taped together, and explained himself by noting that the only people he'd really be defending himself against would be teenagers who

---

4. Jane Jacobs, *The Death & Life of Great American Cities* (New York: Random House, 196), 159.

tried to come onto the deck of the schooner at three in the morning to drink. He didn't need to have a gun for them—a fierce Canadian coming at them with a club would be enough to scare them off, although there was also talk of getting a dog.

The world was different—but it does do something to you to know how to handle a dockline right, and to know that it's something that men on that pier have been doing since before Whitman walked down there. I started out by bribing one of the dockline guys with two hot dogs. He was a seventeen-year-old kid who'd been working there since the previous season. He showed me how to do it—to know which line you'd catch first, where you'd stand to catch it, depending on whether the boat was coming in port-to or starboard-to, how to yell at the tourists eating ice cream on the steps until they got out of the way so they wouldn't get hit by the monkey's fist knot at the end of the heaving line you'd haul on eventually to pull the plasticky blue-green dockline up out of the disturbing East River water. He showed me how to run along the outside of the fence, from bollard to bollard, making this 160-foot boat fast.

Even this trade—which was a kind of entry-way to proper sailing—had its own pride. An Italian tourist, a terrifyingly good-looking guy, gave me a smile and said, "You are docklines girl? In my country, I am docklines guy." Must be better paid in Italy, I thought: he was, after all, vacationing in New York.

But maybe he was there as crew, one of the ocean's hitchhikers, and had a day off to explore. People like that are distinctive in their sense of the provisional nature of their life in this one port. They know that they will be leaving, or that they could.

But there's something about being on the waterfront that militates against what we associate with travel now. For the modern, this sense of always potentially leaving a place is the characteristic of the suffocating life of what Samuel Huntington has called Davos Man, the guy who flits from airport to airport, who sees no difference in the departure lounge at JFK and Schiphol, because there isn't one. This is someone who's disembodied, whose jet lag is so bad he doesn't know what time it is ever; whose sense of direction is so bad that he's forgotten that it has something to do with the sun; whose loyalty is to his own personal brand; who lives in symbols.

The sailor may be just as likely to need a passport, but in other ways the two men are poles apart. I, as a good liberal-arts graduate, had lived in symbols when I started sailing; they were, they are, good symbols.

Writing, ideas—these are important, and there's all the difference in the world between a bad or dehumanizing use of symbol and a good one; symbols are a good part of our lives, and we must use them well. Still, to come into a society—a ship's crew—where your value is measured in your physical strength, your memory of how a line runs in the rigging, the speed with which you respond to orders, and your ability to spot actual physical dangers with your actual physical eyes—the fleet of inexpertly skippered 12-meters a half mile away and closing, for example, or one of the McAllister tugs with a barge on the hip heading into Buttermilk Channel—this was a shock. The helmsman I was dealing with was no symbolic helmsman; the ship I was sailing on was, for once, not a ship of state. Everything was real. It was as though I'd lived in the Matrix my whole life and was now unplugged for the first time.

Most of the time in a modern port city those who aren't involved in the maritime trades are able pretty well to ignore the brute fact of the harbor (or, as it might be, the river): those millions of gallons of water that flow in and out like blood pumping every day. A hedge-fund guy could have gone for years, taking the 4, 5, 6 to Wall Street and approaching his office from the Broadway end of the street, without realizing that at the other end of the street is the reason that the city is where it is. He could have stayed in his office and ordered new Sperry Topsiders off Amazon and had them delivered to his Upper East Side apartment and never realized that the whole time there were tides ebbing and flowing and people who caught docklines who went home every day smelling like the East River. But then one day that river might start flowing into the power station that supplies electricity to the air conditioners that cool the servers located under the old Port Authority building on 17th Street where Google has set up its East Coast headquarters, and the power to that building shuts down. Then one day the containers that hold his shoes can't be unloaded in Red Hook, and he's SOL. He knew his business, he knew his tastes, he knew his mind and would doubtless have been able to express his opinions to you over lunch on any number of topics—but in a very real sense he did not know where he was.

If 9/11 refuted the end of history, Hurricane Sandy refuted the hypothesis of the end of nature. When push comes to shove and the fact of our being a port city impinges on us, we are forced to realize that we all—coders and interior designers and bankers as well as plumbers and pilots and garbagemen—make our living alongshore. When we who live in port cities are in danger from the sea, we are all longshoremen.

V

Who are these that fly like a cloud,
and like doves to their windows?
For the coastlands shall hope for me,
the ships of Tarshish first,
to bring your children from afar,
their silver and gold with them,
for the name of the Lord your God,
and for the Holy One of Israel,
because He has made you beautiful.

—Isaiah 60:8–9

But there's more to the waterfront's resonance than the danger of a storm surge. First, the type of conservatism that rejects Sailortown because of its messiness, its instability, is a type that seeks perfection in this world. It is not a measured recognition of the provisional nature of our cities here, the impermanence of all things of this age. Rather, in its hunger for stability—itself a good hunger—it seeks that stability in the quasi-mythical stable communities of the past, the small towns to which the bad city provides the necessary rhetorical foil. Such a conservatism may talk about how very non-ideological it is, how very free it is of the Utopianism that led the Communists (and the Communards) to despise what was in favor of a vision of what would be. But these conservatives have their own *ça ira*: even if it is *c'etait*.

The conservatism that can love a port city is one that allows cities here to be temporary; it is not threatened by the instability of the water's edge. The conservatism that can love an imperfect community is one that knows that we are, or are called to be, citizens of the City of God first; that we are exiles here. But there is a second bit to the conservatism that embraces a port city: it is a conservatism that sees the New Jerusalem as it really is: a multiethnic exuberant rejection of all apartheid, a city full of people from all the nations and, moreover, a city with more Ashkenazim in it than ever were in the tenements of the Lower East Side. During those summers when I was crewing, throughout the long afternoons, I'd see men in their twenties and thirties and forties, sitting on the wooden boardwalk steps outside Pier 17, eating their salads from plastic clamshells they'd bought at one of the dozen joints along Wall Street that cater to the hungry trader who's walking East on his lunch break. They'd buy the salads and walk to the river, take a left, end up at the Seaport. And as they ate they'd look at the boat. "Come sailing," I'd say, and they'd say no, they had to get back to work. I felt somewhat desperate for them: I wanted to rescue them from their plight of being "in finance," of working in an office, of not being a sailor. These were healthy men: any of them could have helped raise the mainsail—if I could, they could—and the more they did it, the stronger they'd get. But sometimes they'd say yes—at least, they'd plan to come back, after work, and I'd feel this sense of triumph. I'd want them to participate, to learn, to look at the sails and try to figure out why we were trimming them in one way or another, try to feel the wind and anticipate having to move out of the way of the jib sheets as they whipped across the deck. I understood that this feeling was really about—or was borrowing a lot of emotional juice from—evangelism. This was the perfect picture of how we are to regard telling people about Christ, seeing them take their first shaky steps into discipleship: a sense of yes, you are being rescued from fruitlessness, you are being initiated into proper, adult, human life: you're not playing anymore, and yet this life is more solemnly playful than all the busywork you can do in Excel. Join the crew, we say when we invite people to know the body of Christ. Come aboard the Ark, we say. Meet your Captain: the one who's worthy of striving to please, worthy of your best effort, the last full measure. I understood that then. What I've only recently realized is the second allegory contained in waterfront life. Here it is, and here is where we can see something particularly poignant in the distinction between the Old Jerusalem and the New: unlike virtually every other major city in the ancient world—and indeed virtually every city before the advent of the railroad—Jerusalem had no waterfront. Babylon, the commentator Alexander McLaren points out, was on the Euphrates, "Nineveh on the Tigris, Thebes on the Nile, Rome on the Tiber; but Jerusalem had nothing but a fountain or two, and a well or two, and a little trickle and an intermittent stream." We might add, of course, the Thames, the Seine, the Hudson. But something is different in the New Jerusalem: something Isaiah saw, something that Saint John, stuck on an island at the end of the world, saw as well, and something that Ezekiel saw very clearly. "The man," reports Ezekiel,

> brought me back to the entrance to the temple, and I saw water coming out from under the threshold of the temple. . . . [N]ow it was a river that I could not cross, because the water had risen

and was deep enough to swim in—a river that no one could cross. . . .

Then he led me back to the bank of the river. When I arrived there, I saw a great number of trees on each side of the river. He said to me, "This water flows toward the eastern region and goes down into the Arabah, where it enters the Dead Sea. When it empties into the sea, the salty water there becomes fresh. Swarms of living creatures will live wherever the river flows. There will be large numbers of fish. . . . [W]here the river flows everything will live. Fishermen will stand along the shore; from En Gedi to En Eglaim there will be places for spreading nets. . . . Fruit trees of all kinds will grow on both banks of the river. Their leaves will not wither, nor will their fruit fail."

"The leaves of the tree," Saint John fills us in, reporting from Patmos, nearly seven hundred years later, identifying these fruit trees with the Tree of Life, "are for the healing of the nations."

That's not a location you can get to if you're going off of Lonely Planet Jerusalem, which as I understand it covers only the present earthly city. MacLaren describes this distinction between the Old and New Jerusalems as a deficiency that will, "in the Messianic days[,] . . . be made good. . . . A mysterious stream shall spring up from behind, and flow out from beneath, the temple doors, and then with rapid increase and depth and width, but with no tributaries coming into it, shall run fertilising and life-giving everywhere, till it pours itself into the noisome waters of the sullen sea of death and heals even them."

In other words, in the Messianic age, as part of the very presence of God among them, which will flow from that City to the world, the people of God are—for the first time—given the gift of a waterfront. Given this imagery, can we call it a coincidence that a good third of the apostles, those firstfruits of God's new people, were drawn from the ranks of fishermen: those who make their living on the water, those who live alongshore?

Part Seven

Philanthropy

Bigness is always suspect. The bigger, the worse.
—MARY KINGSBURY SIMKHOVITCH, *HERE IS GOD'S PLENTY*

Satan Was the First Philanthropist

Jeremy Beer

Warren Buffett, George Soros, Bill Gates, the Koch Brothers, Oprah: all famous for their success in business, all famous, in part, for their philanthropy. What else do they have in common?

They are all in league with the devil.

Such, presumably, would be the judgment of the nineteenth-century American philosopher Orestes Brownson, were he to arise from his eternal resting place (beneath the Basilica of the Sacred Heart at the University of Notre Dame) to write one last 20,000-word article on the topic.

Never one to indulge in understatement (or brevity), Brownson claimed that Satan's "favorite guise in modern times is that of philanthropy."[1] He nominated Robespierre as eighteenth-century philanthropy's most "ardent apostle." "Under the influence of philanthropy," wrote Brownson, "Europe became one vast slaughter-house; kings and nobles, bishops, priests, and nuns, old men and young women, were dragged to the scaffold, and the reign of love was drowned in torrents of innocent blood."[2]

Well. That is not exactly the kind of thing one usually hears from, say, the Association of Fundraising Professionals.

When it comes to philanthropy we are not accustomed to this kind of talk—or, really, to any kind of negativity at all. For most people, philanthropy ranks with puppies and summer vacations in terms of its positive connotations. Our great philanthropists are fêted, admired, revered. We give them awards and they give us checks. They represent the good old-fashioned American Dream. They are, in short, what we aspire to be.

---

1. Qtd. in Walter McDougall, *Throes of Democracy: The American Civil War Era, 1829–1877* (New York: Harper, 2008), 606.

2. Orestes Brownson, *Brownson's Quarterly Review*, January 1855, 49.

What could be wrong with *philanthropy*?

Quite a bit, it turns out. As Brownson pointed out, philanthropy's roots lie in a calculated, deliberate rejection of mere *charity*. Besides a rather embarrassing association with traditional Christianity—where it was regarded as a supernatural virtue that could only be fully attained with the aid of grace—charity to eighteenth- and nineteenth-century reformers was associated with the reactionary view that social evils were ultimately rooted in human hearts. Philanthropy located such evils in the head. Social evils were thus amenable to amelioration via technological reason, given sufficient resources. That is why, explained Brownson, "philanthropy went to work to reform—on a large scale; for philanthropy scorns small beginnings, and proposes always to commence operations on the masses."[3]

An orientation toward charity rather than philanthropy might, Brownson conceded, leave one too ready to accept certain kinds of suffering and injustice as inevitable. But the philanthropic solution—throwing off the shackles of charity to pursue systemic social change—often led to more widespread suffering and graver injustice. "Philanthropy, when acting alone," Brownson concluded, "seldom fails to make matters worse."[4] To his Christian way of thinking, the point of charity was to move hearts toward God, and thus toward neighbors. That is how real reform proceeds.

Brownson realized that this approach lacked a certain pizzazz. "Charity . . . deals not with committees, attends not meetings, and is seen not on platforms, moving or seconding high-sounding 'resolutions,' but addresses herself to the heart of man; for charity is not puffed up, and seeks not to make a noise in the world."[5] One suspects that he would not have been impressed by the Buffett-Gates Giving Pledge.

Nietzsche, as always, understood the game. "Do I recommend love of the neighbor to you?" asked Zarathustra. "Sooner I should even recommend flight from the neighbor and love of the farthest."[6]

Philanthropy's intellectual roots, in short, lie in revolutionary secularism. This fact has contemporary consequences, at least in part because philanthropy's pedigree—specifically, the thinking and practices of the

---

3. Ibid., 48.

4. Ibid., 193.

5. Ibid., 49.

6. Friedrich Nietzsche, *Thus Spoke Zarathustra*, trans. Walter Kauffman (New York: Modern Library, 1995), 61.

dominant players in today's philanthropy sector, or what we might call Professional or Big Philanthropy—can be destructive. And the philanthropy experts and scholars from whom Big Philanthropy's leaders take their cues typically threaten to make matters worse.

Instead of the grandiose projects and utopian visions too often pursued by Big Philanthropy—usually in league with big government—we need a smaller, humbler philanthropy, a philanthropy of accountability and human relationships, a philanthropy of place. Let us call this alternative vision *philanthrolocalism*. But first, a little more about how and why American philanthropy, so often praised without reservation, is in fact pretty screwed up.

The substitution of humanity in general for real, individual human beings as the primary object of benevolence lay at the core of the first modern philanthropic foundations. As William Schambra (among others) has shown, from their beginnings in the late 1800s and early 1900s, the major charitable foundations (Russell Sage, Rockefeller, Carnegie) and their progenitors consciously sought to abandon old-fashioned attempts to alleviate immediate distress for a more focused, scientific, and expert-driven approach that would provide permanent solutions to vexing social problems. At its creation the Rockefeller Foundation devoted itself to serving the "well-being of mankind throughout the world." Rockefeller himself insisted that "the best philanthropy involves a search for cause, an attempt to cure evils at their source."[7]

For the wealthy to simply provide aid to those particular men, women, and children who needed it was no longer good enough. It was time to change the world—just as Rockefeller and the other captains of commerce who started many of these foundations had done with their railroad, oil, munitions, and other business ventures. It was time to attack such problems as crime and disease at their roots. Schambra has shown that eugenics and sterilization programs were vigorously funded for decades by many large foundations precisely because such programs were prototypically "philanthropic" in their focus on the elimination of poverty rather than on helping real, existing poor people.[8]

---

7. William Schambra, "Philanthropy's War on Community," *Nonprofit Quarterly* online, September 18, 2012.

8. *Ibid.*

In this intellectual milieu the term "charity" gradually became discredited. It came to refer, for the most part, to small, reactive, and/or non-strategic efforts to assist the suffering. Charity was the province of simpletons. Sophisticated entrepreneurs, professionals, and scientific experts engaged in philanthropy.[9]

And so it remains today. As a spokeswoman for the $37 *billion* Bill and Melinda Gates Foundation recently explained when pressed about why the foundation chose not to help dozens of homeless sleeping outside its $500 million Seattle headquarters, "We're trying to move upstream to a systems level to either prevent family homelessness before it happens or to end it as soon as possible after it happens."[10]

The family resemblance between the modern concept of philanthropy and the great ideologies of the twentieth century is difficult to deny. As the economist Wilhelm Röpke pointed out in the middle of the twentieth century, it was "frequently in the name of abstract, general philanthropy" that "fanatical and intolerant mass hatred . . . such as national hatred, class hatred, and race hatred" was justified and excused.[11]

Aleksandr Solzhenitsyn knew a little something about that. The narrator of his short story "Ego," set during the Russian Revolution, describes how the practical, small-scale social work of a man named Pavel Vasilyevich Ektov, "a natural-born activist in the rural cooperative movement," was derided by the Leninists then coming to power:

> [Pavel] never took up any of the grandiose, earth-shaking causes of the time. In order to keep true to his beliefs, he had to engage in some bitter debates on how best to remake the life around him and to resist the temptations and withstand the rebukes of the revolutionary democrats: devoting himself to social change by promoting only "small deeds" was trivial; he was not merely squandering his energy on useless work, he was betraying the whole of humanity for the sake of a few people around him; it was cheap philanthropy that would lead to no great end. Now, they said, we have found the path to the universal salvation of

---

9. For this interpretation of the history of philanthropy and charity, see Jeremy Beer, *The Philanthropic Revolution: An Alternative History of American Charity* (Philadelphia: Penn Press, 2015).

10. See Leslie R. Crutchfield, John V. Kania, and Mark R. Kramer, *Do More than Give: The Six Practices of Donors Who Change the World* (Indianapolis: Jossey-Bass, 2011).

11. Wilhelm Röpke, *A Humane Economy: The Social Framework of the Free Market* (Wilmington: ISI Books, 1998), 57.

humanity; now we have the actual key to achieving the ideal of happiness for all the people. And what can your petty notions of one person helping another and the simple easing of day-to-day tribulations achieve in comparison with that?

As the story moves forward, the peasants in Pavel's Tambov province are systematically robbed, raped, murdered, and executed en masse by the communists. Solzhenitsyn clearly wants us to consider whether there isn't a connection between the communists' view of Pavel's charity and their bloody contempt for actual flesh-and-blood human beings.[12]

The communists are gone, but their contempt for "trivial" "small deeds" is conventional wisdom within a professional philanthropy industry that prefers to work at the "systems level." The authors of the entirely representative *Do More Than Give* call for a new kind of "catalytic philanthropy" that produces "systemwide change." But their mind-numbingly predictable call for "proactive problem solvers" who "embrace a proactive, results-oriented, transformative mode of philanthropy" is nothing but mutton dressed as lamb.[13]

Another related critique of Big Philanthropy might start with such questions as this: How is it that we can have a $300-billion philanthropy sector—a sector that has almost tripled in size, adjusted for inflation, since 1970—at the same time that our civic life has become so eroded? Why has participation in community groups and public life declined so much over the same period of time (the last forty years or so) that professional philanthropy has risen so dramatically? What does this say about our priorities, about our beliefs concerning what we owe to those around us?

In short, how is it that the rise of professional philanthropy can be accompanied by such a steep decline in social capital? Something has gone wrong. And it seems possible that that something is rooted in the shift from personal charity to an impersonal professionalized philanthropy that quixotically seeks to "change the world."

Making charity more effective—making it better precisely *as* charity—is one thing. To the extent that contemporary philanthropists and philanthropic institutions are engaged in that project—and, to be fair, many of them are, sometimes in spite of themselves—they make great contributions to our various communities.

---

12. Aleksandr Solzhenitsyn, *Apricot Jam* (Berkeley: Counterpoint, 2011), 21ff.
13. See n. 10.

But such efforts are not valorized by their professional peers. There is immense pressure to conform to the "best practices" identified as such by Big Philanthropy and its advisors. And those practices are often at odds with the deceptively complex and inescapably personal demands of charity and justice.

To give just one example: many larger foundations require their grantees to measure the results of their work, often along numerous dimensions and sometimes using prescribed metrics. Yet the most effective nonprofits are often small, locally-situated shoestring operations unable to meet burdensome assessment requirements. Besides, as Schambra points out, "most nonprofits have developed programs based on the immediate day-to-day encounter with the specific, idiosyncratic communities they serve, hence exhibiting the almost infinite variety of those communities," and thus they are often faced with prescribed metrics that ill-fit their work. Throw in the problem that different funders use "different languages and metric frameworks," and you have created a recipe whereby small (and often innovative) nonprofits find it almost impossible to win grants, no matter how much good they may be doing on the ground.[14]

Philanthrolocalism offers an alternative philosophical foundation for the charitable practices of individuals and institutions. Philanthrolocalism is a philosophy of giving that prioritizes the use of resources to help one's own place, including one's neighbors, community members, churches, businesses, cultural institutions, civic associations, and ecology. Philanthrolocalists seeks to deploy resources to promote human flourishing and civic life in their own local communities. That—not "changing the world"—is their primary concern. If philanthrolocalism sounds as if it is based in the concept of old-fashioned charity, that is no accident.

The first and most basic principle of philanthrolocalism is the common insight that "we are not our own"—more colloquially, that no man is an island. This truism finds perennial expression in our philosophical heritage and in every one of the world's great religious and wisdom traditions. It means that every one of us owes, in part, our achievements, successes, prosperity, and even our very being to others. Except for true egomaniacs, we all know this, which is why our natural response to

---

14. William Schambra, "Mesmerized by Metrics: Is Philanthropy Engaged in Magical Thinking?" Speech given to Wallace Foundation on January 12, 2012, and available at http://www.hudson.org/research/8683-mesmerized-by-metrics-is-philanthropy-engaging-in-magical-thinking-.

success includes an expression of gratitude to those who helped make it possible.

Despite the insistence of countless business biographies, there is no such thing as a "self-made man." That does not mean that one cannot take legitimate pride in one's achievements, especially those that are the fruit of hard work, study, training, discipline, and other virtues. But even the most virtuous person cannot accomplish anything, cannot *become* virtuous, cannot achieve even a limited kind of independence, on his own.

We are the products of others: of the ancestors and families who gave us life and raised us, of the neighborhoods and communities and towns and cities that helped to form us, of the agricultural and ecological contexts that have sustained us, of the schools and teachers that have educated us, of the artists and musicians who have provided us with transcendent insights, of the churches and synagogues and mosques that have taught us about self-limitation and the divine.

The philanthrolocalist acknowledges the fact that we do not make ourselves. Most people, in fact, naturally wish to "give back" to the people and places that helped to form them. Philanthrolocalism affirms and encourages this completely natural and human desire—rather than belittling it or sneering at it, as the culture of Big Philanthropy too often does. Financially supporting our own places is one way we can acknowledge and express our gratitude to that which has made us what and who we are—and to that which continues to sustain us.

A second philanthrolocalist principle is that we have a primary responsibility to look after that which is closest to us. Certain obligations and duties are not chosen but are nevertheless ours by reason of birth and propinquity. That may not be fair, but it is still something that we all instinctively understand, even when we rebel against it.

These two principles are important, because contemporary philanthropists often tend to think of themselves as having no real obligations at all; they therefore fret about having no real guide for their giving. Recognizing this (purported) conundrum, one of the better books published in the field (*Give Smart*, by Thomas Tierney and Joel Fleishman) calls on philanthropists to be accountable to self-imposed "excellence"—not, one notes, to the moral obligations that are theirs simply by virtue of the people and places to which they belong.

A third principle consists of a recognition that the forces of modern life have conspired to fragment and weaken many, if not most, local communities. Despite the benefits they have produced, industrialization, globalization, mass culture, modern warfare, and geographic mobility, to name a few factors, have enriched the lives of a few fortunate places while depleting the vitality of many others. Giving locally is one way we can help rebuild communities across America, counteracting many of the trends that have weakened American democracy and created a very real kind of social injustice.

Now, philanthrolocalists do *not* believe that they should never give to national or international groups and causes. There are many reasons to give nationally and internationally. They do believe, however, that philanthropists ought not to skimp on helping their local communities—their own places—as a result of such giving.

The prioritization of local giving is often denigrated by the philanthropy industry because of a prejudice against rootedness. Most philanthrocrats share their class's suspicion of local communities. They tend to view such communities as bastions of racism, sexism, fundamentalism, and generally dangerous narrow-mindedness. The philanthropist's role is to weaken these communities, thereby making it possible to bring enlightenment to their members.

The value of particular local knowledge, networks, and affections is all but completely ignored by the philanthrocrats. Tachi Yamada, president of the Bill and Melinda Gates Foundation, was asked by the *New York Times* in 2010 what he looked for in new hires. His answer was revealing:

> I've made an observation about people. There are people who have moved. Take somebody who's a child of an Army officer—they will have moved 10 times in their lives. And then there are people who've been born and raised and educated and employed in one town their whole lives. Who do you think is willing to change? I think, in this modern world, you really have to be sure that your work force has the experience of being elsewhere. That experience then has the ability to ensure that you will be comfortable with change.[15]

In other words, despite philanthrocrats' big and brave talk about "changing the world," the one aspect of the contemporary world they have no desire to challenge is the way in which it undermines the possibility of stability, permanence, and placedness. One might think that there are certain unique advantages to be gained by long habitation in a particular

---

15. "Talk to Me. I'll Turn Off My Phone," *New York Times*, February 27, 2010. Online at http://www.nytimes.com/2010/02/28/business/28corner.html.

place, not the least of which are complex knowledge and affection. Why would you care deeply about a place you intend to leave at the next good opportunity? But to people like Yamada, the human attachments that come with such a life make for a bad foundation drone. Probably for a bad "global citizen," too.

An irrational hatred and suspicion of real communities is one reason Big Philanthropy stands opposed to philanthrolocalism. Another is that when they focus on local giving, individual donors and charitable foundations tend not to need extraordinary amounts of guidance from philanthropic experts. It's much easier to spot local needs, to evaluate which local organizations are most effective, and to assess the impact of one's local giving than it is to do any of these things with respect to national and international groups. Sophisticated metrics showing "impact" are made luxuries, not necessities. The questions one asks when one is giving locally also tend to be less abstract—and therefore to be answerable on the terms of everyday logic and common sense.

Finally, philanthropic elites unsurprisingly tend to share the prejudices of their class. Among these prejudices is the belief that to be sophisticated one must transcend the mundane affections and loyalties that drive local giving. As *Do More Than Give* and countless other books and articles make clear, one must think big, scientifically, and universally if one wants to be a *real* philanthropist. Giving in accord with one's natural loves, which are local and necessarily limited, betrays a lack of sophistication.

Away with such mystifications. To practice philanthrolocalism requires neither special training nor adherence to some secret teaching. When you give locally, to whatever organization or institution or cause you wish, you are practicing philanthrolocalism. The primary obstacle to practicing philanthrolocalism, in fact, may be a sense that what you are doing is not "important" or "strategic" enough—that local giving is for rubes. To be a philanthrolocalist, you must educate yourself *out* of the anti-localist prejudices that pervade American education and culture, and relearn the natural human language and sentiments of place.

This is not to say that to be an effective and responsible donor all you need to do is to give locally, and the rest will take care of itself. There are a few core principles that, if you adhere to them, will help you achieve more impact with your giving. For example, the conscientious donor will want to put into place systems that protect his or her donor intent, that evaluate how well or poorly grantees use their resources without burdening those grantees with red tape, and that help the donor build strong trusting relationships with grantees.

That is to name but three principles of a list that could be significantly lengthened. But these principles are generally encapsulated in the wise advice given by the progressive philanthropy scholar Pablo Eisenberg to Owen Lopez when he became the executive director of the McCune Charitable Foundation: "You identify people in community doing what needs to be done; you give them money; and you shut up."[16]

The effective donor need not—and probably should not—want to "change the world." It's hard enough to improve one's own block. Presidents and kings typically fail to "change the world," at least in a positive way, despite the best of intentions. The world—the social world, the world of human behavior, or what we call *culture*—is infinitely complex and infinitely beyond the comprehension of any one person or group of persons. As James Davison Hunter has shown in *To Change the World*, it is therefore inherently refractory to being shaped intentionally and decisively by anyone.[17]

As all localists know, the bigger you think, the more likely you are to fail and to bring about unforeseen consequences, some of which may be negative. It does not reflect poorly on the local thinker's cognitive powers to restrict his philanthropic planning to local matters; rather, it reflects his humility and wisdom.

There are many specific examples of donors acting consciously, intelligently, and creatively to strengthen their own places. For example, David Van Andel has said that his parents, Jay and Betty, "founded the Van Andel Institute in Grand Rapids not because it was the easiest place to establish a biomedical research institute, but because they wanted to share it with the community that had sustained and nurtured them." (It is a measure of the need today for a self-conscious philanthrolocalism that,

---

16. Anne Constable, After 18 Years Leading McCune Foundation and Championing Causes around New Mexico, Owen Lopez Steps Aside," *The New Mexican*, December 10, 2011. Online at http://www.nmccap.org/2011/12/after-18-years-leading-mccune-foundation-and-championing-causes-around-new-mexico-owen-lopez-steps-aside/.

17. James Davison Hunter, *To Change the World: The Irony, Tragedy, and Possibility of Christianity in the Late Modern World* (New York: Oxford University Press, 2010).

as the *Grand Rapids Press* reports, the rising generation of West Michigan philanthropists "tend to be more attracted to global rather than local issues.")[18]

In the economically depressed area of Tamaqua, Pennsylvania, two local foundations have provided extremely generous scholarships for local students to attend local colleges and universities. The result has been that dramatically fewer kids have decided to pull up roots, never to return, and the scholarship opportunities have even led to some families relocating to the area for their children's high school years.[19]

Needless to say, these kinds of efforts could be taken much further. What if a local foundation decided to help pay off local students' college loans if they were to return to their hometown areas after graduation? Such a program would have to be designed with care, in order to avoid creating disincentives for colleges to give financial aid or to keep tuition low. (In other words, if it were to have the same effect as the ridiculous federal student loan programs, then we're better off without it.) But this could be an especially attractive option for the brightest of local kids who amass considerable debt attending liberal-arts schools.

In any case, donors committed to helping a particular area flourish—that is, philanthrolocalists—need to start thinking about how to help keep talent, ambition, and energy at home. A wide dispersal of talent and intelligence is as necessary to the health of our country as is the Jeffersonian ideal of a wide distribution of property ownership.

It is even imaginable that individual foundations and/or professional associations of such foundations could voluntarily adopt benchmarks that provide standards for local giving. Surely this is a much better idea than the National Committee on Responsive Philanthropy's advocacy of governmentally mandated quotas for "diversity" giving. Besides being voluntary, and thus in line with the fine American tradition of free philanthropy, local-giving benchmarks would actually lead to increased real diversity among grantees.

Philanthrolocalism also has strong affinities with other manifestations of the new localist revival, including the buy-local and locavore movements. These movements recognize that industrial agriculture and the mass transportation on which it depends is destructive of the natural

18. "Shandra Martinez, "Grandchildren of Prominent West Michigan Donors Are Shaping the Future of Local Philanthropy," *Grand Rapids Press*, December 11, 2011.

19. Kate Maternowski, "Small Towns, Big Scholarships," *Inside Higher Ed*, May 14, 2009.

world, and hence unsustainable. They believe that local food is typically fresher, healthier, and safer. And they recognize that by shopping and eating locally they are helping to sustain an important part of the local economy.

Philanthrolocalism extends many of the same insights to charitable giving. Because by giving locally we are better able to see the consequences of our own actions, we are also less likely to be destructive. The realm of unintended consequences—the bane of all philanthropists—tends to be narrower and more limited. Eating locally and buying locally can in fact be regarded as expressions of philanthrolocalism.

To practice philanthrolocalism, every donor and would-be philanthropist should ask the following four questions when planning his or her giving:

1. How well will you be able to "see" the effects of your giving—that is, to evaluate its impact?
2. Does your giving reflect the relative strength of the moral claims that others—including your local community—have on you?
3. Does your giving express gratitude to those people, communities, institutions, and places that have made your success possible?

Will your giving strengthen the ability of your community to contribute to the flourishing of its members?

To rebuild our communities and replenish our social capital, we need more people asking themselves these questions before giving. For they are questions inspired by love—charity, *caritas*—rather than by ideological ambitions to remake the world. Surely we know by now that we do better to go into battle with Brownson and Solzhenitsyn on our side than with Robespierre and Lenin.

Philanthropy's War on Community

WILLIAM A. SCHAMBRA

WRITING IN 1952, RAYMOND Fosdick, long-time president of the Rockefeller Foundation, provided this description of its first board meeting in 1913:

> The question which faced the trustees as they sat down to their first meeting was how the broad objective of their charter was to be implemented. What constitutes the "well-being of mankind throughout the world?" A large number of applications had already been received, and it is significant that they were all declined, including one from the YMCA for the rehabilitation of buildings located in Dayton, Hamilton, and Marietta, which had been damaged in the recent floods along the Ohio River Valley. Mr. [Frederick T.] Gates phrased the objection: "The Rockefeller Foundation should in general confine itself to projects of an important character, too large to be undertaken, or otherwise unlikely to be undertaken, by other agencies." This was in line with the emphasis which Mr. Rockefeller himself, six years earlier, had placed on what he called "finalities." "The best philanthropy," he had said, "involves a search for cause, an attempt to cure evils at their source."[1]

Here, at the inaugural gathering of what was at the time the world's largest foundation, was enunciated the doctrine that has governed mainstream American philanthropy for much of its existence. Local communities might approach foundations with requests for projects like helping to repair damage done to beloved and vital village institutions. But the wise far-sighted patricians running the foundations knew that these

---

1. Raymond Fosdick, *The Story of the Rockefeller Foundation* (1952; New Brunswick: Transaction, 1989), 22.

would just be stop-gap efforts to address the most superficial effects of society's problems.

Such niggling small-bore projects, however, were all one could expect from benighted local yokels, entrapped as they were by moral and religious world-views that barely extended beyond the village boundaries. Look at these towns in Ohio—they honestly thought that Christianity had something to teach young men! Happily for the villagers, though, the cosmopolitan patricians now had available to them an instrument that could reach all the way down to the "finalities" so important to John D. Rockefeller. The newly emerging natural and social sciences of the early 20th century enabled us to probe beneath the superficial manifestations of problems and penetrate to their very core, their root cause.

So the first modern American foundations—Carnegie, Rockefeller, and Russell Sage—devoted themselves to developing these new sciences through support for such research universities as Johns Hopkins and Chicago, such think tanks as Brookings, and such coordinating agencies as the Social Science Research Council. The professional elites trained in these world-class institutions would have the expertise necessary to guide, shape, and mold the American people. Psychology and sociology would find the uniform rules of human behavior beneath all of its confusing and superficial diversity so lamentably reflected in America's small communities. Political science would teach us how to reorganize public life according to those rules, moving us away from divisive state and local allegiances, toward an inspiring and ennobling great national community, quietly and rationally administered by cosmopolitan elites according to the unassailably objective principles of scientific management.

Among the most valuable of the sciences supported by the first foundations was the emerging study of human biology known as eugenics. Thanks to the rediscovery of Mendel's laws of biological inheritance at the beginning of the 20th century, we now knew what the root cause of human pathology truly was: namely, bad genes. Nearly every form of human misbehavior or misfortune—from promiscuity to shiftlessness to dipsomania to the all-encompassing "feeble-mindedness"—could be traced back to defective "protoplasm."

And so America's major philanthropies eagerly poured their resources into the promising science of eugenics. Carnegie, Rockefeller, and Mrs. E. H. Harriman (as the widow of the railroad magnate always called herself) provided the funds for Harvard biologist Charles Davenport to establish the Eugenics Record Office (ERO) at Cold Spring Harbor in

New York in 1911. The ERO would be the international center for eugenics research and public policy advocacy until it was finally closed in 1939—when even its philanthropic sponsors could not fail to heed the ominous signals emanating from Germany about the implications of a vigorous eugenics program.

If philanthropy in general was hostile to local community, eugenics was doubly so. Nowhere is this more apparent than in Charles Davenport's magnum opus entitled *Heredity in Relation to Eugenics*, published in 1911 and dedicated to Mrs. E. H. Harriman. Davenport and the ERO may be remembered today chiefly for their concern about the promiscuous importation of defective protoplasm from the villages and shtetls of Eastern Europe, which led to the severely restrictive immigration law of 1924. In fact, however, a larger concern for Davenport was the dangerous accumulation of defective and decaying protoplasm within America's all-too-prevalent jerkwater local communities. As he put it, "negative traits multiply most in long established and stable communities where much inbreeding occurs, while positive traits are increased by emigration, as a fire is spread by the wind that scatters firebrands." Inbreeding (or consanguineous marriage) and the concentration of defectiveness is more likely where people stay put, while "a restless people will show a small percentage of negative traits."[2]

The problem is that when the laudably restless and ambitious move on, as they always had since colonial times, "the weaker minds were left behind to breed in the old homestead."[3] Too many such "old homesteads," in Davenport's view, had been established and maintained in America by groups that tended to cling—perhaps even *bitterly*—to distinctive and exclusive ethnic, moral, and religious ways of life, each of which became a breeding ground for genetic defect.

Even the very geography of America seemed to promote concentrations of defectiveness. Davenport includes in his book a map of the Eastern seaboard, with this caption: "Coast of eastern North America, showing the broken coast line, with islands and peninsulas, each of which is, more or less, a center of consanguineous marriages. Such centers can be picked out by looking at the map." Wherever there's some relatively inaccessible but nonetheless inhabited geographical nook or cranny—some rocky islet, some marshy point, some remote valley, some treacherous

---

2. Charles Davenport, *Heredity in Relation to Eugenics* (New York: Henry Holt, 1911), 182.

3. *Ibid.*, 211.

mountain range—genetic defects tend to become trapped and multiply, like so many diverticular pathogens. Davenport singled out our northernmost coastline for particular opprobrium, noting that "the islands off the coast of Maine show much consanguineous marriage."[4]

Smarting from such shameful depictions in both scholarly and popular literature, the state of Maine decided to take action against one such consanguineous island cesspool the year after the publication of Davenport's book. The year 2012 marked the centenary of Governor Frederick Plaisted's bold effort to solve once and for all the eugenic problem of Malaga Island. Malaga is today a 42-acre nature preserve in the New Meadows River. But until 1912 it housed a thriving community of some 40 residents—whites, blacks, and biracials—most of whose families had lived and intermarried there since the 1840s. Those who have read the Newbery Prize-winning book from 2005 entitled *Lizzie Bright and the Buckminster Boy* will recognize this story.

The islanders eked out a proudly independent way of life through subsistence farming, fishing, lobstering, and odd jobs on the mainland. But to savvy mainlanders armed with the science of root causes, the flimsy shanties, peculiar ways, and especially the mixed blood of the Malaga Islanders all suggested ominous subterranean genetic faults. And so in the spring of 1912 the state of Maine abruptly evicted all the residents of Malaga Island. As befitted a eugenic solution, one fifth of the islanders were sent to the newly opened Maine School for the Feeble-Minded in West Pownal, where most of them lived out their lives as involuntary residents.

No buildings were left standing on Malaga, and—lest former inhabitants entertain notions of having any remaining roots there—even the graveyard was unceremoniously dug up, with the remains thrown into five large caskets and reburied on the grounds of the school for the feeble-minded, where they rest today.

The Malaga Island clearance has justly been described as the most shameful episode in Maine history. However, Malaga is just one episode in the long and tragic story of eugenics in America. It seemed to justify the mandatory institutionalization of hundreds of thousands of so-called defectives—and the involuntary sterilization of some 60,000 American citizens. And that's to say nothing of the inspiration it provided for similar genetic purification programs around the world.

4. *Ibid.*, 190–91.

Today, the governors of the states most enthusiastic about sterilization have apologized for their eugenics programs. North Carolina is moving toward compensation for surviving sterilization victims, and Maine recently deplored its role in the events of 1912. The Maine State Museum's current exhibit "Malaga Island, Fragmented Lives," captures the state's regret.

Nonetheless, the foundations that provided the financial support for eugenics have never issued formal apologies. Indeed, if you look under "e" in the index of any of the leading histories of American philanthropy you will not find the word "eugenics."

In an ironic footnote to the Malaga episode, however, the former grounds of the Maine School for the Feeble-minded, which was known as the Pineland Center when it closed in 1996, have been purchased and redeveloped by Maine's largest private philanthropy, the Libra Foundation. Libra presents a vivid contrast to the giving philosophy of the early Rockefeller and Carnegie Foundations.

Although Libra's endowment comes from Elizabeth Noyce and her portion of the globe-bestriding Intel fortune, it has happily focused its giving entirely within the state of Maine. In its hands, Pinelands today features a working farm, producing its own cheese, natural meats, organic eggs, maple syrup, strawberry jam and seasonal fresh produce. It also has an equestrian center, a much-admired public garden, and building space for lease to small local businesses and nonprofits. As Pinelands' guide puts it, "Tenants enjoy amenities on the campus such as a conference center, cafeteria and"—in a delicious counterpoint to the first Rockefeller board meeting—a "*YMCA.*"

In short, rather than waging war on local community in the name of tracking down root causes, Libra is trying to shore up the cultural and economic underpinnings of local community and do so on the very site of one of the "root cause" approach's most despicable crimes.

To be sure, not all of Libra's initiatives have been successful or popular. Its real estate ventures and its effort to build a self-sustaining Public Market in Portland have come under considerable criticism from Mainers. An effort by Libra in 2000 to open a new center at Pinelands for individuals with disabilities was turned back with particular vigor.

But that's the point. Mainers know precisely where to take their complaints, because Libra is devoted not to the "well-being of mankind throughout the world"[5] but rather to the well-being of this one small struggling state whose residents live and work beside those who run the foundation.

One additional irony of the eugenics movement is worth noting. We are urged today to regard progressivism as the tribune of America's low-income ethnic communities. And yet no one was more enthusiastically eugenicist than such founders of progressivism as Theodore Roosevelt, Woodrow Wilson, and Herbert Croly. They shared Davenport's deep concern about the idiocy of local community life, along with its ignorance, narrow-mindedness, and bigotry. They yearned for an expansive, unified, homogeneous national community, within which all ethnic, religious and moral distinctions would disappear, along with their pathological genetic concentrations.

Yet in the face of that homogenizing and nationalizing impulse it was precisely the tiny island community of Malaga that stood for a degree of racial harmony and intermixture almost unheard of at the turn of the 20th century. And so it has often been throughout American history: the small communities so offensive to sophisticated American writers and intellectuals in fact end up providing the surest refuge for racial minorities, religious dissenters, and cultural renegades.

At any rate, I wish someone from Maine would approach the Libra Foundation with the following proposition. Those lonely graves from Malaga at the back of the Pinelands site should be unearthed once more and transported with dignity and ceremony back to a suitably restored cemetery among the red spruce trees of the Malaga Island nature preserve.

But the cost shouldn't be borne entirely by Libra. It should be shared by the Carnegie and Rockefeller Foundations, as modest down payments against the day they embrace their own shameful past in the war against American communities and begin to reorient their giving accordingly.

---

5. Fosdick, 279.

Part Eight

Technology and Popular Culture

The system of nature, of which man is a part, tends to be self-balancing, self-adjusting, self-cleansing. Not so with technology.

—E.F. SCHUMACHER, *SMALL IS BEAUTIFUL*

Technology, Mobility and Community

Christine Rosen

WHAT IS THE DIFFERENCE between a mobile community and a neighborhood? It wasn't that long ago that we had no need to ask such a question. Neighborhoods and the local communities of which they were a part used to define us not merely physically—as Southerners, or New Yorkers, or Midwesterners—but also emotionally. Mobility was the opposite. To leave the place where you were born was to disconnect from far more than geography. It presented the opportunity to forge a new identity and join a new community elsewhere.

Americans have understood this kind of mobility as a positive thing, tied as it is to notions of exploration and reinvention. Mobility means freedom, as contemporary telecommunications companies frequently remind us in their advertisements. But it is a qualitatively different kind of freedom from that of the past. Consider telecommunications advertisements from just twenty or thirty years ago: Bell System's slogan "Reach out and touch someone," for example, emphasized face-to-face human connection. The company's advertisements assumed that we would prefer to see our loved ones face to face. If we couldn't, the ads suggested, then a conversation on the telephone was the next-best thing.

Contemporary telecommunications companies emphasize something fundamentally different: individual control over the terms of communication. Sprint calls itself "The NOW Network" and promises you the ability to do business, talk to friends, and travel the globe, all "without limits" and on your own terms; AT&T urges us to "Rethink Possible." In many of its commercials people are celebrated for preferring mediated forms of conversation. In one advertisement, two men sit together in a coffee shop conducting a business meeting by sending emails back and forth to each other rather than speaking. This, we are told, is the communication style of the network—far-flung, instantaneous, convenient, controlled—not that of the neighborhood.

But this technology-enhanced mobility hasn't obviated our human need for physical connection and community. The difference today is that more and more of us are seeking those communities online. How do these online communities differ from our real-world communities? How do our relationships change when they occur in the virtual world rather than the physical world? Is our eager embrace of technologically mediated forms of community encouraging us to define community down?

The movement of community from the physical world to the virtual has had undeniable benefits for many of us. Nonetheless, it has also created significant challenges to our traditional experiences of community. Two changes in particular are worth noting: the commodification of community, and the transformation of behavior in public communal space.

Both of these transformations are well illustrated by a new popular activity: mobile geotagging. Mobile geotagging services such as Foursquare and Google Locate, which use GPS tracking to link online content to an individual's physical location, are marketed as community-building services. By bringing the online world's immediacy and broad social networking capabilities into real-world physical spaces, these services, so we are told, encourage people to meet up and form social ties. In fact, sociologists who study online behavior consider geotagging a new kind of social activity, a way for individuals to participate in the "social production of space." Geotagging makes the digital world physical and the physical world digital at the same time.

Here's an example. Socialight, a mobile geotagging service founded in 2005, allowed people to leave virtual "sticky notes" at various locations throughout New York City. Let's say you are curious about a new restaurant in your neighborhood. With Socialight, you could pull out your smartphone, sign in to Socialight, and read someone else's recent musings about the menu. After you eat there, you could leave your own remarks for future users of the service. Socialight's marketing material emphasized its local credentials, encouraging users to see themselves as part of a small, in-the-know network of users who functioned online much like neighbors do in the real world. What's not to like?

The evolution of Socialight offers some insights for answering this question. In 2011 the company was acquired by an organization called Group Commerce, which sells geotagging services to businesses so that those businesses can better track their customers' behavior. Here is how Group Commerce, now renamed Nimble Commerce, described its mission on its website in 2011:

> Imagine a world in which you can walk the streets of New York City and have curated deals automatically delivered to your smartphone based on virtually any criteria—your location, past consumption history, the time of day, or the proximity of your Facebook friends. Imagine that those deals are provided alongside crowd-sourced reviews, as well as related feature articles from your favorite publications (e.g. *The New York Times*) about the neighborhood you're in, the history of the restaurants offering deals (if available), interviews with the chefs, and much more. A compelling vision? Absolutely.

Setting aside the somewhat Orwellian tones of this supposedly "compelling vision," the overarching purpose of businesses such as these is not, in fact, building community but *monetizing* it. The remarks you leave about a local pub become fodder for a company's future pitch to advertisers who want to sell you things. If this is a community, it is a peculiar new form, because it makes products of its own participants.

We mobile citizens wielding our smartphones might think of ourselves as members of a vast virtual community, connected wherever we go and flush with useful information. But the companies that sell us this mobility and control this information see us first and foremost as *consumers*—moving targets whose behavior and buying habits can and should be tracked at a granular level. Their goal for us is not that we form coherent communities; their goal is to capture our attention so that they can commodify our future experiences. And the more attention we give them, the less we have to offer to people in our real-world communities.

Another way our new mobile technologies challenge community is by transforming our notions of physical place. If, as we have been encouraged to believe, virtual communities are as rich and rewarding as physical ones, it is worth asking how our participation in them changes our behavior in physical space: do we act differently when we are in close physical proximity to others, and how important is this for weakening or deepening the bonds of community and social life?

For most of our history, civil society has been rooted in particular physical places—plazas, sidewalks, neighborhoods, cafes, and taverns. My great-grandfather immigrated to the United States from what was then called Bohemia (now the Czech Republic) in the late nineteenth century. As soon as he scraped together enough money he opened a tavern. He could think of no better way to set down roots in his new adoptive homeland than to create a physical space where community could flourish through food and socializing. And for fifty years that is what he did, making his little outpost a local legend for its weekly fish fries and friendly atmosphere.

What happens when these kinds of socializing activities migrate online, or when the online aspect of the activity overlays the physical experience of place, as it does with mobile geotagging services?

The mobile geotagging service Foursquare provides an example. "With Foursquare, you can unlock your world and find happiness right around the corner," the service's website explains. The company created a badge system that encourages users to "check in" multiple times at a particular location. "Check in at a location more than anyone else and you become mayor," the company's website explains. "You don't get a key to the city, but you might get rewards from certain businesses just for being a loyal customer." Check into twenty-five different venues and you get an "Explorer" badge. Check in at the gym enough and earn a "gym rat" badge. And to earn a Foursquare "Local" badge you must check in to the same location more than three times in one week.

What is wrong with this? Aren't these new technologies encouraging us to leave our private worlds and venture out into public space, as Foursquare promises?

Yes and no. Users of Foursquare are encouraged to go out into public space—but they will earn badges only if they publicize their activities in a Foursquare-sponsored location. Foursquare badges are linked to companies and products such as Starbucks, *The Today Show*, the Bravo Network, and *Lucky* magazine. And their badges promote an instrumental and consumerist approach to real-world relationships. There is a badge for "Groupie" but not "Friend," for "Babysitter," but not "Mother" or "Father," for example.

Something else is at work here too: a suggestion that the engineered algorithms of such services offer a more rewarding experience than the real-world alternative. Foursquare, like other geotagging services, encourages its users to use its service wherever they go. "In museums. At airports. On public transportation. During concerts. You never know when you might come across a little planned serendipity," the company's website states. The notion of "planned serendipity" is popular among technology enthusiasts. In an interview he gave in 2010 when he was still CEO of Google, Eric Schmidt claimed serendipity "can be calculated now. We can actually produce it electronically."

How do people actually behave in a world where public space is overlaid with virtual sticky notes, consumer badges, check-ins, and buzzing mobile devices? They might experience individual moments of manufactured serendipity (Starbucks just texted me a coupon for half-off a latte!), but thus far it hasn't led to many serendipitous social interactions. On the contrary, it has dramatically undermined them, as a study of wi-fi use in public spaces by a professor at the Annenberg School of Communication at the University of Pennsylvania demonstrates. In 2010, Professor Keith Hampton and his students observed wi-fi users in public spaces in Philadelphia, New York City, San Francisco, and Toronto. What they report suggests that those who argue that mobile technologies are improving the social life of public spaces are engaging in a fairly elaborate exercise in wishful thinking.

Assessing the wi-fi and mobile phone users in public space, Hampton found that, *contra* Foursquare and Mr. Schmidt, they "were considerably less likely to participate in serendipitous social exchanges of any type." Nearly 80 percent of the users he observed were alone and immune to polite overtures from strangers, prompting Hampton to concede, "a high density of wi-fi use thus appears to reduce public sociability."

Nevertheless, like many techno-enthusiasts, Hampton offered a more Panglossian take on his own findings. He gushed to *Smithsonian* magazine that people with their heads buried in their laptops "are not alone in the true sense," because although they are ignoring the people around them, they reported to him that they *felt* engaged because they were checking into Facebook. "We found that the types of things that they are doing online often look a lot like political engagement," Hampton said, "like sharing information and having discussions about important matters." This might well be true, but should we really call people who are scrolling through the Huffington Post active participants in the public sphere, as Hampton does?

I think not. Although we are still in the early stages of this transformation of public space, it is not unreasonable to be concerned that technologically-savvy citizens who prefer to engage with the private worlds of their screens instead of the public activities of social space might, en masse, have a negative impact on community and social life. As well, when our engagement with virtual communities—on Facebook, LinkedIn, Twitter, or Foursquare—interferes with our ability to interact with others in public space, we risk contributing to an already growing intolerance for the people with whom we must physically coexist—on the bus, waiting in line, in the grocery store. How many of us have witnessed someone talking on a cell phone throughout an entire exchange at a store cash register, never once acknowledging the human being ringing up that person's groceries? How many of us have done this ourselves? Such mundane indignities have a cumulative effect on the quality of public space and public life.

Finally, it is worth asking whether virtual communities can offer the same sort of support and investment in their members that traditional ones do. Communities aren't just places where we have fun and socialize. They are where we raise our children and where we get sick and where we end up when we are old. Foursquare doesn't offer badges for check-ins at your local nursing home.

Critics of our current infatuation with technology are often chastised for downplaying the communal aspects of the Internet, and rightly so. The web's power to connect us has transformed social and intellectual life in many beneficial ways. Physical communities flourish online by connecting their members and keeping them informed of each other's activities. But the ascendant view, which encourages uncritical enthusiasm for the blurring of the line between the real and the virtual, is becoming increasingly impossible to avoid (try to find a college student who isn't on Facebook, for example). It also poses challenges to what it means to be an engaged member of a real community.

Scholars in the field of computer-mediated communication now write about the future as a time when many of us will exist in a state of "polysocial reality"—a world where wearable sensors monitor our physical bodies, sending information back to doctors or family members while we Tweet about our latest purchase and use GPS on our smartphones to navigate to our next destination, which we will promptly geotag. Foursquare and other mobile geotagging services are the leading edge of this trend, but the era of wearable sensors and monitors will soon be upon us.

What does community look like in this new world? It is worth noting that the people who write about this future talk in their work about "humans"—not people, not families, not husbands and wives and children and sisters and brothers. Humans. As opposed to machines—the machines that will nudge and guide and inform us at an increasing rate. The hope of the machines' programmers is apparently that the creators of manufactured serendipity will so perfect their algorithms that we never need worry about missing out on an appropriate experience (or, more likely, an appropriate purchase) and that we never need rely on a tool as crude as our own intuition.

And yet our current online communities have not delivered a new and improved form of community. In many ways they have given us only an unsatisfactory substitute for real community. We talk about "sharing" in our online communities, but what we share Facebook and Foursquare and others monetize. We sign on to these communities to "connect," and yet we do so at the expense of those around us in physical space. On a broader social scale, there is also this paradox: at a time when we are more "connected" to each other than ever before, we are also, as a country, experiencing higher rates of social isolation. (For example, research from the General Social Survey found that between 1985 and 2004 the number of people who reported having no one with whom they could discuss "important matters" tripled.)

Today we store our data and the details of our personal lives in the Cloud, a metaphor that is evocative of both the positive and negative qualities of our online communities. The Cloud is highly mobile and accessible; like a network, the cloud is *everywhere*. The challenge for the future of community is to continue to cultivate places—neighborhoods, parks, taverns, and gathering spaces—where people can come down from the cloud and instead be, definitively, physically, *somewhere*.

Our Hookup Culture

Susan McWilliams[1]

AMONG YOUNG AMERICANS, "HOOKING UP" has been common, both as a term and as a behavioral norm, for more than a quarter of a century. The *Oxford English Dictionary* says the term dates to 1989 (although I first heard it in the early 1990s), used then as it is now to describe fooling around—that is, doing anything from kissing to having what my sister calls "sexy bedtimes"—with someone who is not necessarily involved with you in an established romantic relationship. "Hookup culture," as it is often called, predates even the earliest swells of the Internet. And while the last years have been marked by much ballyhooed technological "disruption" of daily life, nothing seems to have disrupted the dominance of hooking up in the social world of adolescence.

To listen to most pundits, though, you wouldn't know how long hookup culture has been around. Probably in service to sensationalism, media accounts continue to present hooking up as if it is some newfangled post-millennial innovation, like tweets or emojis. But the truly sensational truth is that hooking up isn't all that sensational anymore: the practice is a well-established rite of our passages, and hookup culture is at this point not an exceptional but traditional part of growing up in America. For better or worse, hooking up is a prevalent social standard, and most young Americans today have to navigate hookup culture, whether it be with relish or reluctance or resistance (or some combination of all three).

I think about the college students I teach today, students who were born into a world in which the term and norm of the hookup has always existed. Even with all that seems to have changed about the world in their

---

1. I want to thank Sarah Blumenthal and Amanda Shapiro, both former students of mine at Pomona College, for doing as undergraduates some of the research that I reference in this essay.

lifetimes, and with all the ways in which their college experiences differ from mine, those Y2K babies talk about hooking up much in the same way my friends and I talked about hooking up, back when we were their age, back in a previous century.

In fact, when an advisee recently showed me a campus "hookup chart" that she and her friends had compiled, I was whisked back in time to my own college days. For I must confess: two decades ago, when I was an undergraduate, my friends and I on the campus newspaper staff put together our own "hookup chart," a chart in which we tried to see how many people on campus we could connect with each other via hookup. The answer, an answer that we found more exciting than upsetting, was that we could connect almost half the members of the student body to one another.

As I recall it now, that hookup chart was a work of art for our times, an intricate tapestry of body-fluid-trading that ranged from the romantic to the grotesque, a damning and succinct depiction of what contemporary "social networking" looks like in dimensions that Facebook does not (yet) capture. Under our careful editorial tutelage, the hookup chart went viral. It took on a life of its own. People all over campus started asking us about it, divulging the intimate behaviors of their friends and roommates, proffering news of their own recent trysts, hoping to merit addition to our semi-public record. The hookup chart became an entity in and of itself, a taped-together leviathan that topped out at more than six feet tall and eight feet long: an unwieldy written testament to the unwieldy tangle of bodies and lips that was then Amherst College.

In hindsight, we made that chart for a lot of reasons. Some of those reasons are obvious, like the fact that it's titillating to talk about other people's sex lives, and it's intoxicating to amass other people's secrets, and it's thrilling, sometimes, to reveal secrets of your own. But really, I think, we were trying, in our admittedly clumsy and vulgar way, to make sense of the cultural waters in which we found ourselves swimming. We were literally trying to chart—to plot or organize or see—what all that hooking up amounted to, what shape it took, and what it revealed about the nature of our lives.

My students today are, today, asking the same kinds of questions. That's indirectly evident in their creation of hookup charts (and their occasional presentation of those charts to professors in advising meetings). It's even more directly evident in other ways. For example, a few years ago one of the student groups on my campus organized a professorial panel titled "Hookups: Why We Don't Date," and more than a quarter of the student body attended. During the question and answer component of the event, the line for the microphone stretched toward the door.

My students today, and my friends and I twenty years ago, are not alone in wanting to interrogate hookup culture. Lots of people have tried to make sense of hooking up, especially in the last decade or so. Probably the first person to get a lot of attention for making this effort was Thomas Wolfe, whose novel *I Am Charlotte Simmons* (2004) was heralded as an intimate view of an emerging hookup culture in which hooking up takes precedence over earlier modes of dating and courtship. In subsequent years, a series of more-or-less sociological books on hooking up have been written (interestingly, almost all by women). These include, most prominently, Kathleen Bogle's *Hooking Up* (2008), Donna Freitas's *The End of Sex* (2013), and Laura Sessions Stepp's *Unhooked* (2008).

But most of those works, and others like them, are written or marketed in the tones of presentist sensationalism that I mentioned before. Because they tend to be set up in a tantalizing you'll-never-believe-what-the-kids-are-up-to-these-days mode, they exclaim a lot more than they explain. (Typical in this regard is Charlotte Allen's 2010 cover story in *The Weekly Standard*, "The New Dating Game," in which the author describes a social world in which all the old manners and restraints have fallen away, in which "Cro-Magnons are once again dragging their mates into their caves by their hair—and the women love every minute of it.") To the extent that explanations for the dominance of hookup culture are offered at any length in these books, they tend to circle around a series of relatively predictable claims. Specifically, they suggest that hookup culture has emerged because of:

1. *the decline of religious belief*, which used to encourage people to limit sexual activity outside marriage or formal courtship;
2. *the sexual revolution*, which legitimized sex outside of dating and marriage;
3. *feminism*, which told women to embrace their own sexual desires and act on them;
4. *medical technology*, which makes it easier for women to prevent pregnancy and easier for everyone to treat venereal disease;
5. *legalized abortion*, which means that pregnancies can be made to disappear; and

6. *lenient universities*, where lax administrators all but throw students into bed with each other by offering up coed dormitories and keg parties and free condoms.

There is certainly some truth to all of those explanations—a truth reflected on an early episode of HBO's "Sex and the City," in which one character opines that contemporary womanhood is defined by the ability to "have sex like a man."

Yet these explanations do not explain as well as they might. They smack too much of calling in the usual suspects, and they fail to take stock of the cultural whole.

A more holistic response, I think, comes from moving beyond the idea that hookup culture is a curiosity of the immediate moment, and from moving beyond the impulse to scandalize with stories of sexual excess (oral sex rings! rainbow parties!) that say more about the prurience of older people than the practices of younger ones. When you get beyond that idea and impulse, and see hooking up as more enduringly and banally placed in the culture, you begin to see the extent to which hooking up is almost bound to emerge as a norm among young adults in a large-scale society where mobility is highly prized and cultivated—in other words, a society like ours.

In such a society, young people are schooled early in the lessons of living with transience. Growing up in a country like this one, in which the average person moves twelve times in his or her lifetime and 43 million people move each year, it is hard not to become convinced, pretty early on, that most relationships are bound to have quick-arriving expiration dates. In the United States, such teen movies as *American Pie* (1999) remind us that the culmination of compulsory education—high-school graduation—is a ritual of separation. Everyone who attends an American high school does so with the expectation that it ends in the breaking apart of a community, not in integration into a community. (This probably explains why all teen television dramas fall apart when the characters graduate high school; for American audiences, it is implausible that a group of high-school friends would remain friends after commencement.) For young people who attend college, the cycle of separation repeats four years later.

Americans learn early—and most of us are reminded often—that the structures of our existence force mobility upon us, whether we would choose to be mobile or not. And it seems to me that adolescents, just as they are all juiced up with the kind of hormones that make you want to touch other people, get hit with that lesson the hardest.

If you come of age in that kind of circumstance, learning that lesson, a certain wariness about the prospects for long-term relationships is pragmatic, is realistic. If all your experiences have led you to believe that relational and community life are ephemeral at best (or to believe that your life is a "series of disconnected emotional episodes," to borrow a phrase from my teacher Hadley Arkes), you have good reason to pursue very short-term engagements with other people, engagements where little if anything is promised beyond the present moment. You have very good reason to develop the kind of superficial friendliness for which Americans are known around the world. And you have very good reason to pursue hookups rather than more serious romances.

Think again about *American Pie*, which is not merely a movie about young people who are about to graduate high school and leave each other but specifically a movie about young people who are trying to have sex before they graduate high school and leave each other. The movie captures so well the fact that in this culture sexuality emerges in the context of diaspora. In going through puberty, the American teenager moves toward what he or she knows is an imminent social scattering. So in the United States, as is so memorably depicted in *American Pie*, your first pursuits or experiences of sex are likely to involve people who you know are not going to be around for long. It's not hard to think that this formative moment creates powerful associations and anxieties for most of us, wherein desire is fraught with a particular kind of anxiety about relational collapse. In that context, it's sensible to try to protect oneself by attaching to other people as minimally as possible—bodily, on the surface—rather than risking the heartbreak and horror of losing the people you have let yourself love, and losing them again and again.

Several years ago I had a research assistant do a series of interviews with college students about hookup culture. One of the things that many of them said was that they were not interested in dating (and certainly not interested in getting married) until they were sure that they could "settle down"—a term they meant often in the literal sense. They expected to move around quite a bit in their twenties, to have to seek additional training and then chase down gainful employment, wherever it might be. They accepted the idea—an idea reinforced by parents, teachers, advisors, and their own observations—that they should be prepared not just to have multiple jobs in their lives but multiple careers, and that those careers would take them in many different directions, to many different places. With those expectations, why should we be surprised that they tended to seek the kinds of short-term entanglements that fit better within the constraints of such a life?

With expectations of transience and impermanence, why should we be surprised that hookup culture has become so dominant, and has had such staying power, among young Americans? And why should we be surprised to see the extension of hookup culture into the lives of older Americans as well?

Consider Ryan Bingham, the character played by George Clooney in *Up in the Air* (2009), a film which resonated deeply with American audiences—racking up box-office dollars, critical acclaim, and a number of industry awards. In *Up in the Air*, Bingham is a middle-aged man whose job keeps him constantly on the road, who more than anything else takes pride in the number of frequent-flyer miles he has been able to accumulate. For him, mobility is the thing, both the means and ends of his being. He equates moving around with moving forward in his life. We are thus not surprised to learn that Bingham's encounters with women rarely last longer than a night, or that he has never even approached the point of getting married. As the movie progresses, it becomes apparent that even if Bingham wanted to pursue the longer-term pleasures of love or the deeper satisfactions of family and household life, the circumstances of his existence are arrayed against their realization. His life is one in which the landscape is always shifting, where bodies are never in the same place for long, where it is hard even to *think* about how to find the grounding necessary for relational and romantic stability. That kind of grounding is oppositional—in a literal as well as metaphorical sense—to being "up in the air."

My purpose here is not to berate or to vindicate hookup culture. Rather, I want to emphasize that if people are interested in understanding the sexual behavior of American young adults, it is worth revisiting the conditions in which we raise those young adults and the lessons that those young adults pick up by cultural experience and training.

Even where there used to be some alternative model for emulation in the American panorama, there is now just the monolith of the mobile. Professional sports teams, which Christopher Lasch lauded in the 1970s for exemplifying the countercultural virtues of rootedness and constancy, have long since become dominated by the movements of free agency and franchise relocation. And among politicians, who used to be derided as carpetbaggers if they were anything other than native sons, transience is now par for the course. In the Election of 2008, for instance, both the Democratic and Republican candidates for the presidency, as Peggy Noonan put it, weren't "from anywhere." Both John McCain and Barack Obama had itinerant childhoods, spent at least part of their lives living outside the continental United States, and had gotten elected to the Senate in states where they had not lived for long. Notably, that last trait did not make McCain or Obama unusual within the United States Senate; more than a decade before, the percentage of Senators born outside the state they represented had reached forty. And for whatever else the technological gadgets of the last fifteen years have done, they have made it easier to be mobile. We call so many of them "mobile devices," in fact, because we understand that their mobility enables our own.

It is not just that the facts of American existence point toward mobility: we have also long acknowledged mobility as an ideal of American existence. Americans tend to talk about mobility as if it is equivalent to success. We associate geographic mobility with achievement; the students whom we deem "the best" in high school tend to travel long distances to attend college. We describe "professional mobility" as a desirable trait, signifying elite status and flexibility. We laud "social mobility." And, of course, we use the term "class mobility" as a way to describe one of the central ideals of American life.

There are lots of good reasons we Americans tend to praise mobility. We praise it because it is our inheritance; as Americans are fond of saying, (almost) all of us come from immigrant families. We praise mobility because we associate it with being free; Hannah Arendt once said that physical mobility is the oldest and most elementary form of freedom. We praise mobility because it exposes us to diversity and variety. We praise mobility because we believe that it affords us certain opportunities and possibilities for self-determination that might not be available to us in more place-bound conditions.

But of course, as many Front Porch Republic writers have said in one way or another, there are serious costs to living in a culture where mobility is so highly valued. One of those is that mobility puts great pressure on (and even works to dismantle) all sorts of human relationships: extended families, long-term friendships, marriages, and so on.

Mobility also shapes our expectations for relationships from the outset. It suggests that few of our relationships are likely to be defined by sustained physical proximity, that physical proximity to any given person is something that will pass quickly. The daily workings of this culture suggest to us that it is normal for physical contact and physical closeness to another person to be fleeting. Hookup culture is what happens when people act on those daily lessons of our culture.

It's an old truth that the strictures of our sex lives are inextricably bound to the strictures of the society in which we live, that the public and the private are never as disconnected as we sometimes imagine them to be. As Plato reminds us in Book Five of *The Republic,* the sexual mores that predominate within any given regime both reflect and reinforce the implicit character of that regime. We live in a regime where mobility and its attendants are prized; therefore, our sexual behaviors both reflect and reinforce those cultural values. The way in which people in any culture pursue and engage in sex is never just about the demands or desires of the body; it's also, always, about the demands and desires of the society in which the body is placed.

Without question, there is a tragic dimension to hookup culture—a dimension that reflects the broader tragedies of the mobile conditions in which we live. Being American means feeling what James Baldwin called "the sorrow of the disconnected," means being beset by what Kurt Vonnegut called a "terrible disease of loneliness."[2]

In recent popular culture that tragic dimension has been best embodied by Nicole Pollan, a young woman whom most American know as "Snooki" on MTV's hit reality series "Jersey Shore." From the very first episodes of that show, Snooki makes it clear that she wants to meet a real boyfriend, maybe even a husband. And yet she often says that she knows she's not going to meet that one special guy by hooking up with random people after downing multiple shots of Jaegermeister, or in the grim and sticky corners of the nightclubs that you can tolerate only if you're wasted. But she keeps going to those clubs, and she keeps hooking up with random people, because that seems to be the best if not the only option she's got.

When, more recently and somewhat off-camera, Snooki did find a boyfriend, got engaged, got married, and got pregnant (though not quite in that order), media commentators were quick to note the improbability of it all—and to opine, correctly, that to succeed in this domestic venture, Snooki would to have to stop being Snooki. In order to increase the

---

2. James Baldwin, *Giovanni's Room* (New York: The Modern Library, 1956), 97; Kurt Vonnegut, *Palm Sunday: An Autobiographical Collage* (New York: Random House, 198), 180.

likelihood that her marriage and family could thrive, she would have to turn her back on precisely those behaviors and habits that brought her so much public attention and popular success.

She's both an emblem and a victim of the culture, as to varying degrees are we all.

Before it took on its present connotation, "hooking up" was a term popularly used in the years after World War II, when television operators began using the phrase "hook up" to describe the act of connecting two or more broadcasting systems for the short time needed to broadcast a common program.

In the present formulation of the term, I suppose the implication is that people are the equivalent of separate broadcasting systems, with otherwise different programs, who only have a short time to "broadcast in common." It's a term of technology rather than a term of spirit or soul, a term that implicitly frames our ideas about ourselves in a deeply Hobbesian way: as mechanical, stand-alone, perfunctory beings.

It's an image, you might say, that captures the spirit of our place and time, a place where and a time when we talk about "connectivity" rather than camaraderie, where we occasionally plug in as we all move along, mobile devices in hand—mobile devices that whisper to us, every time we stare into their screens, that when it comes down to it, all we can rely on is the iWhatever, not ever the weTogether.

Part Nine

Beyond the Corruption of Moth and Rust

The object of a religion or a philosophy is not to make men wealthy or powerful, but to make them, in the last issue, happy: that is, to fulfill their being.

—HILAIRE BELLOC, *SURVIVALS AND NEW ARRIVALS*

Life Under Compulsion: Rejecting the Glorious Liberty of the Children of God[1]

Anthony Esolen

IN THE DIM YEARS of the sixth century, when the half-barbarian Germans had perforated the Roman Empire in the west, Saint Benedict drew up his Rule, a counteroffensive, a plan for battle. I am not claiming that he understood it as such, in any political sense. But in the midst of that crumbling civilization he sheltered in his citadel what civilization is ultimately for: the freedom of the human spirit to contemplate the everlasting things, and to share with others the fruits of that contemplation. If we consider it in that light, it was no accident at all, but the foreseeable consequence of the work of Christian prayer, that Saint Benedict's monks would preserve and hand on to future generations the great expressions of human freedom made manifest in the poetry and philosophy of the pagan world. It was not the first time, it would not be the last, that, in her devotion to God—a devotion made possible by the grace that at once satisfies all that is human in us and raises us beyond ourselves—the Christian Church should do for man what he could not do for himself.

What did the world understand then, if not conquest? What does it understand now? Our barbarians do not scale our city walls with fire and sword. Their weapons are more impressive than that. Now all the massed ordnance of technology and advertising and broadcasting, all the manifold lies told by economic and political determinists, all the self-compelled ambitions of scientists whose livelihoods depend on homage to the daemon demanding, "Farther, more," all of those engines of

---

1. First published in *Life Under Compulsion: Ten Ways to Destroy the Humanity of Your Child* (ISI Books, 2015). Used by arrangement with the publisher.

compulsion are aimed against the very being of man, to set him free from his humanity, free to sink back into the blamelessness of the beast, or into the inert apathy of a mere object, not above the moral law, but beneath it. The Church alone remains, proclaiming that all created things find their end only in the beatitude of man, because, as Saint Paul mysteriously says, "the creature itself also shall be delivered from the bondage of corruption into the glorious liberty of the children of God" (Rom. 8:21). The Church is for the world, because she is for man; the Church is for man, because she is for God.

That is why we now see that almost the only schools where reverence for humanistic letters is to be found are also places of prayer. This is not because their professors have grown stubborn and antiquarian. It is again the foreseeable consequence of following Christ in a dark age. The air is cleaner in the citadel at the mountaintop, and they who still yearn for it can drag themselves out of the current of the times, fight through the thickets, and climb that mountain, to breathe freely as men, to see, and wonder. That is what our Christian colleges and schools should be about. It is the principle that underlies Cardinal Newman's work, *The Idea of a University*. Newman does not deny that we need tradesmen—we need merchants, and carpenters, and scientists engaged in applied research, and plumbers. But, if I may be allowed the play on words, we need most what we do not need at all. Grant a man a hundred years of health, good food, sexual release, and what passes for important work—grant him that on condition that he remain in a well-decorated basement, with a ceiling fixed over his head, and a painted heaven dotted with painted stars in his room at night—and he will go mad. He needs more than to see. He needs to behold. He needs the heavens.

Let me begin to illustrate the point by bringing to your attention a couple of works of art both human and sacred. Recently, my family and I visited New Bedford, once a jewel of a town with cobblestone streets and colonial houses built by the men who went down to the sea in ships, to hunt the great whales and bring back the whale-ivory and oil and spermaceti. Those ventures engaged maritime peoples from all over the world, including the Portuguese, from Portugal and the Azores and the Cape Verde Islands, many of whose descendants still live in New Bedford and the area around. The museum in New Bedford is filled with their works of art—folk art, as we would call it. The whalers were not exceptionally learned men. One object impressed me most, by its extraordinary delicacy and beauty.

It is a sculptured altarpiece from Cape Verde, gleaming white. The altar is festooned with a riot of flowers, whose petals are rendered with the most exact care. A large monstrance is carved upon the altar, with rays radiating from the center, where stand the letters I H S, the Greek capitals for the first three letters of the name of Jesus. Above the flowers stands the figure of the Lamb from the Book of Revelation, holding his banner with the cruciform insignia. An unfurled semicircle of diamonds provides a canopy for the altar, each diamond bearing a letter, reading *HOC EST ENIM CORPUS MEUM,* "for this is My body," the words of Christ at the Last Supper. To the left of the altar—at a dramatic angle—stands the Cross; to the right, at a corresponding angle, the anchor of hope, dear to the hearts of sailors. That's all that the modern tourist would understand of it; of course a maritime people would value the utility of an anchor. But the sculptor knows better. He is thinking of the promise made by God to Abraham and confirmed with an oath, a promise extended to all of Abraham's spiritual sons and daughters, "which hope we have as an anchor of the soul," says the writer to the Hebrews, "both sure and steadfast, and which entereth into that within the veil; whither the forerunner is for us entered, even Jesus, made an high priest forever after the order of Melchisedec." Hence the anchor and the cross belong together, at the altar where Christ, under the species of bread and wine, is priest and God and sacrifice. The whole work of art nestles in a cradle of branches and leaves. Beneath the altar, in a long scroll, are sculpted, in low relief, words in Portuguese, telling us that the sculpture was made by Father John Silva, in honor of Christ and His Church.

But the most striking feature of this sculpture is this: the whole edifice cannot weigh more than an ounce or two. Father Silva carved it from the spongy pith of a fig tree. With a razor that could make shavings as thin as breath, he must have spent hundreds of hours on that work of love, simply for the joy of it—and, as the Benedictine monks did, to share with other men the fruits of his contemplation. You could crush it in an instant in the palm of your hand; but the human spirit that conceived and executed that work, not the spirit of bondage, but the spirit of freedom, whereby we cry, "Abba, Father!", that spirit we cannot quite crush—though we do our best to thwart it. Secular schools thwart it when they reject beauty and view all works of the human spirit as the compulsions of political determinism. The museum curators themselves did not understand the sculpture; their placards note, obtusely, that Roman Catholicism is still "important" for the culture of Cape Verde. They translate Father Silva's signature, but they do not translate the words of consecration.

That afternoon we drove to the north end of New Bedford, now the rough end of the city, with buildings abandoned or in need of repair, and streets strewn with litter. But it was not always so. In the middle of one old French neighborhood rises the towering red stone church of Saint Anthony of Padua, who was also, as all Portuguese know, Saint Anthony of Lisbon, his birthplace. The doors were locked—I am sure that a hundred years ago we would have enjoyed the freedom of the church, but not in these days when we have lost so many of the ordinary human things. But it is a mighty edifice, with red and white stones set in diamond patterns beneath the towers, and an enormous arch over the main portal, with these words carved in bold relief: *AEDIFICARUNT DOMINO SANCTI ANTONII OPIFICES*: "The workmen of Saint Anthony built [this] for the Lord." The inscription does not say, "The people of Saint Anthony's parish hired a crew of construction workers to build this church," although they did hire two architects and no doubt other workmen too. It says that the men themselves built it—with their own hands and shoulders and backs. They built it for the Lord. "Except the Lord build the house," says the Psalmist, "they labor in vain that build it." We might say more. Except it is for the Lord, such a house will never be built at all. Freely did the men build, as freely as Father Silva carved. The one work of art must weigh a thousand tons; the other, a puff of wind could undo. But they are both works performed in that spirit of liberty that man longs for, and that the Church is the last institution left standing to defend. It is the liberty to love what is beautiful and good for its own sake, not for its utility, and certainly not for the fleeting pleasure it gives to the idle tourist. It is the liberty to be fully human, and it is the liberty to pray.

Now then, how can this defense of what is human and free be made manifest in a Christian university? Newman was careful to keep things and their ends well defined. The object of a liberal education, he said, was not to make a saint, or a merchant, but to make the gentleman, a man whose experience with the humane letters in languages classical and modern would lend him a wide vista for sane and sober judgment. Such a man's mind, says Newman, "is almost prophetic from its knowledge of history; it is almost heart-searching from its knowledge of human nature; it has almost supernatural charity from its freedom from littleness and prejudice; it has almost the repose of faith, because nothing can startle it; it has almost the beauty and harmony of heavenly contemplation, so intimate it is with the eternal order of things and the music of the spheres." My thoughts here turn to Pope Benedict XVI, listening to his beloved Bach, or reading Dante, or thinking about the great saints and mystics of the last two thousand years, while writing a letter whose every word must be handled and turned and weighed, such was his care for the souls and the minds of those in his charge; while the journalists of the world scribbled away, hunters and hunted at once, pressed by the need to produce, tangled in lies and ignorance, and hardly able to write a single sentence worthy of a man of liberal education.

So far, Newman seems to separate liberal from Christian education, and almost imply that you can have that freedom on its natural terms, without the faith. The Lord need not build the house. But that would be to mistake him; and here I owe a debt to the theologian Reinhard Huetter, who has argued that, according to Newman, without theology to make sense of the other fields of knowledge and to unite them, the university itself will cease to exist, though the deceptive name will remain. The university degenerates into a utilitarian polytechnicum, filled with people who make their particular fields of study, their particular crafts, usurp the whole universe. If there is a God, Newman argues, and if by God we mean what not only the scriptures but the great natural theologians among the pagans mean, then He has so "implicated Himself" with the world, "and taken it into His very bosom, by His presence in it, His providence over it, His impressions upon it, and His influences through it," that we cannot shut our eyes to theology "without prejudice to truth of every kind, physical, metaphysical, historical, and moral; for it bears upon all truth."

The implications for the humanities are clear, if one keeps in mind the revelation, known in a shadowy way even by the Greeks, that man is made free, in the image of the God who creates freely, out of love, untouched by the least necessity. Suppose a university professor—whether of politics, economics, literature, history, or the natural sciences—excludes from the outset this truth, that man is free. Such a man, says Newman, would fall to "a one-sided, radically false view of the things which he discussed," taking "his own study to be the key of everything that takes place on the face of the earth." It would not be his study in itself that was untrue. Chemistry is still chemistry, and economics still economics. But his "so-called knowledge," says Newman, would be "unreal," since "he would be deciding on facts by means of theories," exactly what, I might say, the Marxist biologist Lysenko did when he tried to compel the birds and the bees to obey the dictates of dialectical materialism. But the birds and the bees had better things to do, and went about their God-ordained business quite as if there never had been a communist in the world.

The humanities themselves have been partners in crime, conspiring first at their enslavement and then their demise. Return to the altarpiece fashioned by Father Silva. No sane person asks, "What did the priest think to realize by this work, in terms of political power?" Obviously, if you are after political power, there are nearer ways to work than by spending many hours of the day and night hunched over a handful of bark. No sane person asks, "How is this work situated in the perennial fight for the rights of women?" That would be like asking what money you could earn by taking a walk in a garden, or whether green is as tasty as red. The question hardly admits of an answer. It is not at all to the point. Yet that describes most of the "hot," "cutting edge," "trailblazing" work in the humanities, at least if letters of recommendation are evidence, or the advertisements on the jackets of scholarly books. It isn't so much that it is wrong as that it is unreal.

We once interviewed a very nice young man for a position in our English department, to teach medieval literature. He was a Chaucer scholar, without an inkling of what the scriptures and the Christian faith are all about. He wasn't hostile; it's just that he had not had a real education—an education in the reality of the very thing he proposed to study, the poetry of the Middle Ages. He therefore was a walking and talking example of what Newman warned against. When theology is drummed out of the curriculum—and I will say, when all of the noblest aspirations of the human spirit are ignored—then the place it once occupied does not remain empty. The other disciplines rush in where the angels once trod, and those other disciplines deal principally in *things,* or with man only insofar as he can be reduced to a thing. In this young man's case, economic determinism rushed in. He could speak forever about how Chaucer attempted to use his poetry to make for himself a nice career at court. It is rather sad when one thinks about it; a young man of sharp wit can imagine nothing more glorious than a career, and interprets the rest of the world accordingly. But to take that view of *The Canterbury Tales* is to be treating of a thing that does not exist; an imaginary economic artifact, and not the actual work of art. It is as if one had been present when Jesus raised Lazarus from the dead, and could think of nothing better to ask than whether Lazarus was a Pharisee or a Sadducee. The headlines of the *New Jerusalem Times* the next day read, "Prophet Raises Man from Dead; Electoral Implications Unclear."

The Church is still, of course, in the business of raising men from the dead; but if she is to do her work, there must be men to raise, that is, beings recognizably human, despite the shoulders bent and the faces smudged by sin. That is where the humanities come in; and for us especially, as it was already for Newman, that means insisting on the very existence of man, and affirming his dignity. We professors of poetry cannot raise men to Paradise, but we can help break them of the compulsions of Hell. We cannot elevate them beyond the human, but we can help restore the human at least. We may be, if it isn't presumptuous to say so, fellow workers upon the mountain of Purgatory. And it is to that brilliant work that I turn now.

To us who have nearly lost any sense of what the study of poetry, history, and philosophy are for, Dante has given us an inestimable gift in the very structure of his realm of purgation. Purgatory is not beneath the earth. It is not above the earth. It is *upon* the earth, and it is a mountain, ascending toward the heavens. It is the essence of man's life on earth to be so oriented; we cannot be more true to the earth and to our common humanity than when we climb that holy mountain. That is why, at the beginning of the *Purgatory*, Dante does not tell us exactly where we are, and does not have his pilgrim namesake speak with Virgil, *until* he first directs our gaze heavenward:

> Sweet sapphire of the morning in the east,
> gathering in the starlit face of Heaven,
> pure from the zenith to the nearest ring,
>
> Renewed my joy in looking on the skies
> as soon as I had come from the dead air
> that had saddened my heart and dimmed my eyes.
>
> The radiant planet fostering love like rain
> made all the orient heavens laugh with light,
> veiling the starry Fishes in her train.
>
> I turned to the right hand, and set my mind
> to scan the southern pole, and saw four stars
> no one has looked on since the first mankind.

> The heavens seemed delighted in their flame!
> O widowed region of the northern stars,
> you who have been deprived the sight of them!

The pilgrim here beholds three beautiful things of heaven, and the three combine to instruct us not only in where we are going, but *how* we are to go; Dante holds before our gaze not only the glory of blessedness, but also the sweetness of the human journey. The first object is the color of the early morning sky, its rich sapphire in the hour before the dawn as Dante looks east, towards Jerusalem and the risen Christ. No doubt Dante wishes us to think of Mary, and the deep blue of her robes as depicted in Christian paintings and illuminations. She, the humble woman of Nazareth, fathoms more profoundly the being of God than does any other creature, as Dante will say in Paradise, and the sky itself, the vault over the humble earth, is meant to be beheld from the earth, and is involved with earth, as God is involved with man.

In that deep blue, Dante beholds the second object of beauty, the morning star, the planet Venus, *che d'amar conforta*, he says, that fosters love. Christ is the morning star that never sets, as is sung in the great hymn of the eve of Easter, the *Exsultet*, but here Dante is thinking also of *all beautiful creatures* that move our hearts to love, and specifically the beautiful woman, Beatrice, in whose praise he wrote his youthful rhymes of love. It is not possible here to separate a supposedly earthly or, to use an ugly word for a cramped idea, secular love from the heavenly love, since Venus herself *faceva tutto rider l'oriente, made all the orient heavens laugh with light*.

Then Dante turns southward, and sees four bright stars that no man has seen since the fall of Adam. Dante takes care in the Purgatory to let us know that these stars represent the four cardinal virtues, temperance, courage, prudence, and justice, the four that Virgil swears to have followed without fault. They prepare us for the dance of the four virtues at the summit of the mountain, after Dante has been washed clean in the River Lethe; those ladies will lead the pilgrim to their three fellows, Faith, Hope, and Charity, so that the poet may finally behold the *second beauty* which Beatrice has not yet shown him—the beauty of her joy; her smile.

If we follow Dante's cue, we see that we cannot, in the end, talk sensibly of earth without looking to heaven. To put it another way, we cannot have a really *human* study of history or poetry or philosophy, or any of the natural sciences, while remaining fixed under the low ceiling of materialism; when we cease to look up, we cease to look at all.

That is why, I believe, Dante accompanies the restoration of health to sinful man with the restoration of poetry—the poetry of love. Beneath the protected realm of Limbo in Hell there are no discussions of poetry at all, or of art. In Paradise, theology reigns triumphant, and poetry, though not forgotten, recedes from our attention. Not so in Purgatory. In Purgatory—again, that infirmary where we recover what is most human—Dante meets poets and artists and singers everywhere, and even at the top of the mountain, in earthly Paradise, without any prompting, Matelda graciously suggests that the ancient poets

> in their melodies of old
> may have dreamed on Parnassus of this spot,
> singing about the happy age of gold.
>
> For here the human race was innocent;
> forever spring, and fruit upon the vine.
> This is the nectar which the poets meant.

Her words bring a gentle smile to the lips of Virgil and Statius, who stand behind Dante, listening quietly.

I do not believe that Dante's concentration upon the nature and the aim of poetry is incidental; I do not believe he said to himself, "Hell does not deserve it, and Paradise is beyond it." Consider Dante's notable meeting with a poet whom he criticized severely, Bonagiunta of Lucca. Dante and Virgil and Statius are making their way along the terrace of gluttony, when one of the emaciated spirits looks intently upon Dante, prophesies that he will derive some comfort from a good woman in Lucca when his fellow Florentines drive him into exile, and then asks him the question that nobody in Hell ever asks:

> "But do I see the introducer of
> the new songs, and the verses which begin,
> 'Ladies who have intelligence of love'"?
>
> Said I to him, "I'm one who takes the pen
> when Love breathes wisdom into me, and go
> finding the signs for what he speaks within."

Bonagiunta is deeply satisfied with this response, and affirms that *that* allegiance to the indwelling Spirit of love was what he and his fellow poets lacked; it was not their manner that caused them to miss the *dolce stil novo, the sweet new style*, but their failure to turn to Love for direction. Bonagiunta had satirized the *stilnovisti* for inserting into their love poetry terms borrowed from the schools, from theology and philosophy. Here Dante makes him correct himself. Terms may be used artfully or clumsily, but the whole orientation of poetry is toward love—and love turns our gaze heavenward.

I should like to turn now to what I think is, in the *Purgatory,* the sweetest and most surprising moment of healing for the humanities. Dante had hinted, in the *Inferno,* that his best friend and fellow poet, Guido Cavalcanti, may be destined to lose the good of the intellect. You may recall how Cavalcanti's father, in Canto 10, suddenly interrupts Dante's conversation with the Florentine powerbroker, Farinata, to ask about his son. If here, he says, you are traversing this dungeon

> *through power of genius at its height,*
> *Where is my son? Why is he not with you?*

Shall we call Cavalcanti a Baconian, a believer in untrammeled human power, with no aim beyond the domination of nature? He seems oblivious to any danger to his son's soul; it is enough for Cavalcanti, proud father that he is, that Guido show the brilliance of his mind, his *ingegno,* his *power of genius.* The contrast between that view of humane study and Dante's may be seen in the first lines of the *Purgatory,* when Dante says *la navicella del mio ingegno,* his *little ship of ingenuity,* his *little bark of inborn powers,* now must hoist the sail to speed through better waters; and again we recall that there is no sailing without the stars to guide us.

So Dante must correct the old man. He is *not* traversing through Hell through power of genius at its height. He is being led through Hell by his companion, Virgil, for the sake of *one your Guido, maybe, held in scorn*—for Beatrice, as I read it, or Christ; for Guido Cavalcanti had written most pessimistically of love, calling it an irresistible and ultimately destructive force. But Guido's father hears none of that; he hears only the past tense of Dante's verb, *held,* and slumps back into his tomb, assuming that Guido has died, that the sweet sunlight has ceased to strike his eyes. It does not occur to him to consider that if Guido has died and if he is not in Hell, then he is in a place where he beholds that sweet sunlight still, if not a light that is infinitely sweeter and brighter. Cavalcanti's obtuseness here, his shortsightedness, the smothering of the imagination of one who was by all accounts a most intelligent man, is well represented by the lids that will seal the coffins of these heretics at the Last Day, when, as Farinata says, *the future ends, and judgment shuts the door.*

University life, even the study of the humanities, is like the death within death that Cavalcanti and the materialist heretics will experience in those cramped little tombs, unless it is open to the skies. But Dante was not willing to let that judgment against his friend remain. He still held out hope that Guido could be redeemed. And here I must cite Guido's sweetest poem, a simple and intensely erotic pastoral lyric, not philosophical, not tormented with doubts. Here are the initial couplet and the first stanza:

> *In un' boschetto trovai pastorella,*
> *Piu che la stella bella, al mi' parere.*
> In a small grove I found a shepherdess,
> lovelier, in my eyes, than a star above.
> Blond hair she had and woven in little curls,
> love in her eyes, and rose-flush in the cheek;
> she led her lambs to pasture with her staff;
> her feet were shoeless, glistening with the dew;
> and she was singing as if she were in love.
> She was adorned with all that gives delight.

It is an exquisite work, as witness the delicate internal rhyme in the first couplet—with a caesura following that word *stella*, star; the heavenly object that Guido's father will nevermore behold. *Cantava come fosse innamorata, she was singing as if she were in love;* that is the key line. She was singing. There is no singing in Hell, but there is plenty of singing all up and down the mountain of Purgatory. *Cantare amantis est,* says Augustine; singing is what the lover does, and therefore song draws near to the heart of prayer. It may not be a holy thing to write a song in honor of a beautiful woman, but it is a human thing, and, like the mountain of Purgatory, it points toward a beauty and a love beyond itself.

And that is why Dante will not leave his friend's poetry behind. Matelda, that lovely guide in earthly Paradise, has, as we have seen, suggested to the ancient poets that their dreaming of the Golden Age had as its object the land she now walks. That canto ends with the smiling of Virgil and Statius—their pagan poetry is brought into the great song of love; and in the next canto it is Guido's turn. For Dante begins with these words: *Cantando come donna innamorata: Then as a woman sings who sings in love.* Guido had written, of his imaginary shepherdess, *Cantava come fosse innamorata,* using the subjunctive mood: she was singing *as if she were* in love. Dante has replaced the subjunctive with the indicative: *Cantando come donna innamorata: Then as a woman sings who sings in love.* The implication is clear. *This woman is indeed in love, and that is why she sings.* She is in love both with the sweet earth, whence she culls her flowers, and with the Lord of earth and heaven. She is Leah the active, to Rachel the contemplative. She is the forerunner John, to the savior Christ. She brings Dante to the place where he will look upon Beatrice.

Why study poetry, or any of the humanities, in our educational mills, if it means only toil in the harnesses of utility? And that is what it must be, without the stars above to guide us. I say again: the Church is for man, because she is for God. Dante's great poem, and the soaring towers of a stone church in New Bedford, raised up by that extraordinary creature known as a man in prayer, and that delicate sculpture by a priest dwelling in the reflected light of eternity, they all testify to where true freedom is to be found.

Defining Conservatism Down

D.G. HART

WHAT MAKES AN EVANGELICAL Protestant conservative? If voting for Republican presidential candidates qualifies, then evangelicals are among the most conservative Americans, since their support for the GOP regularly hovers around seventy-five percent. But voting impresses traditionalist conservatives much less than thoughtfulness or way of life. And when it comes to reflections on the best way to nurture human flourishing within a well-ordered society, born-again Protestants disappoint.

Jeffrey Hart, longtime senior editor at the *National Review,* certainly detected something amiss in the way that president George W. Bush applied his born-again faith to domestic and foreign policy. "[T]he evangelicalism of the Bush presidency," Hart wrote, "presents American conservatism with a perplexity, and perhaps with a problem."[1] The perplexity stems from the enthusiasm and populism that characterize evangelical piety, characteristics that spook conservatives. In fact, the tension between evangelicalism and conservatism is so prominent that Columbia University historian Alan Brinkley judged evangelicalism to be conservatism's "greatest problem." In an essay from 1994, "The Problem of American Conservatism," Brinkley described evangelicals as a "segment of the contemporary Right whose demands are considerably more radical and whose critique of the contemporary world derives not from elitist notions of tradition and morality but from what, for lack of a better term, might be called deep-seated cultural and religious fundamentalism."[2]

---

1. Jeffrey Hart, *The Making of the American Conservative Mind:* National Review *and Its Times* (Wilmington, Del.: ISI Books, 2005), 351.

2. Alan Brinkley, "The Problem of American Conservatism," *American Historical Review* 99 (April 1994), 423.

If evangelicals are mistaken to think of themselves as conservative, they are not entirely to blame. For close to a century, evangelical leaders have insisted that born-again Protestantism is deeply conservative, perhaps not politically but at least religiously. This claim has the ring of truth thanks to the realignment of Anglo-American Protestantism (i.e., the largest denominations of English descent—Congregationalists, Episcopalians, Presbyterians, Baptists, and Methodists) that began during the 1920s at the time of the so-called fundamentalist controversy. From roughly 1920 to 1945 the largest Protestant denominations developed liberal and conservative wings, with conflicts among Presbyterians and Baptists spawning new small conservative denominations. The form of conservative Protestantism to emerge was often thin. But because the leaders of the mainline Protestant churches regarded conservatism as sectarian and divisive, they were generally happy to let fundamentalists have the word *conservative*.

What may confuse contemporary readers, whether they have a background in evangelical circles or not, is that both liberal Protestants (also known as modernists) and fundamentalists claimed to be *evangelical*. Both sides used the word in an older sense as synonymous with Protestant. In the sixteenth century Lutherans were originally known as the *evangelicals*. In the eighteenth century at the time of the awakenings associated with George Whitefield and Jonathan Edwards, *evangelical* also referred to those Protestants passionate (read: enthusiastic) about conversion and evangelism. In the nineteenth century, *evangelical* stood for all Protestants who were Trinitarian and not members of a novel sect (like the Mormons or Unitarians). For that reason, as much as it would upset contemporary usage, liberal claims to be evangelical were common down to the 1940s.

But after World War II, *evangelical* became synonymous with conservative (Protestant) thanks to a group of dissatisfied fundamentalists who wanted to put behind the negative associations of the 1920s and develop a positive reputation. These younger leaders founded a number of important institutions to give some coherence to the movement. The first (1942) was the National Association of Evangelicals, which functioned as a vehicle for cooperation among a variety of denominations (from Pentecostal to Lutheran) and independent congregations who were opposed to the liberal mainline Protestant institutions. Another was the creation of *Christianity Today* (1956), which served as the intellectual vehicle for evangelical opinion and theology and provided a magazine that would do for conservative Protestants what *Christian Century* did for liberals.

But what gave evangelicalism its greatest coherence was not an institution but a person—Billy Graham. During the 1949 Los Angeles crusade, Graham emerged as the great twentieth-century urban revivalist, and evangelicalism found its poster-boy. Here was a man with whom average born-again Protestants could identify and follow, from his evangelistic meetings around the world to his meetings with political figures. Graham's evangelicalism was also *conservative* in the sense that it received and passed on the practices of revivalism, begun in the eighteenth century by Whitefield, perpetuated in the nineteenth century by Charles Grandison Finney, and kept burning during the late nineteenth and early twentieth centuries by the likes of Dwight L. Moody and Billy Sunday. Revivalism was also apparently conservative since it was a form of ministry that the theologically liberal denominations had abandoned.

These Protestants—from the fundamentalists to the new evangelicals—were precisely the constituency that comprised the Moral Majority, founded by Jerry Falwell in 1979 with major assistance from operatives in the Republican Party. Falwell's organization, in turn, became the vehicle by which evangelicals came to think of themselves as American conservatives. They had, after all, opposed liberalism in the churches since the 1920s. Now through their support for Ronald Reagan and other Republican candidates, born-again Protestants would oppose liberalism (sometimes referred to as "secular humanism") in United States government and culture. Either way, Protestants who associate with evangelical congregations, publications, schools and colleges, and parachurch ministries regard themselves as among the most conservative of Americans.

As important as twentieth century religious developments were for identifying evangelicalism with conservative Protestantism in the United States, nineteenth century developments were crucial for preventing American conservatism from developing a tight grip on born-again Protestants. The form of Protestant faith that blossomed in the antebellum era inaugurated a new era in Christian history in which evangelicalism abandoned most of the teachings and practices that characterized Protestant churches at the time of the Reformation and prevailed into the seventeenth century. The result of the Second Great Awakening was a two-party system in American Protestantism that pitted an individualistic, moralistic, and millennialist faith against a churchly, sacramental and

Augustinian piety, with the former constituting the mainstream (Anglo-American) of Protestant churches in the United States.

In 1843, John Williamson Nevin, professor at the German Reformed school in south central Pennsylvania, Mercersberg Seminary, wrote one of the most powerful critiques of mainstream American Protestantism ever penned by someone who did not convert to Rome. Ten years later Nevin did consider following the path trod by the likes of Orestes Brownson and Isaac Hecker, but chose finally to remain a Reformed Protestant. Part of the reason for Nevin's refusal to switch was his own effort to recover the churchly sensibility of such older Protestants as John Calvin. In addition, that effort to hold on to historic patterns of Protestant devotion in the face of evangelical innovation led Nevin to write *The Anxious Bench*, a smallish pamphlet that targeted the revivals of the nineteenth century awakenings whose prime mover was Charles Grandison Finney.

In his conclusion to *The Anxious Bench*, Nevin contrasted two styles of Protestant devotion. The bench referred to Finney's new-fangled measure to produce converts: a seat near the front where a person experiencing the weight of guilt could go for spiritual counsel and prayer. It became the basis for the evangelical altar call. In Nevin's mind, the bench stood for a shallow system of Christianity in which faith was presumed to authenticate itself. "With very little instruction, and almost no examination, all who can persuade themselves that they are converted, are at once hailed as brethren and sisters . . . and with as little delay as possible gathered into the full communion of the Church." According to Nevin, the alternative to the religious system represented by the bench was that rooted in catechism. In the case of Nevin's German Reformed Church, the catechism could refer narrowly to the Heidelberg Catechism. But he had more in view when drawing this contrast. The catechism stood for a churchly pattern of devotion in which people became Christians not in a moment of torment but over the course of a lifetime. In sum, the catechism symbolized "patient perseverance in the details of ministerial work," that is, in the "agencies, by which alone the kingdom of God may be expected to go steadily forward."[3]

What is particularly notable about Nevin's analysis is the argument that revivalism was profoundly at odds with older Protestant practices. Nevin's rendering of revivalism would become practically unintelligible in the twentieth century when awakenings and conversions were

---

3. John W. Nevin, *The Anxious Bench* (Chambersburg, Pa.: *Weekly Messenger*, 1843), 55, 56.

synonymous with "old-time" religion. In the 1840s, however, his argument was arguably more plausible, since such ethnic Protestants as German Lutherans and Dutch Reformed Protestants found the enthusiasm and anti-formalism of revivalism to be dangerously novel. Even so, revivals were a century old in America thanks to the imprimatur of Jonathan Edwards and George Whitefield.

This meant that two kinds of Protestantism were in conflict during the period when the United States itself was dividing along sectional lines. Anglo-American Protestants had generally appropriated the styles and assumptions of revivalism into their ways of doing church. For lack of a better word, these were "low-church" Protestants who associated anything sacramental or liturgical with Roman Catholicism. In contrast, many ethnic communions, Lutheran and Reformed (with the Oxford Movement influencing some Episcopalians), held on to forms of ministry that reflected sixteenth century patterns of Protestantism. Mark Noll put the differences well when he contrasted the newer forms of Protestantism spawned by Finney with an older style maintained by the Puritans:

> Although Puritans stood against Catholic and Anglican formalism, salvation for the Puritans was still mediated by institutions—family, church, even the covenanted society; in evangelicalism (at least in American forms), salvation was in principle unmediated except by the written Word of God. Puritans protested against nominal ecclesiastical life, but they still treated institutions of church and society as given; American evangelicals created their own communities, at first ecclesiastical, then voluntary. Puritans accepted authority from designated leaders; American evangelicals looked to authority from charismatic, self-selected leaders. Puritans fenced in enthusiasm with formal learning, respect for confessions, and deference to traditional interpretations of Scripture; American evangelicals fenced in enthusiasm with self-selected leaders, individualistic Bible-reading, local grassroots organizations, and intuitively persuasive reason.[4]

These differences between paleo- and neo-Protestants are important for trying to understand why evangelicals, allegedly the most conservative of believers, are the proponents of some of the most novel forms of worship

---

4. Mark A. Noll, *America's God: From Jonathan Edwards to Abraham Lincoln* (New York: Oxford University Press, 2002), 173–74.

known to the history of Christianity, forms that include praise songs, bands, and stand-up pastors.

The religious differences between evangelical and ethnic Protestants also turned out to have significant political consequences. Interpreters of nineteenth-century political culture have identified a strand of politics that carries an indelible evangelical imprint. According to Robert P. Swierenga, evangelicals were

> New Testament-oriented, antiritualist, congregational in governance, active in parachurch organizations, and committed to individual conversion and societal reform in order to usher in the millennial reign of Jesus Christ. Pietists did not compartmentalize religion and civil government. Right belief and behavior were two sides of the same spiritual coin.

The Second Great Awakening in fact spawned a two-pronged political program. First, evangelicals created a "benevolent empire," a system of voluntary parachurch agencies to spread religious awareness and improve morality, from temperance and anti-slavery societies to Sunday schools and tract societies. Second, they entered the political mainstream by joining the Whig Party, which "viewed government positively, trusted the governors more than the governed, and believed in absolute law based on eternal verities." The Second Great Awakening was about more than saving souls. It also involved establishing the kingdom of God in the United States.[5]

In contrast, ethnic Protestants tended to vote for the Democratic Party and opposed the consolidation of government and promotion of cultural uniformity that Whigs advocated. An important reason for this different political affiliation was the ethnic Protestants' understanding of the church. The church for them was a place for assisting members in their pilgrimage from birth, confirmation, marriage, child-rearing, and vocation to death. Clergy ministered chiefly through the means of grace, namely, word and sacraments, and these rites strengthened the faith of members as they prepared for the world to come. In other words, the church was not an agency for social reform or nation-building, nor was faith a means for making good American citizens. Instead, the church was a spiritual institution with sacramental means for otherworldly

---

5. Robert P. Swierenga, "Ethnoreligious Political Behavior in the Mid-Nineteenth Century: Voting, Values, Culture," in Mark A. Noll, ed., *Religion and American Politics: From the Colonial Period to the 1980s* (New York: Oxford University Press, 1990), 152, 153.

ends. The Democrats offered a vision of American society most conducive to the ethnic Protestant understanding of the church. Because the Democrats generally favored a limited, populist government, as opposed to using state power to legislate social behavior, they also provided the greatest insurance that the United States government would not encroach on churches, parochial schools, or the lives of ethnic Protestants.

Although traditionalist conservatives recognize in the folk ways of ethnic Protestants an admirable alternative to the consolidation and centralization of national life that the Whig and Republican parties championed, contemporary evangelicals, whether on the Left or the Right, almost never do. In fact, Jim Wallis, the founder of *Sojourners* and author of *God's Politics: Why the Right Gets It Wrong and the Left Doesn't Get It* (2005), and Michael Gerson, speech writer for George W. Bush, self-identified evangelical, and author of *Heroic Conservatism: Why Republicans Need to Embrace America's Ideals* (2007), both look back to the moral crusades of the antebellum era as high water marks for evangelical political engagement and influence. Wallis, who concludes his book with a chapter entitled, "We Are the Ones We've Been Waiting For," laments that he was born in the wrong century. "Before the movement was humiliated as a result of the famous Scopes trial in 1925, fundamentalism was often socially allied with the Left." In the nineteenth century, evangelicals and fundamentalists led in abolishing slavery and fighting child labor. But in the twentieth century, fundamentalism became "an increasingly conservative and isolated enclave of faith."[6] Likewise, Gerson the Republican invokes such nineteenth century evangelicals as Lyman Beecher and Harriet Beecher Stowe, who were "religious idealists." So fond is Gerson of the era that he has no trouble appealing to the abolitionist, William Lloyd Garrison, a political radical who was part of the network of revivalist voluntary associations until the late 1830s when he cut those ties. Without "the demands of a conscience rooted in faith," Gerson writes, "America would be a different and crueler country." Meanwhile, Gerson faults traditionalist conservatives for lacking "a piece that is shaped by conscience"—the very piece that makes conservatism heroic.[7]

The point is not to mock evangelical assessments of the Second Great Awakening and its moral crusades but to note how born-again Protestants invariably fail to look beyond morality or religious experience

---

6. Wallis, *God's Politics* (New York: HarperSanFrancisco, 2005), 67.
7. Gerson, *Heroic Conservatism* (New York: HarperOne, 2007), 115, 272.

and consider the health of mediating structures such as families, neighborhoods, community associations, and local schools for cultivating a healthy society, which in turn nurtures responsible and restrained members of that society. Arguably, the overriding factor that colors such historical judgments is eschatology, a factor that accounts for evangelicals' abiding sympathy for a moral idealism that borders on radicalism. Unlike the ethnic Protestants, who possessed an Augustinian outlook that distinguished the fortunes of God's kingdom from national well-being, evangelicals in the nineteenth century and today read the progress of salvation in the pages of newspapers and social statistics, in the affairs of government agencies and the occupant of the White House.

This is another way of saying that evangelicals conceive of secular and sacred history in ways that inevitably immanentize the eschaton. Conservatives are almost constitutionally predisposed to reject the utopianism that comes with seeking earthly manifestations of eternal realities. Evangelicals are disposed in precisely the opposite direction—to see the affairs of nations and societies as signifying the fortunes of heaven and hell.

If observers and conservatives only know evangelicals by reference to their twentieth-century background, they miss a telling piece of religious history. What is remarkable about evangelicalism's nineteenth-century past is not the excess or ideology to which its moral urgency and religious idealism were prone. Instead, what stands out is a form of Christian devotion and a perspective on history that runs directly contrary to the restraint and sobriety that informs traditionalist conservatism. As long as evangelicals refuse to embrace the sort of dispositions of which Russell Kirk wrote in *The Conservative Mind*, born again Protestants and conservatives will have only the Republican Party in common. At the same time, anyone who thinks that evangelicals are capable of adding a dose of Kirk to the dispositions of Lyman Beecher or Jerry Falwell is arguably misguided. Moral idealism and millennialism are essential ingredients to evangelical piety. The real key for evangelicals becoming conservative is for these believers to find a version of conservative Protestantism more compatible with American conservatism.[8]

---

8. On what such a conservative Protestant faith might look like, see D. G. Hart, *The Lost Soul of American Protestantism* (Lanham, Md.: Rowman & Littlefield, 2002).

Imagination and Memory Deformed: The Gnostic Resentment of Embodied Life and its Limits

Mark Shiffman

Modern Consciousness

To think of yourself as modern is to think of yourself in distinction from what is not modern—namely, what is ancient, in the past, passé, and generally "on the wrong side of history." It is to turn away from the past in preference for what is current and then to see the present as poised to give way to the future that present momentum is already sweeping us toward.

Being modern, then, means living in a certain disposition of memory and imagination. The past, the world as it has hitherto been, is remembered primarily as that which is to be done away with, while imagination envisions future possibilities never before realized that will be brought about by human ingenuity. Modern consciousness dwells always in a juncture between two sets of images: one set seen as shining possibilities and the other as destined to be replaced by them as the old world undergoes dissolution in the face of the world to come.

In other words, modern consciousness is Gnostic consciousness. One of the primary attitudes of Gnosticism is anticipation of the dissolution of the previously given bad old world and liberation into a new and purified one. So, to be more precise, the distinctly modern disposition of memory and imagination is a Gnostic disposition. This disposition is antithetical to the understanding of imagination and memory found in the classical philosophical tradition and amplified in the Christian theological tradition, as the following discussion will attempt to show.

Anyone who resists the momentum and enthusiasms of this modern consciousness is readily accused of wanting to live in the past. No doubt someone unimpressed by the promised wonders lying in store in the still-to-be-unlocked future might be inclined to some nostalgia for the many goods that have been destroyed in the pursuit of those wonders, and may even simply reverse the direction of the utopian imagination. But the notion that dissenters can only be trying to jump off the train of history is one of the characteristic illusions of modern consciousness.

To be anti-modern, however, is not to live in the past; it is to deny the premise of the accusation of wanting to live in the past. Against the modern optimism that nihilistically destroys all actual goods in pursuit of imagined possible ones, the principled anti-modern will counterpoise hope, which is founded on long experience of goods available to us if only we have the eyes to see them. This hope is necessarily at home with the presence of tragedy, because the excess of available goods means there will always be conflicting priorities for lives lived within humane limits. The Gnostic imagination knows only the acceptable collateral damage of the "creative destruction" by which the future is conjured into being and in the wake of which the past is soon relegated to the dustbin of dim memory.

These broad generalities are meant to provide a general sense of the parameters of the following analysis. This examination of memory and imagination, and their relationship to the body, place, tradition and history, both as classically understood and as deformed by Gnosticism, is offered in the hope that it will provide some clearer understanding of the delusional visions that seek to abolish the sort of humane limits we need if we are to be fully human.

Aristotle on Imagination

Aristotle is the first western author to attempt a lucid examination of what imagination and memory are, and for him imagination is primary. While contemporary parlance treats imagination as a particular mode of consciousness that especially occupies itself with possibilities, for Aristotle imagination (*phantasia*) covers most if not all of the range of what we refer to as consciousness.

According to Aristotle, imagination is "that through which some image comes about for us."[1] "Image" (*phantasma*) does not refer strictly to visual forms but to anything that represents something else experienced, remembered, or thought. Words, figures, symbols can all serve as images. Imagination thus enables us to capture and retain images of what we have encountered through the senses, as well as to form abstractions and concepts and reflect upon them. Because it works with what is given in the senses as the basis of image-formation, imagination as Aristotle understands it is something inherently connected to the body. Remembering is a mode of imagining, treating images as referring to particular past occurrences;[2] and memory makes each of us "who" we are, which is a particular embodied soul.

It is *through and in* images that we are able to apprehend what is intelligible, so that imagination and intellect are distinct both notionally and experientially, even though our ability to contemplate intelligible principles depends on our ability to use images as vehicles for attending to them. Intellect is active only in those moments of insight when I can recognize that I am apprehending something *more* than a set of symbols manipulable within a set of rules.

This would mean, for example, that in most "knowledge" of modern science intellect is almost never at work, except in original insights or in the learner's momentary participation in them. Kepler's sudden realization that the numerical data recording the motion of Mars fit perfectly on an ellipse is an act of intellect; my "knowledge" that planetary orbits are elliptical is only an act of imagination. The manipulation of symbols and formulas according to set rules, and more importantly the *representation* of the natural world in terms of these symbols and formulas, is an activity of imagination.

Aristotle recognizes intellect at work in the study of nature most clearly when we are able to apprehend *what* something is, the form that is the principle of the order and unity of a natural being. In this experience there is a stretching beyond imagination, something other than "representation" in "concepts" or "ideas," a contact with the real being of something as its form is taken into the intellect. When we understand knowing in terms of model-construction, or working according to experimental procedures within a paradigm, Aristotle would regard such

---

1. *De Anima* III.3, 428a1.
2. *Ibid.*, 450b20.

"knowing" as confined to imagination. Model-construction describes the "how" of things; for Aristotle imagination, on the level of which concepts and models reside, is permeable to intellectual communion with the "what" of things, their natures and forms, which provide the true knowable foundation of order. Imagination is concerned less with possibilities than with what is.

St. Augustine on Memory

Imagination, then, concerns not only images of distinct things but also the relationships among those images and representations, including relationships established by intellectual insight but "stored" in the images. This feature of imagination, its ordered and associative structure within which images have their meaning, leads Saint Augustine to accord primary status to memory rather than to imagination. Where Aristotle tends to reflect on the isolated appearance of images, Augustine takes greater interest in the retention that separates images from sense impressions and holds them within a larger structure of meaning. Memory, for Augustine, is not primarily understood as imagination considering images with reference to time; rather, as the condition of our own personal continuity, and of the ongoing relating of things within our personal drama of understanding, it is what makes the sense of time possible.

Let us begin with this last point. In *Confessions* Book 11, Augustine struggles to say what time is. His best effort to make sense of it is in terms of a kind of stretched tension of the mind (*distentio animi*).[3] Our soul is held open in expectancy toward the future, which is constantly arriving into the present and then immediately taking its place in the memory: "The mind expects, attends, and remembers, so that what it expects passes by way of what it attends to into what it remembers."[4] Memory is the foundation for all three of these acts, because we can only expect on the basis of what memory has enabled us to conceive and desire, and we can only attend meaningfully because memory allows us to recognize and contextualize what presents itself to us. Thus memory plays the central role in giving time its structure. Contrary to the typically modern notion that time flows forward from past into future such that the future is constantly displacing the past, Augustine sees that the anticipated future

3. *Confessions*, 11.26.33.
4. *Ibid.*, 11.28.37.

is always flowing into the remembered past and constantly augmenting the vast storehouses of memory.

The arriving future takes its place in the remembered past, however, only to the extent that we attend to its arrival in the present. This attentiveness depends upon the will. Augustine illustrates the failure to attend to and remember the present by drawing upon the experience of walking through a landscape while our will is directing our thoughts elsewhere. We cannot walk without stumbling unless we perceive where we are passing, but that perception does not become memory without the will directing attention toward it.[5] Thus we can navigate the landscape without taking in any distinct impression of it and so without remembering anything about it.

Memory, by structuring what we experience into a meaningful order and carrying forward with us the representation of that order, constitutes our understanding of the world. Consequently, only if that world is lovable (i.e. considered good) does the will direct our attention to it in a way that takes in its rich texture, its beauty and complexity and depth, and continually works it into the memory of an intelligible whole of distinctly intelligible parts. Thus a Gnostic consciousness, enamored only of the possible but not yet actual, does not seek to adjust its memory to an ever-richer reflection of a given world it considers bad. It moves through the world as if through an indistinct landscape. Its remembered world must continually become thinned out and more schematic—a symbolic structure part of whose function is to buffer the soul from the given world.

Augustine's world of memory is constantly open, through questioning, to the effects of contact with the intelligible principles ordering the world we are trying to take in. Two things especially that we find in memory are fertile sources of that questioning: happiness and God. Happiness, as that for the sake of which we choose and act, is the primary object of our will; thus what we take happiness to be orders our will in all its more proximate objects. With reference to the order of willing, happiness is the highest good. With reference to the order of being and knowing, God is the highest good, because He is the ultimate source of all that exists and is good and knowable. The right ordering of memory requires the recognition that, in the structure of our world of meaning, happiness and God must coincide as the highest good we seek. The ongoing process of conversion in heart and mind involves the constant reordering of

---

5. *On the Trinity*, 11.8.15.

memory so that all paths of association in our desiring and our rational understanding lead to God, the true source of the meaning and order of everything.

All creation reflects the goodness of its source. The beauty, especially, of all created things both beckons us to love and question them and points us to their Creator, the source of their being, goodness and beauty.[6] Everything that we encounter through embodied existence is therefore a lovable reflection and reminder of God's goodness, worthy of receiving our attention and finding its proper place in the structure of meaning that is memory—including the marvelous gift of our body itself and the embodied relationships with others that it makes possible.[7]

Only as embodied beings who take the world in through the senses do we have imagination and memory in the first place. The life of an embodied being is a drama played out within a structure of meaning at the core of which is the quest for happiness. Its particularities, including place, history and language, as well as one's own life drama, give contour and limitation to our remembered worlds. The pursuit of more adequate understanding of the given world must therefore be social, in dialogue with one's contemporaries and predecessors, as an ongoing encounter and adjudication of landscapes of meaning. This participation within a historically particular dialogical tradition is, however, not self-enclosed, because memory and imagination are permeable to true principles of order available to intellect.

Such is the heart of the classical and Christian understanding of imagination and memory. The Gnostic understanding is quite different. Only in modern Gnosticism do these differences attain explicit articulation; but we can see their contours sketched implicitly in the Gnostic "Gospel of Thomas" in a way that justifies the use of the same description for both historical developments.

Gnosticism Old-Style

The short Coptic writing known as "The Gospel of Thomas" has come to be one of the classic texts of the recent Gnostic revival among scholars of

---

6. *Confessions*, 10.6.9–10.
7. *Ibid.*, 1.7.12,

Christianity.[8] Much of the content has strong Gnostic implications,[9] but it is above all in its form and style that it exemplifies the Gnostic sensibility regarding imagination and memory.

The text contains no narrative of the life of Jesus but is simply a collection of sayings. It begins simply: "These are the hidden words which Jesus the Living-one spoke and Judas Thomas Didymus wrote. And he said: 'Whoever finds the interpretation of these words will not taste death at all.'" Over a hundred more sayings follow, which almost all begin abruptly with "Jesus says." There is no context, locale, story, drama, birth, healings, suffering, dying or rising, only sayings.

The text presents us with a very disembodied Jesus, whose words alone matter. These words do not occur within an embodied dialogue with the suffering, in the heat of the midday sun or over a shared meal, in the celebration of a marriage or under threat of beatings, in Galilee or Jerusalem. They drop from a remote higher consciousness straight into the soul of the listener to resonate there alone, and their detachment from all context engenders a similar detachment in the hearer. Precisely this detachment from any defining context makes the Gnostic vision appealing to the modern individualist.

The underlying motivation for this detachment is release from the limitations of the flesh. The rich structure of embodied memory is meant to give way to an ecstatic transcendent state beyond its limiting ties: "A person old in days will not hesitate to ask a child of seven days about where life is, and he will live; and many who are first will be last and last first, and they will end up in oneness."[10] This shedding of lived memory would seem to lead to the "emptiness" that Saying 28 tells us we were born into the world with and must recover, and the erasure of all distinctions (including male and female) that Saying 22 tells us is the precondition for entering into the Kingdom.

Thus the very form of the text is a-cosmic, a severe abstraction from the order of the world that, for Augustine, it is memory's task to

8. See especially Elaine Pagels, *The Gnostic Gospels* (Vintage, 1989) and *Beyond Belief: The Secret Gospel of Thomas* (Vintage, 2004). The Coptic text was discovered in Egypt in the 1940s and published in a scholarly edition in the 1970s, and the original is generally considered to date from the second century.

9. Some parts of the text, such as "Saying 28," which speaks of Jesus appearing in the flesh, go against the Gnostic grain, though they are usually susceptible of Gnostic interpretations (in this case, the interpretation that his flesh is merely an outward appearance).

10. Saying 4, my translation of the Greek version.

elaborate, envision, maintain and continually correct. The word *kosmos* occurs with some frequency (in Coptic as well as Greek versions), but always as something to be negated. This is most stark in Saying 10: "I have set fire to the *kosmos*, and behold I am watching over it until it burns up."[11] The Gnostic wish for dissolution of the given world is reflected in the withering of the rich concreteness with which memory at its fullest encounters and absorbs that world.

According to the orthodox Christian teaching, the incarnate God did not shrink from absorbing the concrete texture of the world into himself, even to the point of allowing it to pierce his flesh. The "Gospel of Thomas" never explicitly denies the Incarnation, but its form renders the Incarnation irrelevant. These sayings could be spoken at any time, in any place and to anyone. Access to the timeless wisdom they claim to convey requires none of the details of Jesus' life and sufferings. The irrelevance of the Incarnation to interpreting the Sayings implies a tacit rejection of the principle St. Irenaeus had to defend against the Gnostics: apostolic succession. There is no advantage to having been a witness to how Jesus lived and related physically, personally, to those around him. His words, not his person, constitute the revelation, and they could be anyone's words. The text thus removes itself from involvement in tradition, the ongoing unfolding of a revelation of divine personhood through teaching kept faithful to the witness of those who had the fullest embodied experience of that revelation.

For this same reason the text breaks itself free from any relationship to the history of the Hebrew covenants. When Jesus asks the Apostles to whom they might compare him, Peter says an angel, Matthew a philosopher, and Thomas says that words are inadequate; no one proposes any figure from the Hebrew prophetic tradition.[12] The only character from Biblical history mentioned at all in the text is Jacob, and it is unclear whether this is in fact the Jacob of Genesis; indeed, the promise that the destiny of the disciples is to go to "Jacob the Righteous, for whose sake sky and earth have come to be," suggests a figure more mythical and mystical than historical.[13] The irrelevance of the Incarnation entails the irrelevance of Jesus' birth in the lineage of Jacob and as heir to the history

---

11. In Saying 27, the kosmos is something from which we must fast, and in Saying 56 it is a corpse.
12. Saying 13.
13. Saying 12.

of the covenants with Abraham and Moses, none of which is required for interpreting the "knowledge" Jesus' words impart.

The "Gospel of Thomas" thus communicates through both form and content the Gnostic disposition: it focuses the imagination on a promised future state of "higher consciousness" in the service of which it dissolves the concrete complexity of lived memory and situated meaningfulness. This amounts to the dissolution, in memory, of the shared world as a rich context in which to seek the good.

We can identify three distinct moments in the Gnostic dissolution of the world represented in this text: 1) it directs the hearer away from the concreteness of embodied life and toward ecstatic experience that replaces embodied love and responsibility; 2) it rejects the sense of tradition that presupposes the relevance of embodied presence and dialogue, through which wisdom grows as memory is gradually reconfigured to anchor us better in given reality; 3) it consigns to oblivion the entire history of human accomplishment, failure, and partial insight that provides an inheritance within which the words and acts of Jesus would make sense, so that those words and acts would both carry forward and transform a flawed but invaluable accumulated culture of meaning.

But these three moments also characterize the phases of the rebirth of Gnosticism in its distinctly modern character. Recognizing the analogy helps us see more clearly how these very modern developments harbor within them the spirit of ancient Gnosticism and are animated by a resentment of the limits of embodied life.

The Three Waves of Modern Gnosticism

The tide of modern Gnosticism's rising cultural dominion in the west comes in three waves: 1) the origin of the sexual revolution in the medieval celebration of passionate love; 2) the radically revised understanding of knowledge of the world underlying modern physics; and 3) the futurism of modern revolutionary politics. In the scope of this essay we can only sketch the outlines of these developments as they relate to imagination, memory and embodiment, in the hope that this will bring added clarity to the cultural dynamics of Gnosticism in our midst.

Among the last inheritors of the direct tradition of ancient Gnosticism was the sect of heretical Christian ascetics known as the Albigensians or Cathars. According to a brilliant cultural analysis by Denis de Rougemont,[14] the Albigensian heresy inspired Provençal courtly poetry, the primary vehicle by which the Gnostic disposition subsequently conquered the European imagination. Dwelling on the suffering poet's intense love for an inaccessible lady, these songs are too short to situate that passion within a richly articulated life-drama.[15] Like the "Gospel of Thomas," their form decontextualizes the passion for world-transcendence: everything but the beloved becomes meaningless, so that the lover tires of life and wishes for death.

The chivalric myths of obstructed adulterous love shaped by this courtly rhetoric of passion thus express the Albigensian rejection of procreative love and marriage upheld as a Christian vocation and social institution by the Catholic Church. The necessity of veiling this animating heresy leads the western literary tradition to develop this theme of passionate love in forgetfulness of its origins, so that adulterous passion could increasingly present itself as merely an antidote to the confining limits of bourgeois respectability. Removed from the context of the clash between heterodox and orthodox arguments over the religious value of marriage and embodiment, romantic literature becomes fuel for the fantasies of rebellious bohemian aestheticism. Thus that peculiarly western development, sexual liberation, has its spiritual roots in the death-enamored nihilism of Gnosticism's ecstatic attempt to transcend the confines of embodied love.[16]

The sexual revolution accordingly inherits a great obfuscation from the literary tradition, in that it presents itself as a celebration of the body when in fact it represents an insistence upon the absolute demands of the will to use and abuse the body as it wishes. Its justification for treating the

14. *Love in the Western World* (Princeton University Press, 1983), which the reader should consult for a more expansive treatment of the present topic.

15. One might contrast the literary forms employed by one of the great Christian inheritors of this tradition of vernacular poetry. Dante's early *Vita Nuova* begins his response to courtly love by situating a series of short love songs within a longer narrative of his encounters with Beatrice and their effects on his life, and his later *Commedia* further situates that drama within a richly imagined and historically dense world. Dante deliberately re-embeds the poetry of love within the world of memory from which Troubadour song abstracts the experience of transcendent passion, just as he insists that the soul is defective and frustrated when unnaturally separated from the body. (See *Purgatorio* XXV.95–108, *Paradiso* XIV.43–66; my thanks to Kevin Hughes for drawing these passages to my attention.)

16. For a more extensive treatment of Rougemont's thesis in relation to western nihilism, see my lecture "The Myth of Romantic Love": https://www.youtube.com/watch?v=jubh2PeVkY8 (University of Chicago, 13 Nov. 2014).

body arbitrarily is strengthened by the second wave of modern Gnosticism: the scientific objectification of nature. One of the most familiar and effective forms of this objectification is the coordinate grid developed by Descartes and used by modern physics to re-configure our imagination of the world of bodies. In Gnostic fashion, the Cartesian grid provides a decontextualized view from nowhere that belongs to no embodied being, a representational schema generated by imagination and interposed between mind and world. Its aims, however, represent a new and decisive twist on the Gnostic resentment of worldly limits: instead of fleeing into pure spirituality, we can construct models of the world's processes that will allow us to exert our wills over nature. Knowledge liberates when it generates power.

This notion that knowing consists in model-construction, which is embedded in our modern understanding of science, turns imagination from a structure of meaning bringing us to greater communion with reality into a pure instrument of will, a symbol-schema by which thought can exercise its power most efficiently. Descartes grounds this radical reconception of intellect and imagination in his famous universal doubt, which begins with a complete erasure of embodied memory: none of the content or form of his previous structure of meaning is at all trustworthy. Starting from an initial position of suspicion and alienation, he reconceives the world in terms of what we cannot avoid imagining it as having, namely quantifiable spatial relations. The imagined world is evacuated of substantial beings whose forms give them unity and distinctness (and thus goodness, beauty and lovability), in favor of calculable abstractions constructed by our imagination. Since imagination is no longer the means by which intelligible principles reach our intellect from the world, but rather the construction of a world-schema out of the concepts of our own minds, the alienation from situated and embodied personhood also involves alienation from the great tradition of dialogue that had grounded itself on the possibility of communion with and through the shared world. Imagination is henceforth about the future to be built; method subordinates the organization of memory to the project of constructing a powerful model of the world.[17]

17. I have treated these themes in greater detail in "Descartes, Algebra and Alienation" (http://www.frontporchrepublic.com/2009/06/algebra/) and "The Modern Reduction of Intellect to Imagination" (https://www.academia.edu/5165341/The_Modern_Reduction_of_Intellect_to_Imagination). See also Jacob Klein, "The World of Physics and the 'Natural' World" in *Lectures and Essays* (St. John's College Press,

The transgressive Gnosticism of passion and the organizing Gnosticism of reason both turn away from embodied memory of the given world toward an imagined future. The political revolutionary channels the two impulses into the redemption of human history, proving the nobility of his passion by wrenching himself from the remembered world and dying for another one constructed in imagination. Third wave Gnosticism is the politics not of informed experience but of youthful idealism, the unhampered belief in pure possibility of the seven-day-old child of the "Gospel of Thomas." It demands the unwavering conviction that all obstacles history has left strewn in the way can be eliminated; it is thus well served by inexperience and an imagination unmoored from actual embodiments of order.[18]

For the tradition stemming from Aristotle, the excellent political practitioner requires practical wisdom kept on target by the habituated moral virtues. Practical wisdom involves richly endowed memory: long experience of practical choice, the ability to size up the concrete situation based on extensive knowledge of particulars, the capacity to recognize analogies amidst complexity, and a structuring hierarchy of ordered goods. It requires the ability to imagine things as they are, and to recognize opportunities and threats within the given order. It is fed on political history, illustrating practical choices made in response to inherited historical constraints. Gnostic politics, scorning history and cutting off "the dead hand of the past," treats its ideological model as a schematic program for dismantling the given in favor of what is imaginable. If it attains the totalitarian form toward which it inclines, the destruction will be intense and focused; but political liberty, if it is no more than a counterbalance of conflicting futurisms, may prove far more effective at

---

1985) and Leon Kass, "The Permanent Limitations of Biology" in *Life, Liberty and the Defense of Dignity: The Challenge for Bioethics* (Encounter Books, 2004).

18. As Eric Voegelin, the great analyst of Third Wave Gnosticism, puts it in his characterization of Marxist dogmatics: "In the clash between system and reality, reality must give way. The intellectual swindle is justified by referring to the demands of the historical future, which the gnostic thinker has speculatively projected in his system." See *Science, Politics & Gnosticism* (ISI, 2004), 34. Voegelin famously described this new vision of history as an "immanentization of the eschaton," which is to say a heretical form of Christianity in which the ultimate salvation promised by God outside of earthly history becomes the responsibility of human beings to accomplish on earth. See Voegelin, *The New Science of Politics* (University of Chicago Press, 1987), 107–132.

steadily razing obstacles to its competing visions of history's fulfillment than at nurturing sustainable institutions.[19]

As this brief survey suggests, love, embodiment, inherited context, and the demands of institutional continuity lie at the heart of the conflict between the Gnostic and Classical-Christian dispositions. The persistence of sexuality and fertility as central themes of Gnostic politics should thus come as no surprise. Far from reflecting a Christian obsession with sexual taboo and control as commonly alleged, this preoccupation arises from the fundamental Gnostic requirement: rejection of the given constraints of embodied love, and of its consequences in the form of responsibilities and institutions through which reality impinges upon the freedom to dwell in imagined possibilities.

Imagination that declares its independence from reality becomes thin and poor. Habituation in the rhetoric of passion, the schematic modeling of reality, and the futuristic imagination of history dissociates consciousness from situated embodiment in the given world. Buried within these practices and the embrace of their consequences lies a theological principle: rejection of the goodness and lovability of the created world. Love motivates attention to persons and things in their distinctness and complex meaningful relations, and thus it constitutes a meaningful world of memory responsive to the given world and those with whom we share it. Gnosticism, by disdaining the given world, seems to confine consciousness to a kind of idiocy within its symbol-world, enamored only of its own reductive consistency. Through enthusiasm for the banal productions of technological innovation, erotic novelty, and consumer rollouts, or the passing frisson of inventing one's identity (sustained beyond its novelty only by angry insistence that others recognize it), Gnostic consciousness seeks distraction from its own tedious poverty and from what continually deepens that poverty: its destruction of the shareable world.

---

19. For reflections on the similar economic and social effects of communist and free-market Gnosticism, see my "Crunchy Pope, Part II: Against Gnostic Economics" (http://www.frontporchrepublic.com/2009/04/crunchy-pope-part-two-against-gnostic-economics/) and "Brave New World Reconsidered: A Tale of Two Gnosticisms" (http://www.frontporchrepublic.com/2009/06/brave-new-world-reconsidered-a-tale-of-two-gnosticisms/).

Afterword

Jason Peters

IN SUCH TIMES AS have precipitated this collection of essays—troubled times, let us call them—a man ordinarily disposed to goodness might find himself given to cynicism or even despair. He must resist both, despair especially. Spenser figured it as a subtle-tongued "man of Hell" with "greazy Locks, long growen" and cheeks hollow from not eating, a "cunning thief" living in a "darksome cave" poised to offer a length of rope or a rusty knife to such passers-by as might prove susceptible to his poisonous insinuating persuasion.[1] A generation later Bunyan made despair a giant, and the thing about giants is that they are big. They are also strong. (Bunyan's, too, recommends suicide by knife or noose or poison.) But they are sometimes known for their stupidity as well, which is a point in our favor so long as we ourselves are not. At any rate, I would remind anyone inclined toward despair (and cynicism), as I myself sometimes am, that hope, which is a virtue, makes for a better disposition. It is like obedience. I may find no *reason* to hope, just as my children may find no reason to obey, but there is at least this much to say in favor of obedience: it leads unfailingly to happiness—as Dante and others have taught us—as surely as disobedience does not. And so it is, I think, with hope.

And about hope I wish at the moment to make only two modest points. One is that it is not the same thing as optimism, which no one is required to practice, because it is not a virtue. Optimism is a kind of affected sanguinity, a therapeutic mood you have to stir yourself into. Hope, by contrast, being an actual virtue, *is* required of us; at least we should require it of ourselves. I doubt very much that the Savior was brimming with optimism as he rode into Jerusalem on the foal of an ass.

---

1. *The Faerie Queen*, Book I, Canto IX.

And I wonder if it is because we do not adequately distinguish between hope and optimism that we are too readily disposed to despair—which, let us not forget, has been called the unpardonable sin. Why it should lie outside of pardon I am neither learned nor good enough to say. Perhaps it is as offensive to God as "enriched" white bread is to a baker. Certainly each is its own punishment. "None else to death this man despayring drive, / But his owne guiltie mind deserving death."[2]

I would no more require optimism of a man than a diet of lima beans and liver. You cannot look around you and be optimistic: not about presidential elections, which are staged distractions that keep us from attending to matters close at hand; not about education, which in the lower forms is all standardized tests but no standards, and in the higher forms an expensive exercise in narcissism; not about the endowments of soil and water, which, to guess from our careless use and incoherent reasoning, exist in infinite supplies on a finite planet; not about the "financial world" masquerading even into its death throes as an economy; not about the state of marriage, which is now a training ground for faithlessness and divorce; not about the integrity of the family; not about the health and well-being of children; not about our catastrophic suburban living arrangements designed to be run on a dwindling energy supply that there are no replacements for; not about architecture or civic design; not about the availability of good food; not about literacy or the state of letters; not about the various therapeutic charades formerly known as religion, once a haven from this debased culture but now, more often than not, an extension of it.

No. There is no reason to be optimistic. But the alternative to optimism is pessimism, not despair. Despair is nowhere indicated. It has no place in our lives. If you've stood on the sidelines of a flag football game or sat in the bleachers while fifth-grade spastics affect to play basketball, and I hope you have, you probably know what it is like to be pessimistic. But who has ever despaired at the Little League ball park with its smiles and joys and chatter, or at the farmers' market with its oregano and laughter and girls in summer dresses? That cunning old cave-dweller Despair, or, if you prefer, that giant Despair (depict him how you will), belongs across town, on the other side of the tracks, at the multiplex movie theaters, seducing the teenagers and the adolescent adults who are trying to fight off acedia and ennui in the very place where these maladies incubate.

2. *Ibid.*

And this brings me to the second point I want to make about hope: just as (it seems to me) we do not sufficiently distinguish between hope and optimism, so too do we tend to prefer using "hope" in its transitive form. No golfer says, "Let's make a tee time for eight o'clock and hope," because the golfer, always engaged in an act of futility, requires an object of the verb: let us hope "for good weather" or hope "the others show up on time" or hope "they haven't top-dressed the greens recently." And when at last he steps to the tee, he doesn't just hope; he hopes that he doesn't slice his ball into the trees. Of course, this is perfectly legitimate, because "hope" is a noun but also a transitive verb. I myself hope "for the resurrection of the dead" and express this hope frequently.

But used intransitively "hope" names not an object but a disposition or a condition of the soul, and it is this use that interests me at the moment. To hope rather than to hope *for* is to understand that

> the discipline of ends is no discipline at all. The end is preserved in the means; a desirable end may perish forever in the wrong means. Hope lives in the means, not the end. Art does not survive in its revelations, or agriculture in its products, or craftsmanship in its artifacts, or civilization in its monuments, or faith in its relics.[3]

So wrote Wendell Berry in 1970.

To see that hope is in the means is to understand how it increases as people behave hopefully and in ways that make it possible at all, as at Little League games and local farmers' markets. People who are actually interested in what their children are doing, who are concerned about where their food comes from, who want to live in communities built to human rather than to mechanical scale; people who prefer their front porches to amusement parks, who consider themselves citizens instead of consumers, who know where they are and who respect the limits of their place; people who prefer actual faces and books to Facebook, who value self-control over government control—such people hope *for* but they also *hope*. They recognize, even if only intuitively, that hope is in the means, not the ends, and that to live hopefully is to take up the burden of enlarging and increasing hope. (Eliot: "I said to my soul, be still, and wait without hope, / For hope would be hope for the wrong thing."[4]) What you

---

3. *Discipline and Hope* (1970; Shoemaker & Hoard, 2004), 125.

4. "East Coker" III, 23–4 in T.S. Eliot, *The Complete Poems and Plays 1909-1950* (New York: Harcourt, Brace & World, 1971), 126.

feel in the air at the ballpark or the market or in the well-built human environment or on the front porch or in the backyard garden is not a warm fuzziness. It is not optimism. It is the hope that always increases as men and women behave hopefully. I would call all this an operation of grace coming to us, as grace does, by physical means—that is, sacramentally. None of these places is the source of hope, mind you, just as none is the source of grace. But such places and the people in them, their work and their talk and their presence, are the means and vehicles of an agency we stand in great need of, as life marked by the larceny of 2008 and the circus-show of 2016 fairly well demonstrated.

And so I would modify Berry's language slightly. If agriculture, craftsmanship, civilization, and faith do not survive in their revelations, products, artifacts, monuments, and relics, neither do they endure apart from them. The objects of these disciplines are probably as important as the objects of hope used transitively. And this, maybe, is the principal flaw in such productions as Hawthorne's "Artist of the Beautiful," a story that survives in material form but seems to suppose that art may detach itself from material circumstance. Discipline and art are transitive after all; they must "cross over" to their objects. But we must also be disciplined and hopeful even when a child of strength reaches up, crushes the mechanical butterfly, and leaves it in a heap of glittering fragments.

In my opening sentence I called the times "troubled," as indeed they are—as indeed they ever have been. "Trouble" pretty much captures what we're in all the time. The human condition is troubled and troubling by default, and it has never been our portion to eradicate the trouble (much less "rid the world of evil"), only to mitigate it. And this time Hawthorne had it right: Georgiana's birthmark, that "blemish" that resembles a tiny crimson hand, is not superficial; it goes to the heart. Remove it, and you'll be down a wife—not to mention the object of a clodhopper's scorn. But, troubled though the times be, and as durable as complaints against them have been (*O Tempora! O Mores!*), we are still much better served by an intransitive hope than by mere optimism. On this point I have found the words of C.S. Lewis instructive. Addressing other troubling times, the threat of annihilation by the atomic bomb, he wrote:

> The first action to be taken is to pull ourselves together. If we are all going to be destroyed by an atomic bomb, let that bomb when it comes find us doing sensible and human things—praying, working, teaching, reading, listening to music, bathing the children, playing tennis, chatting to our friends over a pint and a

game of darts—not huddled together like frightened sheep and thinking about bombs. They may break our bodies (a microbe can do that) but they need not dominate our minds.[5]

The essays in this book recommend this very hopefulness; they recommend the "human things" by the doing of which we preserve our humanity and perpetuate hope in troubled and troubling times, there being no other times in which "human things" have ever been, or are, or ever will be done.

---

5. "On Living in the Atomic Age," in *Present Concerns*, ed. Walter Hooper, (New York: Harcourt, Brace, Jovanovich, 1986), 73–4.

Contributors

Andrew V. Abela is Provost of The Catholic University of America. His research work on the integrity of the marketing process, including marketing ethics, Catholic Social Doctrine, and internal communication, has been published widely, and he is the co-author of the award-winning *Catechism for Business* (Catholic University Press, 2014). Prior to his academic career he worked at Procter & Gamble, McKinsey & Company, and the Corporate Executive Board, and he holds a B.Sc. from the University of Toronto, an MBA from the Institute for Management Development (IMD) in Switzerland, and a Ph.D. in Marketing and Ethics from the Darden Business School at the University of Virginia. He and his wife Kathleen live in Great Falls, Virginia, with their six children.

Jack R. Baker is Associate Professor of English at Spring Arbor University, where he is the resident medievalist and Director of the Christian liberal arts curriculum. He is the co-author (with Jeffrey Bilbro) of *Wendell Berry and Higher Education: Cultivating Virtues of Place* (University Press of Kentucky, 2017). He lives in Spring Arbor, MI with his wife and three children.

Jeremy Beer is a principle partner at American Philanthropic and president of the American Ideas Institute. He is the author of *The Philanthropic Revolution: An Alternative History of American Charity* (University of Pennsylvania, 2015) and the editor of *America Moved: Booth Tarkington's Memoirs of Time and Place, 1869-1928* (Front Porch Books, 2015). He is at work on a biography of Oscar Charleston, baseball's greatest forgotten player. He lives in Phoenix, Arizona.

Philip Bess is Professor of Architecture at the University of Notre Dame and project director of *After Burnham: The Notre Dame Plan of Chicago*

2109, a collaborative effort by students, alumni and faculty of the Notre Dame Graduate Urban Design Studio. He is the author of *City Baseball Magic: Plain Talk and Uncommon Sense about Cities and Baseball* (Knothole,1991), *Inland Architecture: Subterranean Essays on Moral Order and Formal Order in Chicago* (Interalia/Design Books, 2000), and *Till We Have Built Jerusalem: Architecture, Urbanism, and the Sacred* (ISI, 2006). He lives in South Bend, Indiana.

Jeffrey Bilbro is Associate Professor of English at Spring Arbor University. He is the author of *Virtues of Renewal: Wendell Berry's Sustainable Forms* (University Press of Kentucky, 2018), *Loving God's Wilderness: The Christian Roots of Ecological Ethics in American Literature* (Alabama, 2015), and the co-author (with Jack R. Baker) of *Wendell Berry and Higher Education: Cultivating Virtues of Place* (University Press of Kentucky, 2017). He lives in Jackson, Michigan.

Suzannah Black received her BA from Amherst College and her MA from Boston University. Her work has been published in *First Things*, the *Distributist Review*, *Ethika Politika*, *Providence*, and elsewhere, including Front Porch Republic. She is a founding editor of Solidarity Hall. She blogs at radiofreethulcandra.wordpress.com and tweets at @suzania. A native of Manhattan, she now lives in Queens.

Allan Carlson is Editor of *The Family in America: A Journal of Public Policy*. His books include, most recently, *Family Cycles: Strength, Decline & Renewal in American Domestic Life, 1630-2000* (Transaction, 2016). He resides on a farm in Winnebago County, Illinois.

David Cloutier is associate professor of theology at The Catholic University of America in Washington, DC. He is the author of *Walking God's Earth: The Environment and Catholic Faith* (Liturgical, 2014) and *The Vice of Luxury: Economic Excess in a Consumer Age* (Georgetown University Press, 2015). He edits the group blog catholicmoraltheology.com and serves on the Board of Directors of The Common Market, a food cooperative in Frederick, Maryland. For now he lives in Ward 3 of Washington, DC.

John Cuddeback is Professor and chairman of Philosophy at Christendom College. He is the author of *True Friendship: Where Virtue Becomes*

Happiness (2010) and a homesteader who raises heritage breed pigs. His website dedicated to the philosophy of family and household is BaconFromAcorns.com. He lives with his wife and their six children in the shadow of the Blue Ridge on the banks of the Shenandoah.

Katherine Dalton is a free-lance writer and editor. She took her first publishing job in college at *The Yale Literary Magazine*, then a national magazine based at Yale. She has worked as an editor for *Harper's* and *Chronicles* magazines, written for publications ranging from the *Wall Street Journal* to *Elle* to the online site Front Porch Republic, and is a contributor to the books *Conversations with Wendell Berry* (University Press of Mississippi, 2007) and *Wendell Berry: Life and Work* (University Press of Kentucky, 2007). For twelve years she and her family lived on a farm in New Castle, Kentucky. They now live 30 miles to the west in her hometown of Louisville.

Patrick Deneen is David A. Potenziani Memorial Associate Professor of Constitutional Studies at the University of Notre Dame. He is the author of *Why Liberalism Failed* (Yale, 2018), *Democratic Faith* (Princeton, 2005), and *The Odyssey of Political Theory* (Rowman & Littlefield, 2000). He is also the co-editor (with Joseph Romance) of *Democracy's Literature* (Rowman & Littlefield, 2005) and co-editor (with Susan McWilliams) of both *The Democratic Soul: A Wilson Carey McWilliams Reader* (University Press of Kentucky, 2011) and *Redeeming Democracy in America* (University Press of Kansas, 2011). He lives in South Bend, Indiana.

Anthony Esolen is Professor of Medieval and Renaissance Literature at The Thomas More College of Liberal Arts. His books include *Ironies of Faith: The Laughter at the Heart of Christian Literature* (ISI, 2008), *Life Under Compulsion: Ten Ways to Destroy the Humanity of Your Child* (ISI, 2015), and *The Politically Incorrect Guide to Western Civilization* (Regnery, 2008). He is also a translator of Dante and Lucretius. He lives in Warner, New Hampshire.

Michael P. Federici is Professor and chair of the Political Science and International Relations Department at Middle Tennessee State University. He is the author or editor of five books, including *The Political Philosophy of Alexander Hamilton* (Johns Hopkins University Press, 2012).

Richard M. Gamble is Anna Margaret Ross Alexander Professor of History and Politics at Hillsdale College in Michigan. From 2011 to 2016 he served as Director of the college's Honors Program. He is a contributing editor for the *American Conservative* and a member of the editorial boards of *Humanitas* and *Modern Age*. He is the author of *The War for Righteousness: Progressive Christianity, the Great War, and the Rise of the Messianic Nation* (ISI, 2003) and *In Search of the City on a Hill: The Making and Unmaking of an American Myth* (Bloomsbury Academic, 2010). He lives in Hillsdale, Michigan.

D. G. Hart is Visiting Professor of history at Hillsdale College. He is the author of several books on the history of Christianity, including most recently *Calvinism: A History* (Yale, 2013). He lives with his wife and their three cats in Hillsdale, Michigan.

Bill Kauffman is the author of eleven books, including *Poetry Night at the Ballpark and Other Scenes from an Alternative America* (Front Porch Books, 2015), *Dispatches from the Muckdog Gazette* (Henry Holt, 2003), and *Look Homeward, America* (ISI, 2006). He also wrote the screenplay for the movie *Copperhead*, directed by Ron Maxwell (2013). He lives in Elba, New York.

Susan McWilliams is an Associate Professor of Politics at Pomona College. She is the author of *Traveling Back: Toward a Global Political Theory* (Oxford, 2014) and co-editor (with John Seery) of *The Best Kind of College: An Insiders' Guide to America's Small Liberal Arts Colleges* (SUNY, 2015). She is also the co-editor (with Patrick Deneen) of *The Democratic Soul: A Wilson Carey McWilliams Reader* (University Press of Kentucky, 2011) and *Redeeming Democracy in America* (University Press of Kansas, 2011). She lives in Claremont, California.

John Médaille is the author of *Towards a Truly Free Market* (ISI, 2011) and *The Vocation of Business* (Bloomsbury Academic, 2007). He is a businessman with experience in management at large corporations and as an independent real estate agent. An instructor at the University of Dallas, he has served five terms as a city councilman in his hometown of Irving, Texas.

CONTRIBUTORS

Mark T. Mitchell is Professor and chairman of Government at Patrick Henry College and the founding president of the Front Porch Republic. He is the author of *The Limits of Liberalism: Tradition, Individualism, and the Crisis of Freedom* (Notre Dame, 2018), *The Politics of Gratitude: Scale, Place, and Community in a Global Age* (Potomac Books, 2012), and *Michael Polanyi: The Art of Knowing* (ISI, 2006). He is also the co-editor (with Nathan Schleuter) of *The Human Vision of Wendell Berry* (ISI, 2011). He lives and farms in Purcellville, Virginia.

Jason Peters is Dorothy J. Parkander Professor in Literature at Augustana College (IL). He is the editor of both *Wendell Berry: Life and Work* (University Press of Kentucky, 2007) and *Land! The Case for an Agrarian Economy*, by John Crowe Ransom (a Front Porch Republic book published by the University Press of Notre Dame, 2017). He lives in Williamston, Michigan, with his wife and three children.

Pete Peterson is the Dean and Senior Fellow of Pepperdine University School of Public Policy. He is a national speaker and writer on citizenship, public-sector reform, and the conservative movement. His columns have appeared in *The Wall Street Journal, Los Angeles Times, San Francisco Chronicle*, and *Real Clear Policy*. He lives with his wife and daughter in Santa Monica, California.

Jeff Polet is Professor of Political Science at Hope College. He is the co-editor (with David Ryden) of *Sanctioning Religion? Politics, Law, and Faith-Based Public Services* (Lynne Rienner, 2005). He is currently working on a book on how Christian theology has shaped American politics. He lives in Grand Rapids, Michigan.

Christine Rosen is senior editor of *The New Atlantis*. She is author of *Preaching Eugenics: Religious Leaders and the American Eugenics Movement* (Oxford, 2004), *My Fundamentalist Education* (PublicAffairs, 2005), and *The Extinction of Experience* (W.W. Norton, forthcoming). She is also the co-editor (with Naomi Schaefer Riley) of *Acculturated* (Templeton, 2011). She lives in Washington, DC.

William A. Schambra is a senior fellow at the Hudson Institute in Washington, DC. He has written extensively on the Constitution, the theory and practice of civic revitalization, and civil society in *The Wall Street*

Journal, *The Washington Times*, *Policy Review*, *Christian Science Monitor*, *Nonprofit Quarterly*, *Philanthropy*, *The Chronicle of Philanthropy*, and *Crisis*. He is the editor of several volumes, including *As Far as Republican Principles Will Admit: Essays of Martin Diamond* (AEI Press, 2011). He lives in Alexandria, Virginia.

Mark Shiffman is Chair of the Department of Humanities and Classical Studies at Villanova University. He is a scholar of Greek philosophy, especially Plato, Aristotle and Plutarch, and the history of western thought more generally. His writings on Christianity, politics and culture have appeared in *First Things*, *Communio*, and *Commonweal*, as well as on Front Porch Republic. He lives in the Mount Airy neighborhood of Philadelphia with his wife and two sons.

R. J. Snell is Director of the Center on the University and Intellectual Life at The Witherspoon Institute. His most recent book is *Acedia and its Discontents: Metaphysical Boredom in an Empire of Desire* (Angelico, 2015). He lives in Havertown, Pennsylvania, where the businesses still keep the liturgical year, particularly St. Patrick's Day.

Jeff Taylor is Professor of Political Science at Dordt College. He is author of three books: *Where Did the Party Go?* (University of Missouri, 2006), *Politics on a Human Scale* (Lexington Books, 2013), and *The Political World of Bob Dylan* (Palgrave, 2015). He lives in Sioux Center, Iowa.

James Matthew Wilson is Associate Professor in the Department of Humanities and Augustinian Traditions at Villanova University. A poet, critic, and scholar, he is the author, most recently, of *The Fortunes of Poetry in an Age of Unmaking* (Wise Blood, 2015) and *Some Permanent Things* (Wise Blood, 2014). He lives in the village of Berwyn, Pennsylvania, with his wife and children.

Lightning Source UK Ltd.
Milton Keynes UK
UKHW041850310123
416242UK00007B/358